WISDOM'S BOOK

The Sophia Anthology

Edited and Introduced by
Arthur Versluis

PARAGON HOUSE
St. Paul, Minnesota

First Edition, 2000

Published in the United States by
Paragon House
2700 University Avenue West
St. Paul, MN 55114

Manufactured in the United States of America.

Library of Congress Cataloging-in-Publication Data

Wisdom's book: the Sophia anthology / edited and introduced by Arthur
    Versluis.-- 1st ed.
        p. cm.
    Includes bibliographical references and index.
    ISBN 1-55778-786-7 (cloth) -- ISBN 1-55778-783-2 (pbk.)
    1. Spiritual life--Christianity--Miscellanea. 2. Wisdom--Religious aspects--
Christianity--Miscellanea. 1. Versluis, Arthur, 1959-

BV4501.2.W5738 2000
248--dc21
                                                                            99-046724

                    10 9 8 7 6 5 4 3 2 1

For current information about all releases from Paragon House,
visit the web site at http://www.paragonhouse.com

But the noble Virgin shows us the Door, and how we must enter again into Paradise.

—Jacob Böhme, *De Trib. Principiis,* xx.§40

CONTENTS

Introduction

This is not an ordinary book that you hold in your hands, but a living record of a hidden tradition in Judeo-Christianity, a tradition whose traces can be found throughout history, from the most distant antiquity to the present. This tradition reveals a spiritual record of men and women who have come to know with complete certainty that they are Wisdom's children, guided by Sophia, divine Wisdom. And in this book we see the modern traces of their spiritual experiences, a revealed hidden tradition in Christianity of special significance today, a tradition which we may equally call the Sophianic, the theosophic, or the Wisdom tradition.

Most people are familiar with conventional Christianity, with the numerous Protestant sects, with the various forms of Roman Catholicism and Eastern Orthodoxy, but not too many have yet heard of the Sophianic school in Protestantism which, completely non-sectarian, is centered on inward spiritual realization and on the guidance of the holy Sophia. I suspect that this omission in the history of religion and literature is no accident, nor is it happenstance that the works represented in this book are only now, at long last, readily available. For until now, most of the works included here were hidden away in private collections or national libraries; some have never before been available in published form. But perhaps the time has finally come for the Wisdom tradition to become more widely known.

Who is Sophia? The name "Sophia" is Greek for "Wisdom," and is the root for the words "philosophy" (love of wisdom) and "theosophy," the Wisdom of God. Sophia has always been seen as feminine, and is described in the Book of Wisdom as "a holy and intelligent spirit, unique, yet manifold, subtle, free, lucid, pure, clear, harmless, loving the good, eager, beneficent and kind, steady, inerrant, free from care, all-powerful, all-seeing, and all-permeating, through intelligent, pure, and delicate spirits. Wisdom moves more easily than motion itself, pervading all things because she is pure." Sophia is a "flawless mirror" of the divine, the means through which God creates, permeating the entire cosmos, and called the "glory of God."

Although both Sophia and Christ are often seen in vision in anthropomorphic form, and are spoken of by the great French theosopher Louis-Claude de Saint-Martin, for instance, as beings of holiness, purity, and light, the theosophers—those who have direct experience with Christ and Sophia—also speak of them as principles.[1] Hence Christ is often called the "Repairer" by Saint-Martin, because in principle Christ acts to restore to integrity what has been rent asunder by sin, repairing the divisions between people, between people and nature, and between people and the Divine. And Sophia is not the "Fourth" added to the Trinity so much as the medium in which the Trinity exists, for how could the Trinity, or the cosmos, for that matter, exist without divine Wisdom?[2]

To answer the numerous delicate theological questions regarding the nature of Wisdom, however, would require at the very least a work of its own, and one is always faced, in this field, with its inexhaustibility. More than any other aspect of the Judeo-Christian tradition, the Sophianic stream is perennially creative, always reappearing in new forms, even if the nature of these forms is always ultimately similar. We can certainly expect that our own age, and times to come, will produce new Wisdom literature too. One might even say, to use the unusual title of a book by Jane Leade, that the Wisdom tradition is akin to a "Fountain of Gardens"—that is, an inexhaustible fountain out of which countless spiritual gardens appear and blossom.

Wisdom in Antiquity

What are the historical origins of the Wisdom tradition? Certainly there are parallels between the *magna mater* divinities of antiquity and Judeo-Christianity, and particularly between Isis, Sophia, and Mary, the latter two representing aspects of the divine feminine as it appears in Christianity. But was there a direct continuity between the extant traditions of antiquity and Judeo-Christianity? Some will insist on the uniqueness of Judaism and

Christianity; others will insist just as vehemently that Judaism and Christianity did not exist in a vacuum, and in fact both absorbed much from their "pagan" ambience. Undoubtedly the truth includes aspects of both perspectives.

But in Judaism by the time of Christ, there was a developed Wisdom tradition, and in fact some scholars now argue that this tradition was central to Christ's mission. Among the works of the Wisdom tradition we can name as paramount the Song of Solomon and the Book of Wisdom. The Song of Solomon is perhaps most important for its conjoining of erotic and spiritual language; here, as indeed throughout the Wisdom tradition, the language of a lover speaking to his beloved is also the language for speaking of the Divine. Such language may often seem scandalous, or be labelled "heretical," but it is the single most vivid and living current in Judeo-Christian spiritual literature.

also Sirach Proverbs

However, the Book of Wisdom is the most revealing of the Judaic Wisdom works because it discusses extensively the path to Wisdom, the rewards of such a path, the ways Wisdom functions in creating the cosmos, and most of all, Wisdom's nature. There is one famous passage that I must draw attention to here: it is that in which Wisdom is called the "artist of all things," and in which we are told that those who know her know all the secrets of nature and man. A "reflection of everlasting light," she is "the flawless mirror of the divine active power, and the image of his goodness." Furthermore, "unchanging, she renews all things; age after age she enters holy souls and makes them friends of God and prophets, for God accepts only those who make their home with Wisdom."

To this passage the later theosophers return again and again; one finds allusions to Wisdom as the "flawless mirror of the divine active power" throughout the early modern and modern tradition. This definition is precise and extremely important, above all because it reveals the nature of Wisdom as the mirror of the Divine, "pervading all things because she is pure." In other words, Wisdom is not only the means by which the cosmos comes into being, Wisdom permeates the cosmos—and therefore can be described as the mediatrix between the cosmos and the Divine, herself divine, and the vivifying power of life and manifestation. Thus the statement that Wisdom "renews all things" and makes holy souls "friends of God and prophets" takes on far more levels of meaning than we might at first glance have thought.

Above all, the Wisdom tradition for these "friends of God" entails a resanctification of the cosmos, for if Wisdom pervades all things because she is pure, then although both man and the cosmos can be seen in their present condition as ruptured from their paradisal origin, still Wisdom permeates them and so, no matter how great the decadence of man and the suffering in the natural world, the lineaments of paradise can be glimpsed in us and all around us. The prophets are those who call us away from disintegration and back toward reintegration, toward a resanctified relation to humanity, nature, and the Divine.

But if this is the Judaic Wisdom tradition, what happened in the early Christian era, when various Gnostic sects appeared, many of whom affirmed more radical versions of this Sophianic mysticism? Here again the question is difficult to answer, not least because, even though we have numerous newly discovered Gnostic texts, our views of Gnosticism have been filtered through centuries of opprobrium by more conventional, historicist Christian apologists. Still, without question Sophia played a far more central role in Gnostic Christianity than in more dogmatically oriented sects. What's more, this role became fairly complex, mainly because the Gnostic traditions, being mythologically rather than historically oriented, created a profusion of myths, and even several Sophias, including the Fallen and the Heavenly Sophia.

Fundamentally, however, as Kurt Rudolph suggests, the Gnostic myths of Sophia grow out of the earlier Wisdom tradition, and represent a new development of it,[3] particularly of the resanctification and restoration of humanity and the cosmos that characterizes the entire Wisdom tradition. It is true that Gnostic movements often emphasized the split between the fallen cosmos and paradisal realms, or the alienated and divided nature of man in this cosmos, but so too did the Old Testament prophets insist on the deviatedness of contemporary humanity, for whom nature is desolate and unsanctified. The extent of Gnostic dualism and its parallels to secular existentialism have been over-emphasized[4]; rather, most and perhaps all of Gnosticism represents variations in the Wisdom current that stretches from antiquity up to the present day.

It is important, in thinking about the Wisdom current in the

European heritage, to recognize that we are not looking at fixed doctrines, but at the intersection of a living *mythos* with human imagination.[5] This is why the Sophianic tradition may be glimpsed in so many works that may not precisely be called 'theosophic,' but still represent points at which images of Sophia appear anew in literature. We can trace Wisdom throughout the medieval European tradition, appearing, for example, to Boethius in prison, and to Dante as Beatrice in *La Vita Nuova* and the *Divine Comedy*, again to the troubadours, figured in their poems, so that even though the Gnostic tradition of Sophia *per se* does not seem to have continued, the divine feminine nonetheless appears time and again, often apparently conjoined with an actual woman.

This conjunction between an actual woman and divine Wisdom is, as we have seen, visible throughout the Wisdom tradition, from the Song of Solomon, through the troubadours, right up to the present. Such a conjunction has been from the beginning controversial and even scandalous in the eyes of the orthodox, but at the same time it expresses a deep and abiding need for human beings to see the archetypal or transcendent through another human being, as through nature. The Sophianic tradition continually reflects this necessity of 'grounding' the transcendent in the immanent, in what we have also called the "resanctification" of nature and of humanity. Unlike historocentric Christianity, which despite its own traditions, often tends toward implying a vast distance between the Divine and man, or the Divine and nature, the Wisdom tradition from antiquity to the present is centered explicitly and precisely upon eliminating such alienation, and upon restoring the paradisal relationships between man and woman, and between humanity and nature.

Modern Christian Theosophy

The works in this anthology, with the exception of the central passage "In Praise of Wisdom" from the Book of Wisdom, entirely belong to the Christian theosophic school whose inception is around the time of Jacob Böhme (1575-1624), marked clearly by the appearance of his voluminous writings. This collection in *Wisdom's Book* is especially important because it reveals the breadth and depth of this theosophic school, many of whose writings have

never before been available except in rare editions or even only in
manuscript form.

Although Christian theosophy certainly existed before the time
of Böhme—the term itself has its origins very early in the Christian era, among the more gnostic Church Fathers and among the
Neoplatonists—the selections of writings in your hands represents
a particularly modern movement that begins early in the seventeenth century, as a kind of complement to Protestantism. This is
of immense and thus far unrecognized importance in the history
of European spirituality. All too often, Protestantism has been mis-
represented as merely 'protest' against the excesses of institution-
alized Roman Catholicism, or, one might say, as grim women in
long dresses and grim men in black coats and hats who occasionally killed people. But with theosophy we find a strikingly different aspect of Protestantism: here we find the animating essence of
non-sectarian spirituality.

This non-sectarianism characterizes virtually the whole of theosophy, and every author whose work we see in this selection. In
fact, it is both noteworthy and revealing that in the whole of theosophy one finds so little sectarianism, and that even when, in
the late seventeenth century, the theosophic circle in England surrounding Jane Leade called themselves 'Philadelphians', they were
reproved by other theosophers on the Continent, and themselves
said that they did not approve of such sectarianism as is visible in
Lutheranism, Calvinism, and so forth. In general, it is a theosophic
principle that one ought to remain in the tradition to which one was
born, while inwardly following the path of spiritual awakening.

There is, according to theosophy, great importance in not forming a sect, mainly because, as Johann Gichtel (1638-1710) pointed
out numerous times in his letters, the founders of sects generally
mean well, but their organizations congeal into anti-spiritual in-
stitutions, forming a kind of 'astral shell' that separates their members from authentic spiritual realization. One comes, all too soon,
to take the rituals or the doctrines as more important than that of
which they are only an expression and to which they are means.
What is worse, according to Gichtel, eventually the sect sinks to
wholly serving the *spiritus mundi*, or spirit of this world, religion
then coöpted into nothing more than justifications for worldly
accumulation. We can see numerous instances of these deviations

in the present day.

Of course, it may be alleged against theosophy that it represents an extreme of spiritual independence, and tends toward what we might call spiritual anarchy. But in practice what we find, generally, among the theosophers is an extremely retiring, even ascetic way of life, a life of prayer or meditation and very little in the way of proselytizing or even public contact—one might even say, a kind of Protestant monasticism or, at the very least, conservatism. Indeed, virtually the only departure from this, again Jane Leade's Philadelphian Society, met with such public censure that as a test case, it does prove the rule. What is more, while theosophers certainly disagree with one another on various points, sometimes vehemently, there are nonetheless enough points of agreement to allow us to map their territory with considerable certainty. All of this suggests that, although theosophers insist on independent experiential verification of their spirituality, it would be more accurate to characterize them as spiritual experientialists than as spiritual anarchists.

This emphasis upon direct spiritual experience marks the whole history of modern Christian theosophy, particularly from Jacob Böhme in the early seventeenth century. Böhme's voluminous writings, although certainly shaped by his later learning and his spiritual friends, drew upon his own direct visionary experiences, and in many respects are unparalleled for their creativity and for their insights into hidden aspects of the cosmos. This corpus—including a whole complex terminology all its own, a cosmology and metaphysics, and an intensely devotional visionary spirituality—represents the touchstone for virtually the whole subsequent Western European Sophianic tradition.

Around the time of Böhme there were other Sophianic circles, including that whose existence is documented by the manuscript and series of letters under the title *Aurora Sapientiae* (1629), published in excerpt for the first time ever in this collection, and testament to a theosophic circle in England with connections to the Continent. By the 1650's one saw the appearance of a theosophic circle around Dr. John Pordage, originally a clergyman who lost his post due to false and hysterical charges, and who subsequently lived a very retired life with his wife and a few others, bent on meditation and later, during the 1670's, on writing down his visionary experiences and insights. Pordage was the first in the theosophic school to devote an entire treatise to Sophia, a kind of diarium, part of which is retranslated here for the first time—for unfortunately, only German translations remain of nearly all Pordage's extensive corpus of writings.

By the late seventeenth and early eighteenth centuries, theosophy had blossomed into numerous circles, perhaps most notably one around the cantankerous and saintly Johann Georg Gichtel, the "hermit of Amsterdam," who never married, and spent much of his life in prayer and reclusion. Gichtel wrote thousands of letters of spiritual advice, later collected by his friend and confidante Johann Ueberfeld and published along with a hagiographic volume under the title *Theosophia Practica* (1722) a complementary set to Gichtel's edition of Böhme's writings, which Gichtel entitled *Theosophia Revelata* (1682/1730). Gichtel is without doubt one of the most profound of the theosophers, and in his work we find striking parallels to other esoteric traditions of the world, most notably Buddhism, for Gichtel includes an esoteric physiology.[6]

At roughly the same time that Gichtel's circle, the Angelic Brethren, flourished in Amsterdam, Jane Leade—successor to Pordage—founded her Philadelphian Society, mentioned earlier. But Gichtel (like many Continental theosophers) saw Leade as too entranced with visionary revelations, and too chiliastic; while he was no stranger to direct revelation, Gichtel saw Leade's visions as revealing that she had not penetrated beyond the astral or subtle realm into transcendent illumination. Leade also held the doctrine of universal restoration, that one day all beings would be saved, even the demonic, something that Gichtel could not countenance. It's not surprising, then, that Leade's group did not meet with a warm reception in Germany or the Netherlands, but one should note that these theosophic circles were aware of one another and communicated by letters and messengers, as various extant collections attest.[7]

Relatively little remarked, but also important, was the appearance of several theosophic, or theosophically influenced communities in North America, especially in Pennsylvania around the turn of the eighteenth century. Comprised mainly of German immigrants who sought to escape the kind of persecution that Gichtel faced before he fled to Amsterdam, one group settled along the Wissahickon River and, devoted to Sophia, lived quasi-monastic lives, while another later group settled at Ephrata and built a community there. Such communities in Pennsylvania produced a little-mined trove of Sophianic, or Sophianically influenced literature that is worthy of study in its own right as a theosophic branch. Many works of the early modern theosophers in this collection were taken to Pennsylvania, studied, and republished. But all of this I discuss extensively in my book *Wisdom's Children: A Christian Esoteric Tradition*.

If the early history of modern Christian theosophy is well represented by communities, theosophy is nonetheless composed of individuals, an individual history that is represented in this anthology. For even these communities or circles were centered around extraordinary individuals like Böhme, Pordage, and Gichtel; and many theosophers were rather more like Louis-Claude de Saint-Martin (1743-1803), the great French writer whose work was published under the *nom de plume* "the unknown philosopher," and who brought theosophy directly into combat with modern materialism and nihilism. Saint-Martin, whose wonderful correspondence with the Swiss Baron Kirchberger is well worth the purchase, saw himself as a "spiritual Robinson Crusoe" in revolutionary France, and such a description might hold for more than one theosopher.

Indeed, each figure in this selection represents a unique facet of theosophy, a different refraction of the tradition. The Kabbalist aspect of theosophy is certainly represented in the works of Friedrich Christoph Œtinger (1702-1782), just as the magical, pansophic current is visible in the works of Georg von Welling (1655-1727), and a purely mystical vision is revealed in the remarkable 1678-1679 journal of Anne Bathurst. The nineteenth century was not devoid of theosophers either, most notable among whom are Johann Jacob Wirz, center of a small devoted community in Germany, and Franz von Baader (1765-1841), undoubtedly the greatest European philosopher of the nineteenth century, whose work represents a brilliant series of insights into diverse fields ranging from science to medicine, from esoteric physiology to culture and literature.

And one finds theosophy's influence stretching into the twen-

tieth century as well, not only in such Russian authors as Sergei
Bulgakov and Vladimir Soloviev—who, having read the works
of Böhme and other Western European theosophers, developed
an Eastern European Sophiology that drew upon the Eastern Orthodox tradition—but also in the renowned philosopher Nicholas Berdyaev, who even wrote an introduction to a work of
Böhme's, and certainly drew upon theosophy for his own writings.[8] Then too, there is Leopold Ziegler, arguably the preëminent
German theosopher of the twentieth century, and author of numerous books that act as bridges between Asia and Europe, particularly between Buddhism and Christianity. Finally, Peter
Koslowski has also brought theosophy into a contemporary and
even 'postmodern' context.

Clearly, given even this brief historical survey, we can see that
the Wisdom tradition is not limited to this or that era, a matter of
dead documentation, or of only academic interest, but rather is
striking for its continued renewal. This particular collection of
writings demonstrates incontestably that there *is* a modern Christian theosophic tradition, and that this Wisdom tradition has generated not only devout and spiritual writings but also profound
insights and some of the highest flights of speculative illumination that Europe has yet produced. *Wisdom's Book* opens the door
to unexpected riches of the spirit.

Major Aspects of Sophianic Spirituality

It may come as a surprise to many—who have heard the word
"Sophia" appear in various contemporary books on or discussions of feminist spirituality—to discover that there has been such
an extensive preëxisting tradition. For many today, the word
"Sophia" may represent a blank space into which one can project
one's own longings or expectations. But the Sophianic tradition
represented in this collection is indeed a single tradition, even if
some of its representatives did not know all their predecessors or
contemporaries. For Sophianic spirituality has certain primary
characteristics that recur historically again and again.

The characteristics of Sophianic spirituality are slightly different than those of Böhmean theosophy as a whole, which I have
discussed in detail in a number of places. In brief, the Sophianic

tradition represents a paradigm with certain common elements that reappear even if various groups are wholly unaware of one another, including 1) the focus upon the figure of divine Wisdom or Sophia, the "mirror of God," generally conceived of as feminine, 2) an insistence upon direct spiritual experience or cognition, meaning insight into the divine nature of the cosmos and into transcendent realms, 3) non-sectarianism, and 4) a spiritual leader who guides his or her spiritual circle through letters and oral advice.[9] Another characteristic, not really represented in the selections that follow, is "reading nature as a spiritual book via the visionary faculty," which I have suggested as a primary characteristic of Böhmean theosophy as a whole. I have replaced this characteristic with "non-sectarianism" here because "reading nature" can be seen as a subset of 2), "an insistence upon direct spiritual experience or cognition."

The first of these characteristics is, of course, a reliance on the guidance of divine Wisdom. But contrary to what one might think, Wisdom is not necessarily personified here. Occasionally, as in the case of Jane Leade for instance, Wisdom does appear in vision in a woman's form. However, the theosophers are quick to affirm that fundamentally, Wisdom is neither male nor female, but transcends all such designations. From a theosophic perspective, to cling to the view that Wisdom is feminine and must have feminine form is to miss the fundamental nature of Wisdom, which is "pure," "flawless," and like a "mirror." Wisdom is the emanation of the Divine, the pure element or tincture that surrounds the Divine and that pervades all of nature.

This being said, of course, it certainly remains the case that Wisdom, throughout the theosophic tradition, is spoken of as feminine. Indeed, in one of the most charming of all the works in this collection, Johann Wirz personifies Wisdom as a mother, as a sister, and as a wife. But as we travel through this visionary tale, we begin to realize that underlying it is the recognition that Wisdom is everywhere, and pervades all things: we simply needed to be guided through the progressive stages of realizing this. And likewise, throughout the theosophic tradition we find that Wisdom appears or is depicted in feminine form as a guide, but also sometimes as a lover, or a sister—but what remains foremost are the qualities that these relationships represent. Such relationships are not literal but metaphoric ways of describing what is in fact beyond language.

Here we find a second primary characteristic of the Sophianic tradition: it focuses on a specific path of spiritual transmutation or awakening. It is true that the range of authors we see represented here do not describe such a path in the same way—some, like Anne Bathurst, are solely interested in chronicling their own spiritual experiences, while others, like John Pordage, are more inclined to detailed spiritual cartography and, occasionally, to a letter of advice on the spiritual path. And still others, like Franz von Baader, are more drawn to the intellectual implications of Sophianic spirituality. But all of these authors nonetheless not only presuppose but insist upon a path of Sophianic spiritual awakening that comes through prayer and interior attention and, sometimes, through inner vision.

Perhaps surprisingly, visionary encounters with divine beings (for instance, Wisdom, or Sophia) are not necessarily characteristic of Sophianic spirituality. It is true that many of our authors had such experiences, but certainly not all of them did, at least so far as we can tell. Certainly it is the case that the circle surrounding John Pordage and Jane Leade did tend to have visions, but even here this was not emphasized as central to the spiritual path: in his letter on the philosophical stone, a work of spiritual alchemy, Pordage did not directly refer to visions at all. Rather, the spiritual work in question has to do with the stages of spiritual awakening expressed in terms of planetary symbolism; one moves toward a state of gnostic illumination. Thus we might distinguish a kind of visionary spectrum that ranges from visualizing certain symbols or images, to having inner vision that perceives spiritual principles or realms, to having encounters or dialogues with spiritual beings on a visionary inner field of perception. The Sophianic tradition encompasses all of these possibilities.

While it may or may not be visionary, the Sophianic tradition is certainly non-sectarian, our third primary characteristic. During the era when theosophy was emerging in its modern form, around the turn of the seventeenth century, one saw an enormous degree of religious strife in Western Europe. Protestantism in particular carried in its wake considerable sectarianism under its various denominations: Lutherans, Calvinists, and so forth, each insisting that their dogmatic formulations alone were correct. By contrast, because the Sophianic tradition insisted upon individual and community spiritual practice and awakening as its center, its adherents were explicitly non-sectarian. Johann Gichtel, for example, advised his followers to remain in whatever denomination they were born to, for what matters is inward illumination, not outward form or dogmatic adherence. And indeed, although theosophy emerged in a Protestant context with its founder, Jacob Böhme, more than a few of its members have been Catholic, the most famous of whom is the great nineteenth century theosopher, Franz von Baader.

A fourth characteristic of the Sophianic tradition is that its practitioners tend to form a small circle or community around a leading figure, much like the *tariqah* and *shaikh* of Sufism. Thus, in the early seventeenth century in eastern Germany (near the border of Poland, in a little town called Görlitz) we find a theosophic circle emerging around Jacob Böhme. To the members of his circle, Böhme occasionally sent letters of spiritual advice, and undoubtedly he learned from some of them as well, especially those who were familiar with Jewish Kabbalism. Likewise, in England during this time, we find a circle emerging around the author of *Aurora Sapientiae*, some of whose letters we still have. And later in England, there appeared a theosophic circle around John Pordage, later around Jane Leade; in Amsterdam one finds a group called the "Angelic Brethren" around Johann Gichtel; and in Pennsylvania, one finds the various groups that settled near Philadelphia, including those who founded the monastic community of Ephrata. All of these groups resemble Christian forms of Sufism, the inner lay dimension of Islam, save that some of them had women spiritual leaders.

And the final major characteristic of Sophianic groups and individuals is their focus on a profound cosmology, very much an alternative to the emerging scientific-materialistic view that became dominant from the seventeenth to the twentieth centuries. Here too, although of course there is some diversity, there is also a remarkable unity or coherence of understanding. Sophianic cosmology has its origins in the medieval period, and in the convergence of two primary streams: on the one hand, the alchemical-spagyric medicinal tradition of Paracelsus and of medieval alchemy; and on the other hand, the high Germanic gnostic tradition of Meister Eckhart and Johannes Tauler. These two primary streams merge in the work of Böhme, where they take on a form that in turn recurs throughout subsequent theosophy.

Here, of course, we hardly have space to detail theosophic cosmology, but we can sketch its general outlines.

Sophianic Cosmology

Although it is true that the materialist-rationalist paradigm—which produced the modern world and all its technological power—has certain advantages, it is not the only way of understanding the nature of the cosmos. Indeed, given some of this paradigm's destructive effects in the natural and social realms, i.e., ecological disruption and social fragmentation, many people today are searching for other ways of understanding the cosmos and our human place within it. But as of yet, while many people have looked to indigenous traditions, to Asian religious traditions, or even to modern physics for alternatives to materialism-rationalism, relatively few have looked a bit closer to home, to the very time and place (Western Europe during the past several centuries) where modern technocracy emerged, to see if there were also alternative ways of seeing the world here. Only now, it seems, have we begun to rediscover the hidden wealth of the Western esoteric traditions.

Here, of course, our focus is not on Western esotericism generally, but on one primary stream within it: Christian theosophy. Christian theosophy takes on its representative form in the work of Jacob Böhme, whose voluminous works, with their unfamiliar Latin-based terminology and complex structure, are too much to explicate here. Here, instead, we will simply examine some primary elements of Böhmean theosophic cosmology. Böhme's cosmology has at its center the *ungrund*, a word that literally means "unground," but also signifies that which is prior to all existential manifestation—including the manifestation of God. The *ungrund* is equivalent to the Godhead of Meister Eckhart, and to the *En Soph* of Kabbalism: it is the primal origin or foundation of all existence. Out of the *ungrund* emerges the two fundamental qualities that are to pervade the entire cosmos: wrath and love. Wrath precedes love, inasmuch as it is also the principle of differentiation; love is the principle of union or reunion, and of course separation must precede reunion.

But the physical cosmos does not yet exist: as the "third principle," it comes into being only as a function of a series of "falls." The first of these falls is that of some of the angelic powers, led by Lucifer, and this descent from divine harmony is followed by another. Originally, Adam, the primordial androgynous human, lived in paradisal harmony with Sophia, his eternal divine companion. But Adam too falls from grace, and when Sophia, or Wisdom, must leave him, is divided into two: man and woman. Here Eve or woman is not blamed for the fall, as in less esoteric forms of Christianity. Out of this division emerges the temporo-spatial world as we now know it, in which we live only briefly, not for eons, and where we encounter suffering and evil. This physical cosmos is the juncture, so to speak, of the visible and the invisible; it is the field of combat between the Luciferian and the divine powers, between wrath and love. And thus it is the place where human beings can ascend or descend, can become vehicles either of love or of wrath.

Now the physical cosmos, in the theosophic view, is not merely physical but also supraphysical. Everything in the cosmos emerges as the interplay of principles, forces, or energies, which can be expressed in terms of the three alchemical principles of Mercury, Salt, and Sulphur. These three principles, whose nature is that of quick liquid, crystallization, and fierce flaming, or water, earth, and fire, inform everything in existence. It is possible to see "inside" the nature of things, and even to restore them to their paradisal or primordial original nature. For each thing in nature bears a particular divine signature as well; and the purpose of human existence is to incarnate the divine on earth, to restore once again the paradisal balance that once existed between humanity, nature, and the divine.

The restoration of paradise takes place through individual spiritual practice and illumination. Here the term "restoration of paradise" does not mean that the earth is literally transformed into the garden of Eden, but rather that fallen humanity is regenerated or renewed, and lives up to its original potential as the companion of Wisdom. For it is through Sophia, or Wisdom, that humanity is restored from a fallen condition, at the mercy of various psycho-emotional forces, to a regenerated or paradisal state. This path of restoration is sometimes expressed in terms of "courting" or "wooing" Sophia, and in the terms of Johann Gichtel and later, Johann Wirz, becoming her friend, her companion, and finally her husband. These metaphoric terms are, of course, not to be understood literally, but as the expression of spiritual stages that are as valid for women as for men. What matters is the path of transmutation itself, in which one's various bodily centers and psycho-emotional energies are transmuted into their divine, pristine natures.

Thus the theosophic cosmology cannot be separated from the individual spiritual path. The importance of understanding the hidden or supraphysical aspects of the cosmos lies not in gaining power over the cosmos, but in why we live in a state of disharmony with the world and the divine, and how we can restore our true, paradisal condition once again. The importance of understanding the hidden nature of the macrocosmos lies in ourselves. For all the energies that inform the cosmos also inform us. And to restore our own illuminated, harmonious inner spiritual life is to play our part, the only part we can play, in restoring this illuminated harmony in the cosmos as a whole.

But according to theosophy, there are forces in the cosmos that do not want us to follow this path of spiritual awakening. Sometimes in later theosophy, particularly that of Johann Gichtel, these forces are represented as the *spiritus mundi*, or "spirit of this world." The *spiritus mundi* corresponds, in some respects, to the demiurge of the ancient Gnostics: it is the power of selfishness, of acquisitiveness and of power-over. The *spiritus mundi* whispers in our ear that "I" deserve riches and fame and power; and if we spurn such advances in favor of the spiritual path, then according to the theosophers, we are tested or even attacked by it, that is, by those in the human world who serve it. This explains, say the theosophers, why so many who follow the path of Wisdom are denigrated, attacked, and even tortured and killed. Here one thinks, for instance, of the virulent attacks on Böhme by his local minister during his own lifetime, or again, of the crowds armed with sticks and stones who attacked Jane Leade and her followers in London nearly a century later.

Clearly theosophic cosmology differs radically from materialist-rationalist cosmology in that it centers not on acquisition or power-over, but on the human path of spiritual awakening. The theosophic cosmos is seen in this light, and as a result is rendered in some respects "transparent." That is, someone engaged in a spiritual path is progressively able to see more deeply into the principles or energies that inform everything in existence. Modern consumerist society, of course, from a theosophic view is seen to correspond quite exactly with the reign of the *spiritus mundi*, with the selfishness of greed, jealousy, anger, and desire for power over things and people. If an organization, even a church, contributes to or engenders these emotions in people, then it belongs to "Babel" and is not only unhelpful but positively harmful on the spiritual path. In theosophy, in other words, cosmology is inseparable from spirituality.

Feminism and Sophia

Undoubtedly one of the most powerful socio-political movements of our time, feminism also engendered a strong critique of mainstream Christian theology and traditions. This critique—founded in opposition to the male-centered history of Christianity—became also an affirmation, oftentimes of reconstructed ancient or pagan goddess or magna mater religions, but in any case of an emphasis on the feminine over the masculine. Thus it is not surprising that many feminists found the figure of Sophia in Judeo-Christianity to be extremely important in reconstructing that tradition in a more feminist image. Out of these efforts came such books as *Sophia: The Future of Feminist Spirituality* (1986), or Elizabeth Schüssler Fiorenza's *Jesus: Miriam's Child, Sophia's Prophet* (1995).[10] But as we look closely at these books, we discover something rather surprising: they have absolutely no references whatever to the actual Sophianic tradition as represented in this book.

How could this be? one wonders. How could numerous books emerge on the figure of Sophia, even on Sophia as the future of spirituality, yet there appears not an inkling of the preëxistent theosophic tradition of Böhme, Gichtel, Pordage, or Leade? The answer may lie in part in the previous inaccessibility of this tradition: many of the writings in *Wisdom's Book* have never been published before, and have remained ensconced in private libraries or elsewhere, known only to a handful of scholars. Some of this neglect was also due to the strong prejudices against "enthusiasts" or gnostics, prejudices left over from the vituperative battles of several centuries past between rationalist-materialist camps and those more open to such alternative worldviews as those represented by alchemy, Kabbalism, and, yes, theosophy.

Of course, there is much in the theosophic tradition that would be entirely amenable to contemporary feminism. For instance, it is certainly the case that the theosophic circles were considerably more open to the possibility of a woman leader than any of the mainstream Christian traditions of the last several centuries. The English Philadelphians, for instance, around the turn of the eighteenth century, were led by the prolific visionary Jane Leade, and women were prominent throughout the history of that movement, even when crowds attacked them armed with stones and sticks. And certainly in the manuscript writings of Anne Bathurst, published here for the first time ever, one finds ample material for the study of a woman's spiritual journey around the turn of the seventeenth century. What is more, the prominence of Sophia in the writings of men in this theosophic tradition also may have unexplored significances.

Yet it may also be that the actual Sophianic tradition may prove somewhat inconvenient for a socio-political feminist perspective. For one thing, our theosophers, be they male or female, are singularly uninterested in worldly affairs. They care not a whit for achieving socio-political power or status, and indeed, as we can see from our discussion of Sophianic cosmology, from the viewpoint of theosophy much of feminism belongs to the realm of the *spiritus mundi*, i.e., to the realm of this-worldly distraction from the spiritual life. What is more, the vast majority of the theosophers, again male and female both, insisted on living a chaste, virginal life, so that what might today be depicted as misogyny or misandrony, is in fact not at all the hatred or fear of one sex for the other, but rather akin to the monastic inclination found in religions around the world to separate the sexes and avoid distraction during intense spiritual endeavors.

One of the dangers in working with the theosophic tradition in scholarship today is that people try to remake it in their own images. It is all too tempting and easy to look back in history and find there support for our own contemporary biases or expectations, rather than looking at works like those represented in this collection in order to understand precisely what their authors had to say. The more thoroughly one studies the Sophianic tradition represented here, the more one recognizes that these writings emerge from an esoteric spiritual perspective *fundamentally* different from the perspectives of most of us in the modern world. Thus, rather than reconstructing Böhmean theosophy in the image of modern physics or psychology or even feminism, it may be more fruitful to try and understand the Sophianic tradition sympathetically, and from the inside. This is the premise underlying this collection, in which these authors are allowed to speak for themselves, more than one for the first time ever in an English publication.

The Virgin Sophia

From the beginning to the end of this collection, virtually every author's work is concerned with living a "virginal" life in order to realize wisdom, and it is important to recognize what this means. It was Jacob Böhme in the seventeenth century who first and perhaps most extensively wrote about the spiritual and cosmological significance of Sophia in relation to the Fall of humanity and spiritual regeneration, and our final selection by Nicholas Berdyaev in the twentieth century is still engaged in recognizing the implications of this relationship. While it is not possible here to offer a complete survey of this central theme, we can certainly offer an outline in order that readers can better understand what underlies so many of these writings.

According to Böhmean theosophy, humanity (Adam) was created as a luminous, androgynous being, and it was only after the Fall of humanity that man and woman as sexual beings came into existence. Before the Fall, humanity (Adam) was wedded to the Virgin Sophia, meaning that humanity existed in union with the Divine. This union was sundered when humanity fell into differentiation, the outward sign of which is the duality of man and woman; this also entails being subject to time and the cycle of birth and death, as well as to emotional forces like greed, anger, desire, and jealousy. In other words, humanity has fallen away from Wisdom. But there exists a path back to Wisdom.

This path back to Wisdom means that we are called to live a virginal life, "virginal" here having a greater meaning than simply sexual chastity. According to theosophy, we are called toward our original state of virginity, meaning the transcendence of dualistic fixations that include the whole range of emotional energies. On such a path, many of the theosophers insist on sexual chastity as an important component, but as Jane Leade put it in her *Fountain of Gardens*, we are also called away from "the shoar of mortal Things."[11] On 15 December, 1678, she records a particular insight into the uniting of the *"Contrarieties* in Nature," only after which " Opening and Spiritual Parly" was she "cast as into a *Trance,* and had all [her] outward Senses drowned, and was brought by the Spirit into such a place, that was as the Scene of another World."[12] This place was the "Magia-School," or "the school of the magi," or the "theosophic college," which exists in a realm "clear as crystal," inhabited by angelic beings with "clarified Bodies."

This realm of the "theosophic college" of which Leade wrote is above time and space as we currently conceive of them, and is entered by going into the "Watch-Tower of the silent Mind." Like a *"Holy Island"* beyond the "Coast" of this world, entering it is "a restoring to the Cœlestiality of that Kingdom, to which ye have been Alienates." Thus the first rule is to *"unlearn* and *unknow* all, which the wise rational Spirit hath in its refined Morality disciplin'd and exercised our Senses in."[13] We are called to "fly above" the elemental regions of the "Sun, Moon, and Stars" and learn "Heavenly Philosophy." No one here can waver between two worlds; one must live either below, in the "leaden" realm of the senses, or rise up to the "Wisdom-School," "New-born in this High & Cœlestial University."

Admittedly, some of the theosophers, notably Johann Georg Gichtel and Louis-Claude de Saint-Martin, thought that Leade was too prone to visionary experiences and had not fully realized the divine Sophia.[14] But this represents a kind of internal squabble within theosophic tradition, and the fact is that what Leade writes in this passage corresponds quite well to the general point here: in theosophy, we are called to a virginal life in a much more profound sense than the word "virginal" usually entails. The theosophers, beginning with Böhme, often spoke in terms of a "marriage" with the Virgin, which is a different way of referring to the reunion with Sophia that has a long and venerable history. In any case, whatever the metaphor, the theosophers as a whole insist on a path of individual regeneration and reunion with Sophia.

The path to the transcendence of our fallenness is what Böhme calls in his *Three Principles* a "process." It is not simply a matter of intellectually recognizing that we are fallen beings living in a disrupted world: we must go through a path of individual transmutation and awakening. Böhme outlines this "magical process" in his *Signatura Rerum*, or *Signature of All Things*, where he asserts directly that "God must become man, man must become God." (X.53) This process of transformation toward this reunion entails working through stages associated with planetary energies, and is discussed as well in John Pordage's "Philosophical Epistle on the True Stone of Wisdom," included in this collection. Part of this process entails the reunion of the male and female "tinctures" separated by the Fall: the Sophianic path means the restoration of humanity to its unfallen, virginal, androgynous, angelic state.

Thus we can see in at least a little more detail why the Sophianic tradition is not, if taken on its own terms, amenable to an exclusively feminist or, for that matter, masculinist interpretation. Rather, to realize union with Sophia is to realize the transcendence not only of sexual difference, but also of duality itself, and of all the emotional attachments and aversions that it entails. Social, political, or economic issues do not play a role in the Sophianic writings that follow—the diaries and letters included here have nary a reference to the day's external events and conditions. The Sophianic authors included here are interested in realizing Wisdom, and their writings and lives need to be seen in that context. At the same time, these writings do have wider than purely individual ramifications.

Sophia and Contemporary Philosophy

There is no doubt that the theosophic tradition, like all of Western esotericism, is fundamentally interdisciplinary in nature, and has much to say not only for the fields of comparative reli-

gion or the history of Christianity and Judaism, but also for such
diverse areas as science and the history of science, psychology,
art history, literature, and certainly not least, philosophy. Some
of these implications, particularly for religion, the sciences, and
the humanities, I have already outlined in a companion to this
work entitled *Wisdom's Children*. Here, therefore, I will focus on
some of the major implications of the Sophianic tradition for contemporary philosophy.

The very word "philosophy" derives from the word "sophia,"
and conveys a love (*philo*) for wisdom. It is true that in much of
contemporary academic scholarship on philosophy this original
meaning has been somewhat obscured, and perhaps even lost.
More than one contemporary philosopher has declared, echoing
Nietzsche, that modern philosophy is in fact dead, and will remain so unless philosophers return to the original, radical purpose of philosophy: the pursuit and realization of wisdom. But it
is something of an exaggeration to say that there are no major
modern contributions to philosophy when the twentieth century
saw giants like Nicholas Berdyaev, Martin Heidegger and
Nishitani Keiji. What is more, there are also unexplored debts in
such contemporary philosophers as Heidegger not only to Meister
Eckhart and high German mysticism, but also to Böhme and
Böhmean theosophy. Indeed, it may very well be that this aspect
of Heidegger makes him so congenial to Japanese Buddhist philosophers, for instance Nishitani Keiji.

Naturally, we do not have space here to discuss contemporary philosophy in any detail, but there is at least one major figure we certainly must draw attention to. This is Nicholas Berdyaev
(1874-1948), author of numerous philosophical works, including
monumentally important books like *The Meaning of Creativity*, *The
Beginning and The End*, and his autobiographical work, *Dream and
Reality*. Without question, Berdyaev was influenced by theosophy, in particular by Jacob Böhme and Franz von Baader, and
indeed, he even declared himself a theosopher as well as a philosopher in his book *Freedom and the Spirit*. Berdyaev was perhaps
the only major twentieth century philosopher to recognize the import of Böhme's insights for contemporary humanity, and what is
more, Berdyaev was able to convey his understanding in lucid prose.

At the center of Berdyaev's philosophy is the concept of objectification. Modern society, he wrote, derives from the general human tendency to objectify—i.e., to separate into subject and object. Objectification makes possible modern, quantifying scientific knowledge: "I" can study, measure, and manipulate "that." But the "other" remains fundamentally separated from us, and in fact this separation between us and nature, between us and the rest of humanity, as well as between us and the divine, grows ever greater the more we emphasize objectification as our primary mode of knowledge.

Yet there is another kind of knowledge. This other kind of knowledge, which may also be called *gnosis* (a Greek word meaning direct transcendent knowledge), does not derive from objectification but from a different path entirely, which we find in Western esotericism. There was a time, only a few centuries ago, when the sciences and the arts were not separated but united in such esoteric disciplines as alchemy or Kabbala, as well as theosophy. These various traditions had at their center the search for Wisdom, and held that to realize Wisdom means that one must turn inward and come to understand one's object of study (be it the cosmos, as in alchemy, or the divine, as in Kabbala) directly within oneself. Thus this other kind of knowledge is based not in objectification or separation, but in transcendence, or union.

The consequences of objectified knowledge Berdyaev foresaw partway through the twentieth century, but those consequences became increasingly evident as the century went on. One thinks, for instance, of the immense wars and devastation of the past century, of ecological destruction and of social disruption, of the advent of totalitarianism in various forms, and of the emergence of consumerism. All of these have at their root the separation of self and other that is characteristic of objectification: one could not make the decision to strip mine a wooded hill, or dump toxic waste into a waterway, unless one were living under the delusion that one is somehow separated from these actions. Objectification presumes a fundamental barrier between self and other, so that "I" am separate from and can exploit or destroy "that."

The Wisdom tradition represented in this collection, on the other hand, reveals the presence of a fundamentally different kind of knowledge. According to the Wisdom, or theosophic tradition, it is possible for us to progressively realize our essential unity

with humanity, with the cosmos, and with the divine. This essential unity does not obviate the distinction between self and other,
so that, for instance, if I decide that I like your coat or wallet, I can
simply take it. Morality remains, and is if anything intensified.
But in question is the revelation of higher dimensions of consciousness, in which the subject-object or self-other relations assumed
by the objectifying ego-consciousness no longer are seen as the
only kind of relations possible between us and the world.

In other words, the theosophic tradition begins from completely different premises than most of us now take for granted.
Whereas most of us assume, and are trained from birth to assume,
basic divisions between ourselves and nature, ourselves and others, ourselves and the divine, the Wisdom tradition emerges from
the recognition that these divisions are not intrinsic to us as human beings. Inherent in us and in the entire cosmos is an underlying unity, in which the self-other division does not exist. One
way, therefore, to understand alchemy, Kabbala, and the other
currents of the Western esoteric traditions, is to see them as various means of moving toward this essential unity, by way of images, by way of enigmatic literature, by way of the awakening of
inner vision, but above all, by way of prayer. Prayer, here, does
not mean petitioning an external deity so much as obeying the
injunction of Paul to "pray without ceasing." Such unceasing
prayer is in fact our awakening to the fundamental unity prior to
existence that Böhme calls the *ungrund*.

Thus it is with philosophy as it is with cosmology in relation
to the Sophianic writers here: in this school philosophical and cosmological observations emerge from spiritual practice, and cannot really be understood without reference to it. The Wisdom tradition has at its center the view that while intellectual knowledge
is perhaps useful, the one thing needful in life is the actual realization of Wisdom for oneself. Thus, while there are certainly philosophical implications to the Sophianic tradition represented here—
which certainly can be expressed in terms of subject-object divisions—just as there are cosmological, psychological, scientific, and
artistic implications, all of these are subordinated to the most central theme of actually realizing the nature of divine Wisdom inherent in the cosmos and in oneself.

Wisdom

As we can see even from these rather cursory remarks, the Sophianic tradition represented in this collection is far more extensive and profound than one might at first have thought. Here I have outlined the essential characteristics of theosophy, and provided something of an historical context. Yet as we move from this introduction to the works of our various authors, there remains an underlying question that each reader must answer: who or what is Wisdom? It is to Wisdom that this entire collection, and this entire tradition is dedicated, yet when asked directly what is Wisdom, one may very well be at a loss for words. If there is one thing I should like to emphasize here, it is that one should beware of our tendency to grasp, to cling, to objectify Wisdom. For Wisdom will remain beyond all our efforts at objectification.

Indeed, such objectification is the reason that I am here using the word "Wisdom" rather than "Sophia." For as we have seen, the theosophers were extremely careful never to give their spiritual practice a sectarian name, and held that sectarianism invariably creates a kind of mental carapace separating one from actual spiritual practice and awakening. Instead of authentic spiritual work, Gichtel and others held, many people settle for collections of doctrines or beliefs to which they cling and for which they will fight and even kill. It would be totally at odds with the entire import of the Wisdom tradition we see represented in this pages to seek to make of it a sect with dogmatic assertions or a cult devoted to an external "Sophia." An objectified Sophia would be far from the Wisdom we see represented here.

Yet what then is Wisdom? Why is Wisdom represented as feminine? How do we realize Wisdom? To answer such questions, we must turn to these works from the Wisdom tradition itself. But if we go seeking to justify our preconceptions, or to find there this or that self-image, however noble that self-image might appear to us, we will not find Wisdom. It is, John Pordage and Louis Claude Saint-Martin pointed out, only when we have finally ceased our striving to gain control, to "have" Wisdom, to, however subtly, objectify and "gain" her, that we sink into our own inner center and she comes to us. Perhaps it will even be with society as a whole as it is with the individual: that after we have seen the ultimate futility of all our efforts to gain or control the outer world, we turn our attention to the inner dimensions, to the exploration not of outer but of inner space, and to the discovery of who and where we really are. Yet whatever happens in society, we may choose such a path as individuals. To all those on this quest for Wisdom is this book dedicated.

I

In Praise of Wisdom

The most influential section of the Book of Wisdom, belonging to the Old Testament, this passage was cited and alluded to by nearly the entirety of the Sophianic tradition, and is particularly important in the modern Christian theosophic school. It is interesting, and perhaps revealing, that the Book of Wisdom itself was translated by Luther and hence part of the German Protestant tradition, whereas the King James translation of the Bible excluded the Book of Wisdom, so that consequently many generations of English speaking Protestants remained unfamiliar with it. This exclusion suggests a great deal about what was omitted from the dominant conventional forms of Protestantism, and underscores the importance of rediscovering this hidden Sophianic tradition, beginning with its origins in the Jewish Wisdom literature. The Book of Wisdom is cited constantly in the Sophianic tradition, and is central for understanding the origins of this major current in the Judeo-Christian tradition.

In what follows, we find the most frequently cited passages from the Book of Wisdom defining Wisdom from the viewpoint of her suitor, Solomon. This metaphoric relationship, of a suitor and his beloved, is found throughout the Sophianic tradition; yet we also find women, for example Jane Leade, who experience Wisdom personified. In the words of the Book of Wisdom itself, Wisdom is "the flawless mirror of the divine active power, and the image of his goodness. She is one, and can do everything; unchanging, she renews all things; age after age she enters holy souls and makes them friends of God and prophets." There is in this definition no preference of men over women—Wisdom is the mirror of divine power, as such befriends holy souls of either sex, and in the end, cannot be termed either female or male, for she is at once beyond and pervades all things "like a fine mist." This is a poetic and beautiful work, and in some respects stands at the headwaters of the entire Sophianic tradition as it emerged during the modern era.

From
The Book of Wisdom

Hear this O kings, take this to heart; learn your lesson, lords of the wide world; listen, you rulers of the many, so proud of your myriad people. The Lord gave you your authority, and your power comes from the Divine. He will examine your actions and your intent. Although his viceroys, you have not been good judges; you do not adhere to the law or walk in the ways of the Most High. Suddenly and terribly will he descend upon you, for judgement comes hard upon those in high places. The little man may find forgiveness, but the powerful will be called strongly to account; for one who is all men's master bends to none, and is not cowed by greatness. Small and great alike are under God equally, but for the powerful is the sternest inquisition. To you who have great power I speak, hoping that you may learn to be wise and not foolish; those who have kept a holy course will be reckoned holy, and those who have learned their lesson will be able to defend themselves. Eagerly hear me and long for my teaching; so you shall learn.

Wisdom shines brightly and fades not; she is quickly discerned by those who love her, and those who seek her find her. She is quick to make herself known to those desiring knowledge of her; he who rises early in search of her will find her seated at his door. Setting one's thought on her is perfect prudence, and being wakeful for her is the short path to peace of mind. She herself ranges in search of those who are worthy of her, and on their daily path she appears to them with compassion, and in all their aims meets them halfway. Wisdom truly begins with the desire to learn, which in fact is love for her; loving her means keeping her laws; and keeping her laws means immortality, and immortality brings one close to God. Desiring Wisdom leads to kingly stature. If you value your thrones and scepters, you rulers of nations, you must honor Wisdom so that you may reign forever.

Who Wisdom is, and how she came into existence, I will tell you; I will keep no secrets from you. From her beginning I will trace out her course, and reveal knowledge of her in the light of day; I will tell the truth. Pale envy will not travel with me, for the spiteful one has no share in wisdom. The wise are the world's salvation, and a prudent king is the anchor of his people. Learn what I teach, and it will be for your good.

I am but mortal like the rest, descended from the first man, made of dust, and in my mother's womb I became flesh in a ten-month's space, compacted in blood from the seed of her husband and the pleasure that is joined with sleep. When I was born, I breathed the common air and was laid on the earth upon which all tread; and the first sound I made, like all the rest, was a cry; they wrapped me and nursed me and cared for me. No king begins life in any other way; all come into life by one path, and by one path go out again.

Thus I prayed, and prudence was given me; I called for help, and the spirit of Wisdom came to me. I valued her above scepter and throne, and held riches as nothing beside her; I saw no precious stone was her equal, because all the gold in the world compared with her is but a sandpile, and silver worth a pile of clay. I loved her more than health and beauty; I preferred her to the light of day, for her radiance never sleeps. So all good things came to me at once with her, and in her hands was wealth past counting; and all was mine to delight in, for all follows where Wisdom leads, and I was ignorant before, that she is the beginning of it all. What I learned with pure aims, I share without grudging, and I do not hoard the wealth that comes from her. She is an inexhaustible treasure for mankind, and those who profit by it are God's friends, commended to him by the gifts they receive from her instruction.

God has given to me to speak wisely, and according to such gifts of Wisdom to think aright. Thus he guides us on the way of Wisdom, and governs the wise. And then are both we ourselves and our speech in his hand, there also all cleverness and art in all works. For he has given me knowledge of all things, so that I know how the world is made, and the power of the elements; of time, its beginning, end, and middle; the alternating seasons, and how the year's seasons change; the stars' cycles; the nature and kinds of wild animals; how the winds storm, and what people have in their minds; the many kinds of plants, and the power of their roots. I know everything that is secret, for I have been taught by she who is the artist of all things, Wisdom.

For in Wisdom is a holy and intelligent spirit, unique, yet

manifold, subtle, free, lucid, pure, clear, harmless, loving the good, eager, beneficent and kind, steady, inerrant, free from care, all-powerful, all-seeing, and all-permeating, through intelligent, pure, and delicate spirits. Wisdom moves more easily than motion itself, pervading all things because she is pure. Like a fine mist she rises from divine power, a pure emanation of the Almighty's glory, and nothing impure can enter her, even stealthily. She is the reflection of everlasting light, the flawless mirror of the divine active power, and the image of his goodness. She is one, and can do everything; unchanging, she renews all things; age after age she enters holy souls and makes them friends of God and prophets, for God accepts only those who make their home with Wisdom. More radiant than the sun, and surpassing every constellation, she excells the light of day; for day turns to night, but no evil can prevail against Wisdom. She spans the world from end to end in power, and orders all things well.

Wisdom have I loved; I sought her when I was young, and longed for her to be my bride, and I fell in love with her beauty. She adds luster to her noble birth because she lives with God, and the Lord of all has accepted her. Hers is the knowledge of God, and she decides what he shall do. If riches are desireable in life, what riches are greater than Wisdom, cause of all things? If prudence is revealed in action, who more than Wisdom is the prudent maker of all that is? If virtue is the object of human affection, the fruits of Wisdom's labor is virtue; temperance, prudence, justice, discipline, these are her teaching, and in human life there is nothing more valuable than these. If one longs for great experience, she knows the past and the future; she understands argument and logic, she can read signs and augurs, and can foresee the outcome of events. So I determined to bring her home to live with me, knowing that she would be my counselor in good times, and my comforter in bad and worrisome times. Through her, I thought, I should win fame in the eyes of people and honor among the elderly, young though I am. When I sit in judgement, I will prove myself acute, and the great will admire me; when I say nothing, they will wait for me to speak; when I speak, they will attend, and though I hold forth, they will put a finger to their lips and listen. Through her I will have immortality, and will leave an immortal memory to those who come after me. I will rule over many

peoples, and nations will be subject to me. Grim tyrants will fear
when they hear of me; among my people I will be a good king,
and on the battlefield will be brave. When I come home, I will rest
with Wisdom, for there is no bitterness in her company, no pain
in life with her, only gladness and joy.

I considered this and realized that in kinship with Wisdom
lies immortality, and in her friendship is pure delight; that in doing her work is unfailing wealth; to be taught in her school gives
understanding, and an honorable name comes from conversing
with her. So I sought some way to win her for my own. As a child
I was born to excellence, and a noble soul was my lot; or rather, I
was noble, and entered into an unblemished body; but I saw there
was no way to gain Wisdom except by God's gift—and it was a
mark of understanding to know from whom that gift must come.
So I asked the Lord, and prayed to him from the depths of my
heart, saying:

God of our fathers, merciful Lord, who made all things by
your Word, and in your Wisdom fashioned man, to be the master
of creation, and steward of the world in holiness and righteousness, and to rule justly with an upright heart, give me Wisdom,
who sits beside your throne, and do not refuse me a place among
your servants. I am your slave, your slave-girl's son, a weak man,
too feeble to understand justice and law; for let a man be perfect
in the eyes of his fellow-men, if the Wisdom that comes from you
is lacking, he will be of no account. You did choose me to be king
of your people, and to judge your sons and daughters; you told
me to build a temple on your sacred mountain, and an altar in the
city your dwelling place, a copy of the sacred tabernacle prepared
by you from eternity. And with you is Wisdom, familiar with your
works, and present at the making of the world by you, who knows
what is acceptable to you and in line with your commandments.
Send her forth from the holy heavens, and from your glorious
throne bid her come down, so that she may labor at my side and
I may learn what pleases you. For she knows and understands
all, and will guide me well in all I do, and guard me in her glory.
So shall my life's work be acceptable, I shall judge your people
justly, and be worthy of my father's throne. How can any man
learn God's plan? How can he perceive the Lord's will? The reasoning of men is feeble, and our plans fallible; for a perishable

body weighs down the soul, and its clay burdens the mind full of thoughts. With difficulty we guess even at things on earth, and struggle to find out what lies at our feet; and who has traced what is in heaven? Who learned your purposes, unless you gave him Wisdom and sent your holy spirit down from heaven? Thus it was that those on earth were set upon the right path, and were taught what pleases you; thus were they preserved by Wisdom.

II

Robert Ayshford

About *Aurora Sapientiæ*, this rare early English theosophic work and its author, little is known. I discovered it in the collection of Elias Ashmole in the Bodleian Library of Oxford University, bound next to a treatise on meteorology, and knew immediately that it represented a real find. *Aurora Sapientiæ*, or *The Dawn of Wisdom*, represents the earliest theosophic work in Britain, long predating the emergence of the first major theosophic circle around Dr. John Pordage in the 1650's. Dated 1629, this work has no certain attribution, but unquestionably reveals the presence of a theosophic circle in 1620's England devoted to spiritual practice.

Was *Aurora Sapientiæ* written by Robert Ayshford? This we cannot say for certain. But there is some evidence, for after the work itself are appended some "Letters to some good friends," and these seven letters are addressed "To George J." and others, whose surnames are not set down [pp. 41-50]. The last is subscribed "Your servant and brother P. knowen in the grace of God." A fragment of an original letter, written by the same neat hand as this manuscript, has been accidentally preserved between the leaves (and is now fixed on one of the two blank leaves following p. 52), having this subscription—"Youre truly loving friend Ro: Ayshford [dated at] Ayshford the 27 of Aprill 1629." An Ashmolean library cataloguer dryly notes that "This probably was the name of the pretended prophet who was the author of these fanatical compositions."

Of course, there is some discrepancy here. For instance, it does seem strange that the last letter is signed "your servant and brother P.," since if the author were Ayshford, one would think it ought to have his initials. And indeed, Ayshford may have been the copyist. On the other hand, it is not at all uncommon in theosophic history for theosophers to take Latin-based or Hebrew-based names, by which they are known among their brethren. Hence, to give a single instance, Richard Roach (around the turn of the eighteenth century) was called "Onesimus" by his spiritual mentor, Jane Leade. Thus it is equally possible that Ayshford was or was not the author, and final identification is not of immense importance.

Far more important is the nature of the treatise, which shows without any doubt that there was a theosophic circle in England far earlier than we could have guessed, perhaps even during the time that Jacob Böhme (1575-1624), the founder of Christian theosophy, was still alive. What is more, *Aurora* shows no direct references to Böhme, yet has a great deal in common with Böhme's works. Here too, we have a choice. It may be that in *Aurora* we have an extremely early English offshoot of German theosophy; or it may be that we have an original English theosophy independently emerging at around the same time as German theosophy, using similar language. But in either case, it is clear that we have here an authoritative spiritual teacher who, in this work, is elaborating with economy and clarity his own spiritual understanding. Here I offer the first English publication of the beginning of this extremely rare early theosophic work dedicated to the pursuit and realization of Wisdom.

Aurora Sapientiæ

that is to saie
The Daiebreak of Wisdome

Of the three Principles and beginning
of all in the mysterie of wisdome
in which the ground and key of all
wisdome is laid open, directing to
the true understanding of God,
of Man, and of the whole world,
in a new and true triune
wisdome Physisophie, Theologie,
and Theosophie.
tending to the Honour of God, Revelation
of the true wisdome and to the service
of the Sixt Church att Philadelphia
By
Her Minister called by the Grace of
God to beare witness of God and
of Jesus Christ

                    Printed in the yeare 1629

When that great Apostle speaketh of the perfect Wisdom forasmuch as she is hidden in mysteries, he withall declareth that God before the Creation of the World hath ordained her for our Glorie, and that the Chief Rulers and Wisemen of this world knowe nothing at all of her. For God, even from the beginning of the world till this time hath alwaies revealed this wisdom, which hath been hitherto concealed in her mysteries, only to his deare friends, to whom he laieth open his Covenant and his Mysteries. Whence it is come to pass, that this Wisdom never is become Common, but rather hath still remained covered, and hidden from the human eies of all living men. Yea the wise men of God have themselves also concealed her, that the Perles might not come to the Swine, and that which is Holy might not bee cast before the Dogs, so that the Wise of this World knowe nothing att all of her. Yet this Wisdom is such a treasure that she goeth farre beyond Riches, and beyond a faire and sound bodie, yea beyond all things. Nothing is to compare with her. Wherefore all the glorie of this World is to be accounted as dust and sand being of no account in comparison of this Excellent Knowledge of Jesus Christ and of this Mysterie. This wisdome of which we speake hath been sealed up in her Booke, and the waie thereto hath been kept until this last appointed time, even from the times of the Holy Patriarchs, Prophets, and Apostles, and her Dore hath been shut.

But now is this acceptable Time come to us who are the Last of all, that wee might bee the first, so that hee who is Holie, and True, hath given an open Dore to his Church by the Key of David, which is the Spirit in the Mysterie of the concealed wisdom of God. I saie, a Dore To open that no bodie can shut it, by which we enter into the Understanding of all Wisdome, which is in Heaven and on Earth, whereby not only wee receave the Key of Heaven, but also the Key of the Bottomeless Gulfe, by which we put Darkness to shame, and are able to bind Satan, take him prisoner, and leade him up, all which is done by the Name of God, by the Name of the New Jerusalem, being the Cittie of our God, and by the new Name of the Lord, according to the Witnesse of Jesus Christ that great God, which no bodie knoweth, but onlie hee who hath the Spirit of Prophecie, and upon whom the New Name is written with the Godlie Letters of the Word of Life. Seeing then the Daie of Revelation of Salvation is come, let us enter the Dore which is opened unto us. For it is such a Daie that even the Holie Apostle himself desired to see it, and yet he was not suffered to see it, to wit the Daie of the Revelation of the Sonne of Man. But the Lord hath so farre graced us who are the last of all, that we maie receive the pennie with the first, so that the others, or the first, when they shall come, will grudge at it. Let us therefore consider verie well this Word of the Lord, and laie up in our hearts the Goodness of the master of the House, to whom it hath pleased in his greatness that the Last should bee the First, and the First the Last, to the end that wee in pondering it well and acknowledge it rightly, may the more thank him for it. To the end then that your hearts be knitted together in Love, to a perfect Knowledge of God and of Christ, and that ye maie be refreshed at this time, I have according to the Grace which hath been given to mee, by Him who is the Key of David, in the Name of him who is the Holie and True, undertaken to declare the Daie of the Lord by this Daiebreak which Daie we ought to rejoyce, and sing a joyfull Hallelujah and all Creatures with us, yea all the Saints and Angels of God. Praised be he who is, and who was, and who is to come, and blessed be he who cometh in the Name of the Lord. Hallelujah.

Chapter I

Of the Threefold Book of Wisdome

The Wisdome crieth and speaketh in this manner: Go to, All ye that are drie, come hither for water, and though yee have no money come hither, buy and eat. Come hither and buy without money and for nothing, both wine and mick. Hearken diligently at me, and eat that which is good, so shall your Soule become fat in pleasure. But whosoever hath not denied and forsaken himself, with all that is his owne, yea his proper will, he cannot be my disciple. Furthermore, we know that whosoever desireth to learne the Wisdom, hee must first knowe her Mysteries, as in which she witnesseth of herself and by which she is known, that she is triune in every witness of God which is in Heaven and on Earth, according to which also every thing subsisteth in weight, number, and measure, and is a true, holie, and certain Harmonie. According to this Mysterie of Wisdom hath the Spirit of Wisdom propounded unto us threefold Bookes, as in which he hath declared his Wisdom.

The first Booke is that huge Book of the whole World, out of which we can learne and studie our onelie true and certain physiosophia, or Wisdom of Nature by her own Light. By the Letters Word and Witness of this Wisdom we are directed towards God, to wit by all that which is visible.

The other Book is the Booke of the Holie Scripture, out of which we maie learne the onlie true and saving Theologie and Wisdom, tending to salvation. Which also leadeth us to God by a more plain speech.

But the third Book is Man, who is both the sealed and the open Book, whereby we maie learne to understand the theosophia, the secret and hidden wisdome of the Mysterie of God the Father, and of Christ, and of his Church. The beginning and onlie centre of these three Books is that onely right and most holie book that Word, which was in the beginning, of which these three books aforesaid do jointlie beare record, to wit every one in his own Wisdom, in his own Letters and in his own Witness, in a verie fine Harmonie, according to which these three are all one and conspire together, and withall the onlie whole and great Librarie of us all wherewith wee who are the Scholars of the true Wisdome ought to be contented. But no bodie can read and studie in these three Bookes, who hath not received the same spirit, who hath written and made them, and testified himself of the said three Books, which Spirit teacheth his children and Scholars by his unction so that they need not any Master endowed with the name Learning. But God bestoweth this spirit on them, who praie him daie and night for him with penitent, obedient, and faithfull hearts with a humble Spirit and holie Hands. It is only this Spirit of Wisdom, who openeth unto us the meaning and mysterie of everie Booke, who teacheth and instructeth us. For the Spirit of God doth search all things, even the verie depths of God, whereby God hath revealed unto us such things, as no fleshlie Eie hath seen, the Eare hath heard, and which are not entered into any man's heart, to wit a Glorie which surpasseth and which God hath prepared for them who love him. These three Books of Wisdome have been in the centre even from the beginning of the world till this time, sealed up from them which are indued with human Learning and from the Wise of this World, and no bodie can open this Book which is sealed up, much less looke or read in it, but onlie the Lord, and those which are killed with him, and have gotten the victorie over the Beast, which have the Spirit of Prophecie, which is the witness of God, Christ, and the Key of David. But now is the time come, in which these Bookes, who have been sealed up hitherto, are opened, before the Eies of the whole Firmament, so that all Flesh together with one another may see, acknowledge and understand that the Mouth of the Lord speaks. Hitherto hath the Lamb been murdered, Christ extirpated, his Holieness wounded, and his witness hath been trodden under feet by divers false Prophets, Apostles, and Jewes out of the Schools of Satan, in that great Abomination of Desolation, by which the Apostasie from Faith in her Antichrist hath crucifed Christ with the three Languages of the confused Babel of the Sectaries, and hath killed his two witneses. Now shall the Son of Man be exalted againe in an other Language, and in the German Tongue, by Elect and pure Lips to whom is [revealed?] the mouth of the Lord and the learned tongues of the Seven Spirits of God, which are to go forth into all Lands. But this the Axiome of Wisdom of her three Bookes: Whosever can truelie read and understand one Booke in his witness, he can understand the other: for they be all so rich and perfect that in one of them you maie also find the Witnesses of all the others.

Chapter II
Of the Three Principles and the Beginning of All Things

The Mysterie of Wisdom, as it is the Center of all Wisdom, sets before us three Principles, with which and by which we maie consider, dissect, divide, and discern all things according to the Beginning and End of their Subsistence. These three Principles now in their ordination and order stand in this manner: to wit 1. Generalia, as the Nature and the Element 2. Specialia, as the Spirit, the Wind, and the Water. 3. Particularia as Bodie, Life, and Spirit. The one center of these three Principles are these three to wit, Light and Love. All things proceed out of these Principles and by them have all things been made, all things do subsist, are known and declared in them, and with their whole summe are comprehended in their Harmonie. Also one Principle is compared to another, and they are reduced one into another according to the Harmonie, so that where they cease, they begin anew, the one proceedeth out of the other, is known, declared, and justified out and with the others and by the others. The Center of these Principles is so perfect that also according to them we maie consider and know God himselfe. For God is a Light. He is that Life, He is Bodie. According to these Principles hath God also his owne Nature and his owne Elements. He is a spirit who hath his proper Wind and Water, yea hee is himself the Spring of Living Water. He is also a corporeal Word, and hath in himself all Principles, which even hee is himself and withall All in All. This is that Principium Principiorum to wit that corporeal Word out of himself, with and by himselfe subsisting in himself, and Essence of all Essences, the onlie HAIAH IHEIE and the JEHOVAH, who is himself All in All, the Heavenlie Juda Jesse and David, the most highest Adam who is the First and the Last, the Begining and the End, hee who is and who was and who is to come, Jesus Christ, yesterdaie, and todaie, and forever the true Witness, the Beginning of Essence in God, the onelie Highbeloved for ever, Amen. This is that Word which was from the Beginning and in the Beginning, yea the Beginning himself, and yet not such a word which was without Essence, without Bodie, and without Substance. But there is such a Corporeitie in his Flesh that the whole Fulness of Divinitie dwelleth corporallie in it. Of which all Flesh witnesseth, that is to saie, all which hath been made and created in Heaven and on Earth both visible and invisible. This Word is known, witnessed, and justified with, by, out, and in his proper Witness, Names, and Revelation, of the most holie three Witnesses in Heaven, God the Father, the Word, and the Holie Ghost according to the Witness of the revealed onlie visible and corporeal Person of God, in such a Revelation in which Christ Jesus is known, that hee himselfe is the Corporeall, Substantiall and onlie God Father Word and Holie vivifying Ghost, without which no God, Father, Word, and Holie Ghost is nor can bee. For he is even himselfe the personall, visible, substantial, and corporeal Father, the Father of Eternitie, and the Beginning of Essence in God. He is himself that Corporeall Word, the vivifying Ghost, yea the highest Adam, EXATOS ADAM, Summus, Primus, et Ultimus, and the onlie Man, who is the Lord of Heaven, which also is All in All.

Hee is God, and also a Son of God, Hee is a Child and Son and yet withall the Father of Eternitie. He is the Essence and also the Image of God, a visible Image of the invisible God. He is the onlie Man and also the Son of Man which is in Heaven, and to shut up in a few words, he is All in All, according to the Witness Names, Revelation, Essence, Image, Subsistence, and Person of God. According to the likeness of this Image hath the Earthlie man been made. A wonderfull Amen: to wit, both the Beginning and the End, the first and the last, a pretious Mysterie. Therefore is this the Axiome of Wisdom, to wit: Whosoever knoweth rightlie according to the Mysterie of Wisdom the Earthlie Adam and man, and his Eva and Wife, hee knows also the Heavenlie: For the Earthlie hath been made and created according to the likeness of the Image of the Heavenlie, of which the Earthlie is an Image.

Chapter III
Of the Threefold World in the Mysterie of Wisdom

The three Generall Principles are distinguished according to the Mysterie of Wisdom one from another forasmuch as every one of them has his owne proper World, and that with a verie great difference. As God hath first his owne World whose Center is Christ, who is Melchizadech, and is justifie[ably] called Wonderfull. Therefore seeing he himself in all this Mysterie is ineffable, unless he declare himselfe. And indeed the Word is the right Witness of God, yea even God himself. Hee is without Father without Mother, and without Kindred, hath neither Beginning nor End of his daies, and he is himself the Father of Eternitiem from him proceed all God's Children, a Blessed Generation and a Royall Priesthood, by him were all things created, and he is also himself the firstborne of all Creatures. And seeing he himself is the onlie God, there is trulie no other difference between the Father and the Sonne, between God and his Sonne, between the Word and Christ, but only according to the Witness. The Father testifies of the Sone, and the Sonne of the Father, when yet no bodie knows but the Sonne, and to whom the Sonne will declare him. God also is distinguished according to the Names and Revelation, although there is one onlie Witnesse of God, to wit the Word, which no bodie knows but hee who has the spirit of Prophecie, which is the

Witness of Christ, and which Name no bodie knoweth but hee who hath received it, and upon whom it hath been written and which no bodie knoweth but hee who hath seen it and received the Revelation of Jesus Christ. Now as there is one onlie God, and yet three Witnesses for the Revelation's sake, so is there one onlie Witness of God in a threefold Revelation, forasmuch as it witnesseth of the onlie God, who is called Father, Sonne, and Holy Ghost, in the only Corporeal and visible Person of God, who is called Jesus Christ the only God and onlie Angel and the onlie Man, who is Alpha and Omega. The Name and Revelation of this Witness is wonderfull in his Mysterie, and hath been concealed from the beginning of the World till the Daie of the Revelation of the Sonne of Man. So the Godlie World consisteth now onlie in Chirst who is before all which is in Heaven and on Earth, of whom all Flesh beareth witness, that the Word in his Flesh is the Beginning of Essence in God, an Essence before all Essences, an IS before all which is an Image of the invisible God, which is become visible in the Flesh, whose coming forth is from the Beginning of the Daies of Eternitie till this time. O what a Depth of Wisdom, what a pretious witness of the Truth and costlie Word of Secrecie!

After the first Principle and his World followeth now also the other Principle which is the Nature with her world, to wit the Paradisal, the Angelical and Middle World, which according to his Situation lieth towards the Daibreak, that is to say, where meere Light is, above the Firmament and upper waters, next to the Godly World and the forecourt of it, which is the Light, wherein God dwelleth. This Paradise is the Garden which God hath planted before this visible World was, of which Solomon singeth in his Song of Songs, wherein all kind of fruits are and the Tree of Life in the middle of the Garden. This is that holie Mountain of the Lord, upon which the sonne of man shall bee manifested and exalted, where the Lambe and the Sonne of the King as also the Man shall keepe his supper and Great Feast upon which holie Mountain wee shall rise again from the dead, and shall bee carried to meet the Lord in the Aire, when Hee is to come and shall bee alwaies with the Lord, with all them which shall bee partakers of the First Resurrection, Transmutation and Puritie of the Heavenlie Vocation, in the Kingdom of God, in which manie shall sitt at the Table with Abraham, Isaac, and Jacob, but the Heretical Dogs, witches, Harlots, Murderers, Idolaters, Liars, and Evildoers who slander, denie and reject the Sabbath of the Lord in his thousand years, and will not come to his Supper, they must stay without, for the Lord will not knowe them, because they will not knowe him. Therefore the Gospel shall be taken away from the Heathens and unchristians, and shall bee given to the poore, cripple, lame, and blinde Jewes. In this Paradise are Moses, Enoch, Elias, and the Saints who went out of their graves after the Resurrection of Christ. And this is the Heaven the bosome of Abraham, and the Chamber in which the soules of the Just are carried according to that which the Lord speaketh to the thief: this daie thou shalt be with me in Paradise. This is the New World which hath been hitherto concealed.

The third Principle followeth now with his world [this Earthlie World], and this is the Axiome of Wisdom: Whosoever knoweth rightlie and according to the Mysterie of Wisdom the one World, he knoweth also the other, but whosever denieth the one, he denieth also the other, for the Mysterie of Wisdom can never be broken in his Witness. Posito ergo uno ponuntur omnia: Sublato uno, Tolluntur omnia.

III

Jacob Böhme

The most influential or seminal of the theosophic writers was Jacob Böhme (1575-1624), who is certainly also the most well known to many readers, perhaps as the "illuminated cobbler" from Görlitz, a town (symbolically enough) on the border between Eastern and Western Europe. Böhme's spiritual illumination came after a period of despondency, and it resulted in his first book, *Morgenröte im Aufgang, oder Aurora*, written in 1612, and initially only circulated among friends. Although Böhme's extraordinary work provoked extreme wrath in a rather hidebound local Lutheran minister named Gregor Richter, and in fact Böhme was forbidden to write anything further, he eventually developed quite a circle of followers, who asked him for advice, and thus he came to write many more treatises.[15]

Relatively late in his life, Böhme produced a corpus of work that was to inspire virtually the whole of subsequent theosophy, so much so that many later theosophers held that their spiritual lives really began only with their discovery of Böhme's vast body of writings, and even today scientists, philosophers, and literati find inspiration there. In 1618 Böhme began *The Three Principles of the Divine Being*, and between 1619 and his death in 1624, he completed an amazing number of treatises and assorted other manuscripts and letters, including *Forty Questions on the Soul*, *The Signature of All Things*, and the massive *Mysterium Magnum*, a commentary on Genesis, as well as numerous other works, some of which were only published by Werner Buddecke in the mid twentieth century.

It is not possible to sketch here Böhme's writings, which require each reader to work with them individually over an extended period in order to reveal themselves, and because they are multifaceted and have a specialized Latin-based vocabulary rich in neologisms, each reader will see different aspects of Böhme's insights.[16] But we can say that Böhme's writings are based in a fusion of alchemical, Paracelsian, and Hermetic expressions and concepts with what we may call high German mysticism, so that Böhme's works represent a uniquely modern revelation of virtually inexhaustible depth and range. Böhme insists throughout his writings on the necessity that his readers directly experience for themselves the truth of which he writes, and this insistence is at the very heart not only of Böhme's books, but of modern theosophy as a whole, which has as its center and fount of inspiration the *wiedergeburt*, or metanoia, the "turning about in the deepest seat of consciousness," spiritual awakening.

Böhme's writings tend toward a circuitous or even spiralling structure, so that one finds the subject of Sophia or Virgin Wisdom in numerous places, but not as the sole subject of a treatise. The selections that follow come first from Böhme's *The Three Principles of the Divine Being*, and second from his very late book *Christosophia, or The Way to Christ*.[17] The first selections discuss the nature of the Virgin, and the second, beginning with the "Warning to the Reader," focus on how we "woo" and "wed" the Virgin. It is no exaggeration to say that Böhme's writings represent the fountainhead or inspiration of virtually all subsequent theosophy, and the following excerpts are particularly clear and succinct.

On the Virgin Wisdom

I now live under the Spirit of this World in my flesh, and my flesh serves the Spirit of this World, and my heart serves God: My flesh is generated in this world, and has its governance from the stars and elements, which dwell in it, and are the master of the outward life; and my heart is regenerated in God and loves God. And although I cannot comprehend and hold the Virgin (because my mind falls into sins) yet the Spirit of this World shall not always hold the mind captive.

For the Virgin has promised not to leave me in misery, but will come to help me in the Son of the Virgin. I must only hold to him again, and he will bring me again into paradise. I will go forth through thistles and thorns as well as I can until I find my native land again, from whence my soul has wandered, and where my dear Virgin dwells. I rely upon her faithful promise—when she appeared to me—that she would turn all my mourning into great joy. And when I laid upon the mountain toward the north, so that all the trees fell upon me, and all the storms and winds beat upon me, and the Antichrist opened his jaws to devour me, then she came and comforted me, and married herself to me.

Therefore I am only more cheerful, and care not for him; he dominates me no further than over the house of sin, whose master he is; he may take that quite away, and so I shall come into my native land. Yet he is not absolutely Lord over it; he is but God's ape, for as an ape (when its belly is full) prances and imitates all kinds of tricks to make itself sport, and would like to seem the finest, nimblest beast possible, so also does he. His power depends on the great tree of this world, and a storm of wind can blow it away....

Now see the lily, noble mind, full of anguish and afflictions of this world; behold, the holy Trinity has an eternal will in itself, and the will is the desiring, and the desiring is the eternal essences, wherein stands the sharpness (the *Fiat*) which goes forth out of the heart and the mouth of God by the Holy Spirit. And the will that is gone forth out of the spirit is the divine virtue, which comprehends the will and holds it, and the *Fiat* creates it [the virtue] so that in it, as in God, are all essences, and thus the blossom of the light in it may arise and blossom out of the heart of God. Yet this is not God, but the chaste Virgin of the eternal Wisdom and understanding, of whom I often write in this book.

Now the Virgin is present before God and inclines herself to the spirit from which the virtue proceeds, out of which she (the chaste Virgin) is; this is God's Companion to the honor and joy of God; she appears or discovers herself in the wonders of God. In the discovery, she becomes longing after the wonders in the eternal Wisdom, which yet is herself, and thus she longs in herself, and her longing is the eternal essences, which attract the holy virtue to her, and the *Fiat* creates them, so that they become a Substance; and she is a Virgin, and never generates anything, neither takes anything into her; her inclination stands in the Holy Spirit, who goes forth from God and attracts nothing to him, but moves before God, and is the Blossom [Branch] of the growth.

And so the Virgin has no will to conceive or be impregnated with anything; her will is only to open the wonders of God; and therefore she is in the will in the wonders, to discover the wonders in the eternal essences; and that virginal will creates the sour *Fiat* in the essences, so that it becomes a substance, and stands eternally before God, wherein the eternal wonders of the Virgin

Wisdom of God are revealed.

And this substance is the eternal element wherein all essences stand open in the divine virtue, and are visible; and in this the fair and chaste Virgin of divine Wisdom always discovers herself according to the number of infinity, out of the many thousand thousands without end or number. And in this discovering there go forth out of the eternal element colors, arts, virtues, and the fruits of the lily of God; at which the deity continually rejoices itself in the Virgin of the Wisdom; and that joy goes forth out of the eternal essences, and is called paradise, in regard of the sharpness of the generating of the pleasant fruit of the lily in *infinitum*. There the essences of the lily spring up in wonders, in many thousand thousands without number, of which you have a similitude in the blossoming earth.

Beloved heart, behold, consider that this now is God and his heavenly kingdom, the eternal element, and paradise, and it stands thus in the eternal original from eternity to eternity. Now what joy, delight, and pleasantness is therein, I have no pen that can describe it, nor can I express it. For the earthly tongue is too insufficient to express it; all that men say of it is dross compared to gold, and much more inferior. Although the Virgin brings it into the mind, yet all is too dark and cold in the whole man, so that he cannot express so much as one spark or glimpse thereof sufficiently. We will defer it till we come to the breast of the Virgin; we have here only given a brief hint, so that the author of this book may be understood. For we are but a very little drop out of the fountain of the Wisdom of God; and we speak as a little sparkle or glimpse, still high enough for our earthly understanding and for our weak knowledge here upon earth. For in this life we have no need of any higher knowledge of the eternal substance [Essence]. Indeed, if we but barely speak of what has been from eternity, that is enough.

Warning to the Reader

Dear reader, because I am well-meaning, I will not hide from you what has earnestly been shown me: but if you are still in the vanity of the flesh and are not earnestly resolved on the way to the new birth, willing to become another man, then leave these words in your prayers unsaid or they will become God's judgement in you. You should not misuse the holy name of God. Be truly warned that these words belong to the thirsty soul, and if it is right earnest, it will experience what they are.

Guidance to Holy Sophia

How the Soul Should Meet Its Beloved When the Lover Knocks in the *Centrum* in the Soul's Locked Room.

Beloved soul, you must be earnest, without backsliding. You will gain the love of a kiss of the noble Sophia in the holy name Jesus, because she stands before the soul's door and knocks and warns the sinner of Godless ways. So if he desires her love, she is willing, and kisses him with a ray of her sweet love, through which the heart experiences joy. But she does not at once enter into the marriage-bed with the soul—that is, she does not suddenly awaken the corrupt heavenly image that was lost in paradise. It is dangerous for man, because since Adam and Lucifer fell, so this might happen again, because man is strongly bound in vanity.

It must be a true bond in your pledge, if she should crown you. You must first be tested for your sincerity. She takes her ray of love from you and sees whether you will stay true. She lets you cry, and does not answer you with a glimpse of her love. Because should she crown you, you must have been tested: you must taste the sour beer that you have poured into yourself with your abominations. You must first come before the gates of hell and win your victory, and her love in power against the devil's attack, before she will again look at you.

Christ was tempted in the wilderness. If you wish to be like him, you must go through his whole process, from his incarnation to his journey to heaven. Although you cannot do what he did, you must nonetheless wholly go into his process, and the soul's vanity must utterly die in his process. Because the Virgin Sophia weds herself with the soul only in this quality that blossoms in the soul through Christ's death as a new growth that stands in heaven. The earthly body in this time cannot grasp this because it must first die to vanity. But the heavenly image, which was corrupted in Adam, as the true woman's seed—wherein God became man, and his living seed leads to the heavenly being— the heavenly image grasps the true pearl in the way that it came to pass with Mary, in the completion of this bond.

Therefore watch what you do. If you say something, do it, for she wishes to crown you more than you wish for it yourself. But you must stand fast when the tempter comes to you with the world's lust, beauty, and glory, you must throw these from your heart and say: I should be a servant in Christ's vineyard, and not a master, for all that I have is to be used as a servant of God, and I should do with it what the Word teaches. My heart should be like a child in the dust, and I humble.

In whatever position you hold, you must above all be humble, otherwise you will not reach marriage with her, although true humility is first born in marriage to her. But your free will of the soul must stand as a knight; because if the devil cannot conquer the vanity of the soul, [if it won't bite at this lure] then he comes with unworthiness and the whole registry of sins. Then you must war.

You must place Christ's merits above all, for otherwise the creature can not conquer the devil, because here it goes dreadfully with many, whose outward reason thinks "this man is senseless and possessed by the devil." Thus the devil defends himself fiercely in many, because he has a great robber's castle in them, but when he weakens, he must leave his robber's castle. Here truly begins the war, for heaven and hell struggle with one another.

Now if here the soul remains firm and conquers the devil in all his attacks, and ignores all temporal things and wishes the love of the noble Sophia, then the precious knight's crown will be given as a sign of victory. Then the Virgin Sophia will step forth to the soul, revealed in the precious name Jesus with Christ the serpent-treader, as annointed of God. She kisses the soul with her sweetest love in the essence, wholly inwardly, and presses love in its desire as a victory sign. And here Adam's heavenly part is resurrected from death in Christ. Upon this I cannot write; there is no pen in this world that could; for this is the marriage of the Lamb, there the noble pearl is strewn, certainly with great triumph, though it is at first but small as a mustard seed, as Christ said.

When this wedding is complete, the soul should now see what it has promised the Virgin, that the little pearl-tree should grow and flourish; for the devil will soon come with his stormy weather, with godless men, who will mock in scorn and cry out that it is madness. There now must one walk in Christ's process under his cross. Here now for the first time he will know by demonstration what it means when we call ourselves Christians. For here he must allow himself to be called a fool and a godless man, yea, even his best friends, who formerly praised his fleshly lust, will now be his enemies, and even if they do not know why, they hate him. Thus Christ covers his bride under his cross, so that she will not be recognized in this world. Also the devil does this, so that these children of the world remain hidden, and thus more such branches will not grow in the garden he presumes is his. This information I write for the reader with a Christian heart, so that if such things should also happen to him, he knows what to do.

IV

Thomas Bromley

Among those who joined with Dr. John Pordage, the most influential English theosopher, early in the 1650s, were Edmund Brice (dates uncertain) and Thomas Bromley (1629-1691), originally fellows of the All Souls' College at Oxford, who left the academic life for one of spiritual reclusion in Pordage's circle. Of these two, Thomas Bromley was the more important as an author, mainly for his treatise entitled *The Way to the Sabbath of Rest*, which reached a relatively wide audience and was translated into several languages. Bromley's treatise is unique for its frank discussion of spiritual transmutation, and particularly for his willingness to discuss paranormal phenomena as a natural part of a spiritual community's practice.

We know something of Bromley's life mainly from a biography published along with the 1692 edition of *The Way to the Sabbath of Rest*, where we learn that Bromley was born to a noble family in Worcester, attended good schools, and finally became a fellow at All Souls' College, but eventually went to live in the Pordages' house. The leading member of this theosophic circle after Pordage and his wife, Bromley saw his primary work as that of a spiritual guide for others, and this aspect of his work accounts in part for its popularity, for it reflects the very center of the entire Sophianic tradition.

Because of its practical nature, I include part of *The Way to the Sabbath of Rest* here even before the works of Pordage himself, in the hope that it makes a useful introduction to Sophianic spirituality. Here we find the theosophic spiritual path as practiced in the theosophic circle around Pordage and Bromley, outlined in succinct and sometimes startling form. It is perhaps surprising to find Bromley suggesting a kind of clairvoyant sympathy among those who follow this path of illumination together, but he discusses such topics as matter-of-factly as if he were describing the weather. *The Way to the Sabbath of Rest* was a very popular book among those interested in theosophy, and went through a number of editions in England and in America, probably because of its succinctness and clarity.

The Way to the Sabbath of Rest, or the Soul's Progress in the Work of the New Birth
(London: 1678 / Germantown, C. Sower ed., 1759)

I have written this experimental Discourse of the New Birth, not for the Wise and Rich, who think they see, and enjoy enough, but for the Poor in Spirit, who enquiring the Way to Zion, are sensible of their Defects, and breath after a Supply. Let none then come with Prejudice; for that will give a false Tincture to the Eye of the Mind, and prevent the sight of Truth, by a Prepossession that 'tis Error. If any have attained, and enjoy as much, or more than is here expressed, let them bless God for his Goodness, both to themselves and me: If not, let them not be ashamed to learn and practise more than they have already; for, teach a wise Man, and he will be yet wiser. Prov. 9.9 And 'tis no diminishing of Esteem, to grow in true Knowledge, or Disparagement of Age, to gain Wisdom from those that are young; because true Wisdom is the Gift of God, who is no Respecter of Persons, bestowing his Gifts on whom he pleaseth. But think not, I have here chalked out a Way for every one to walk in; for I have only wrote my own Experience: And I know there may be great Variety in Gods Works upon Souls, so that none are to be confined to one exact Path; though all are to be informed, that we must turn, and become as little Children, and be wholly dead with Christ, before we can be as the Angels in the Resurrection, delighting our selves in the Light and Life of Eternity: Therefore the perfect Death should be aimed at by all; for nothing less can fit us for Glory: For, how can any Imperfection enter there, where is nothing but Perfection? or any Thing of Darkness dwell with him, who is Light, and in whom there is no Darkness at all? 'Tis true: Many (from mistaking that Principle, of Gods being the Root of all Things) have endeavoured to reconcile Light and Darkness, Good and Evil, Flesh and Spirit, Christ and Belial; and so to laugh all Mortification and Self-denial out of the Church. But alas! What have the Practices and Notions of Such ended in, but Shame and Confusions of Face? For they have sowed to the Wind, and reaped the Whirl-wind, grasped at an imaginary Heaven and Perfection; but have fallen like Lucifer into Hell and palpable Darkness, having like foolish Virgins spent their Oyl, and received Poyson in their Lamps, and so made themselves unfit to meet and entertain the Bridegroom. Others there are, who come forth in such outward Strictness and Severity, as they are ready to judge all that are not in their peculiar Mode and Form; and so refuse Communion with Some, who have attained much further in the true Death and Resurrection [and are more acquainted with the Renewal of Gods Image, and the State of Restoration] than themselves. And there by many others, who though not owning the first Sort, and much disgusting the last, yet give themselves too much to earthly Indulgements, under the Notion of Christian Liberty, and so make no real Progress in the Change of their Souls. Some of which are cheated with false Notions of their being in Christ; and others of them with sublime Apprehensions of false imaginary Deaths and Ways of Self-denial, which they much feed upon, instead of that Death and Cross, which should work their Spirits and Natures out of Flesh into the true spiritual divine Image. There are another Sort, who are too much offended at Forms, and all usual Ways of enjoying and speaking of God, decrying them as Cheats and empty Things, though they be used never so spiritually and advantageously to those that appear in them; which is a great Mistake, flowing from Ignorance and the Want of a clear Sight, which could not so confine the great and infinite Jehovah within the Limits of no Forms, and exclude him from appearing and working in and through Forms; being it is at his own Pleasure, to shew himself how, and in what he pleaseth. But lastly, a great Part of those that profess Religion, are such who rest too much upon the first Work of Regeneration, and too much eye their first Change, afterward running in a Circle of Duties and Performances, without making that Progress and Growth towards Perfection, which the frequent Exhortations and Examples of the holy Scriptures call and incite us to. Now the Work of Regeneration, renewing both the Will and Understanding, will bring those who persever in it, to a clear Sight of the forementioned Mistakes; by which they will be able to discern betwixt Light and Darkness, (Chaff and Wheat) and come to own the good Seed in all, and endeavour by walking according to the royal Law of Love and Charity, to cherish it. Now this Law of Love is the Rule of Perfection, being the Scope and End of a Christians Progress, a true Conformity to which makes us like God, who is Love, and delights to impress his own eternal Character of Love upon his Children, who are nearer to, or farther from Perfection, as they partake more or less of this essential Love, which is the Spirit and Life of Christianity; without which all Duties and Observances are but as sounding Brass, and perishing Shadows: In which all have their Worth and Use. From the Dictates and Impulses of this Law, I have written this small Discourse, as believing it may be instrumental to undeceive Many, who are wandering in the Labyrinths of Error, yet seek the true Way; and to confirm, strengthen, and direct Others, who are making their Way through the Cross to the Crown of Life. And truly this Subject is of great Concernment to all, because all are capable of the New-Birth; and none without it can ever be happy. To mistake this Work, is very dangerous, because it is the Passage to eternal Rest. The highest heaven is situate in the large Plains of Eternity; yet the Way to it is very narrow: At the Entrance the sharp Sword of Circumcision is placed; on the left Hand there's a Gulf of Fire, on the right Hand a deep Water; at the End there stands a Cherubin with a flaming Sword, whose Office is to cut off the Reliques of all Corruption from the Soul; so that the least Grain of Selfishness or Flesh cannot enter into the Kingdom of Heaven....

We are strictly to watch over the Phantasie, which may easily err in the particular [be drawn to pleasant Images].... For...by such Working of Imagination, we come to slacken the Exercise of the Cross, both upon Imagination it self, which is continually to be restrained, and as much as possible reduced in Subjection to the illuminated Understanding, and also upon the Relicks of the old Man in any other Faculty.

Seeing there may be so much Danger indulging Imagination, even in these pure Objects, we shall find it very requisite, oft to cease from all Imagination, and to act no Thought upon any thing in the Heights above, or the Depths below. I say no thought: Thoughts being but Images, which reach not the Essence of spiritual Objects. But this Practice excludes not that general, constant, intellectual Sight and Apprehension of God, which the Soul, (thus far arrived) enjoys. Therefore I speak not here to those who have not attained a continual, habitual Apprehension of the divine Presence; for if they should strive to cease from their good thoughts, they might fall into a Kind of Stupidity, far worse. But I here give

Directions to those who having attained constant habitual Communion with God, press after Perfection.

And certainly there is no better Way than from the Annihilation of all thoughts, and the Retiring from the Phantasie into the silent Mind, which more fits the Soul for divine Irradiation and spiritual Imbraces; for the more quiet we are, the less Resistance we make against a supernatural Impression, and the easier we perceive the Beginning of divine Attraction, and so yield ourselves to it. And truly, when the Soul hath attained the Power to throw it self (as oft as is meet) into the silent super-imaginary State (which must be attained by the habitual constant Practice of it) it will then come to internal Openings, and intellectual Sights of the invisible World, and many times receive quick'ning Glances from the Eternity, with those strong Infusions of Love, that bring the Soul many Times near to a Rapture. And truly, the Enjoyment we have in this State, fully recompenseth all that self-denial, we pass through to the Attainment of it.

Here then the false Prophet (which is irregular Imagination) comes to be conquered, being commanded by the inward Mind, that now oft draws up the Soul into the Paradisiacal World, from the Motion of Phantasy and Imagination.

Imagination being now overcome, and the animal man mortified, the Soul cannot but clearly discover its Growth into the Image of God, and the Resurrection of the Angelical Man, which now evidently perceives its self springing up in a new Principle, above the Spirit of the World, and its mixt Laws: And here we come to own and receive *new Relations*, contracted in our progress in the New-Birth, and our Tendency from the Spirit of the World toward Eternity.

But we shall here find a *nearer Union and Communion* among those, who have been by one particular Instrument begotten into the Life of Christ, having a peculiar Vein of spiritual Enjoyment running through them; which others, who received not that particular Tincture, do not partake of. And had we lived in the Apostles Times, we should have seen this among the primitive Christians.... [for] amongst those who are thus peculiarly united, we shall see some more closely knit in spiritual Agreement than others, and essenced into one anothers Spirits; as may appear by that great Union which Christ had with St. John, and that particular Affection he bore towards him.

For Grace and the Work of Regeneration do not destroy our natural Signatures, only rectifie them by that Heavenly Principle, which reduceth all our Spirits into the highest Perfection they are capable of, by their primary Model and Frame. Hence it appears that they are more truly Brethren (even according to natural Nature) who thus agree, and correspond in their essences, than they who are ordinarily called so, who are many times very contrary signatur'd. And the reason of this assertion is, in that, when our Natures come to their perfect Rectitude and Restoration by Union with God; this secret Propension and harmonious closing with those that are like essenced, remains; whereas from meer natural Relation there nothing continues; though in those who are related, there may be this Agreement too.

But meer Relation is not the Cause of it, but that secret Law of Influence, which God hath established to Signature some one Way, some another; some in much Agreement and Proportion; others more differing, tho' all representing something of that Variety, which is wrapt up in the Unity of the eternal Nature. I could not but give an Hint of this, because it may open some things concerning Relations, which may lie dark to those who know not the deepest Ground and Root of them.

But I shall proceed to the further Opening of those Enjoyments, which flow from Union with new Relations, which come now to be very dear, because the Ground of the Relation is so pure and good, being not of Man, but of God. Here we shall experience the happy Effects of our pure Union, which produces that Divine Love that none can know, but those that enjoy it. But this will be strongest, where there is most Harmony and Agreement in Spirits and Natures; because the eternal Tincture works upon and thro' every thing according to it's Nature and Capacity: Hence we come to enjoy more from som, than others; and some from us receive more than others. But that brotherly Love and Friendship, which now comes to be renewed in Spirit, far transcends any Enjoyments meerly natural: And whatsoever we parted with, in dying to all earthly Affection and its Objects, we regain in the Resurrection of our Spirits, in this pure Love, which is not Affection, but something above it; not consisting in sudden Out-flowings and Eruptions, but in a constant sweet Inclination and secret Propension of the Spirit, to those which are one with it, in the pure Life: And this Good-Willingness is so great, that from it the Soul could give it's Life [or if there were any thing dearer than Life] for it's Brother; and choose Sufferings, to free Others from them. In this state there will be a sympathizing in Joy and Sorrow; and where the Union is eminently great, there may be some Knowledge of each others Conditions at a Distance, which comes from their being essenced in each others Spirits and Tinctures, which is the Cause of this invisible Sympathy.

And they that are in this near Union, feel a mutual Indwelling in the pure Tincture and Life of each other: And so, the further we come out of the animal Nature, the more universal we are, and nearer both to Heaven, and to one another in the Internal; and the further instrumentally to convey the pure Streams of the heavenly Life to each other, which no external Distance can hinder: For the Divine Tincture (being such a spiritual Virtue, as Christ imprinted into the Heart of the Disciples with whom he talked after his Resurrection, making their *Hearts to burn within them*) is able to pierce through all Distance, and reach those that are far absent; because it is not corporeal, nor subject to the Laws of Place or Time.

Now this is known to some by Experience, who in Absence enjoy such Influences of Spirit and secret Insinuations of spiritual Virtue from one another, that they cannot but value this spiritual Communion above all Enjoyments in the World; which compared to it, seem but like the basest Metal to the purest Gold....

And though some (who think they have passed far in the New-Birth) have experienced this; and may therefore look upon it as a thing not much to be regarded; yet let all such know that the Reason may be, in that they never yet passed clear out of the Spirit of the World, nor overcame their animal Nature by a complete Circumcision and Renunciation; and so were not capable to receive any extraordinary Enjoyment of Visions, Revelations, In-speaking, Prophecies, Unions of Spirits; and being not come into this inward Wilderness, where the Soul is fitted for such Things, and where these spiritual Temptations arise to try it: Whereas being in the outward sensitive Spirit and detained in Flesh and Blood, as *Israel* in *Egypt*, the inward spiritual Faculties of Sensation lie lock'd up, and can have no Knowledge of those spiritual Operations and Enjoyments.

But they that have come so far in the Work of the New-Birth, as to be acquainted with, and to live with these things, must of Necessity die to them, and come to be nothing in them, given up all to God....

After this Death upon the mystical Cross, the Soul in Conformity to Christ's Progress, passed through a State analogous to that of Christ's Descent into Hell, being that Principle, which stands as a smoking Furnace before the Entrance of Paradise, into which none can pass, but those that are dead with Christ, and washed from the Pollution of Flesh and Spirit by the Blood of the Lamb: For whosoever retain the Spots of Guilt, will be kept back by God's Wrath, which in this Principle burns like Fire.

This also is spread (at least potentially, as to its Root) through the whole World; yet invisible to the outward Eye. In this the Dragon and all evil Angels and Spirits are; for Jud. Epist. Vers 6 the Lord reserved the fallen Angels in *everlasting Chains under Darkness*....

Now though the fallen Angels are every where tempting the saints, yet they are always in the chains of this invisible Darkness, which could not be, if this were not every where in this World: whence Ephes. 6,12, it is called, The Darkness of this World. Of which the chief Devils are the *Kosmokratores* or worldly Rulers. And although evil Spirits receive some Refreshment by Mixing with the Souls of Men, which are cloathed with the animal sensitive Nature, and live in the Spirit of the World; yet they are still in Chains under this Darkness, as in their proper Center.

The *dark World* and *Hell* is made up of spiritual Sulphur, Mercury, and Salt, not united and harmonious in sweet Proportion, for then they would be Paradise; but as in Discord and Disproportion, working in contrary Motions through the Absence of that pure balsamic Oil, which flowing from the Heart of God, makes Paradise so delightful....

Now Hell or the dark World may be called the Heart of the Earth. First, In allusion to that large Sphere or Lake of Fire, which according to desCartes and some learned Hermetick Philosophers, is seated in and about the Center of the Earth. Secondly, In that according to the eternal Gradation of Beings and Principles, it may be said to be within, in the middle or Center of it; the Earth and all terrestrial matter being more outward, in the circumference. And though Hell is called Matt. 8.12 *To skotos to exoteron*, the utter or more outward Darkness, yet that's spoken in relation to Paradise and the Eternal World, not in reference to the Earth and this World.

Now Christ having passed through this Principle into Paradise, draws us all after Him....

But we must know, that in our Progress we may many Times be cast into Terror and Anguish; yea feel Hell awakened in us, and afterwards be delivered by some influence of Christ's Spirit, and Infusions of his Love, and yet be short of this Resurrection.... [until] we descend thither without Guilt, in Child-like Innocency, with the Candle of the Lord in our Hands, which is the Pillar of Fire, which alone can lead us through this night into the Day of Paradise....

By this time the soul experienceth the happy State of being freed from the Principle of Selfness, in Returning to God from the Spirit of the World, and sees the real Progress it hath made, from the outward thro' the inward dark World into the internal Paradise, where *Adam* lived before his Fall, and where Christ conversed betwixt the Time of his Resurection and Ascension. In this spiritual Region, the Curse is not manifest, there being a perpetual Spring. Here are the Idea's of all visible Bodies, in much Beauty and appealing Lustre. Here are those bright Clouds, which overshadowed Christ on the Mount, and when he was received up into Heaven; in which he will descend, when he comes again to judge the Earth.

Now the Soul, having attained to the state of this angelical Garden, knows what it is to turn and become as a Child and to attain a secret and quiet Life of Innocency and pure Love, free from those Passions and evil Affections it had formerly groaned under. And here it experienceth what it is to be born of Water and the Spirit, as a necessary Qualification to do the Will of God: And sees it's Conception in the Womb of Wisdom, (which is our new mother) who here distills the milk of the eternal Word, (from the Eternal World) to feed and nourish the Soul. Whither it now travels, as fixing its sight upon that pure River of Water of Life, clear as Chrystal, proceeding out of the Throne of God, and of the Lamb. But now likewise the Soul lives the life of spiritual Vegetation, and grows like a Willow by the Water-Courses, or a Lilly in the Garden of the Lord, being continually refreshed with the Dews of the eternal Heavens and quickned by the Beams of the Sun of

Rightesouness, and cherished with the enlivening Gates of the
Holy Spirit. All that are in this State, are like the harmless Flowers
in a fruitful Garden springing from the same Ground, yet differing in Colour, Virtue, Smell, and Growth, according to their several Natures and Times of Planting; yet all serving to express the
Power, Love, and Wisdom of their Creator, without any Strife or
Contention for Eminent Place or Esteem, being all satisfied with
what God affords them, and their different Capacities fit them.

O what a sweet Harmony is here!

In a word, this is a Life of Stillness, Silence, and spiritual Simplicity, in which the Soul turning it's Eyes from Nature, looks directly forward to Eternity, and strongly breaths after it's Arrival
there....

Here the internal Faculties of spiritual Sensation are more
opened, and give a greater Enjoyment of the first angelical life
which was in Paradise: And we attain the Use and Restoration
ofthese Faculties through our Growth in Regeneration, and as a
Priviledge purchased for us by Christ: So that all Saints shall partake of them, either here or in Heaven, according as their Attain-
ments are. In this State, our internal *Eye* is more unlocked, to behold the paradisiacal World, with those luminous Objects and
Inhabitants that are in it....

In this State likewise we oft *smell* the hot Perfumes of Paradise
and are pierced through with most delightful Odours, which in-
fuse themselves into the tincture of the Heart, create Delight, and
give a plain Feeling and Sense of the Presence of Paradise and
that invisible light World, where there is no Curse or Corruption.
And in a Word, here we *feed* upon the heavenly Manna, Angel's
Food, which is living Bread, that quickens, enlivens, and corrobo-
rates the Soul.... Thus all the spiritual Faculties of Sensation, are
in this Dispensation more opened, and more freely entertained
with their peculiar Objects.

But yet we are not to rest in these Enjoyments, nor to go build
Tabernacles with them; but to look forward, and to press after
perfect Union with the divine Nature in the eternal World: Where
is our true Sabbath of Rest, in the Vision of God, and the perfect
Fruition of his Love forever.

By this Time the Soul begins to draw near the eternal World,
in its fixed Station and habitual Enjoyment, lying under the show-

ers of Love which descend from the Heart of God and the Bosom of Sophia: Here the blessed Tincture of Jesus coming so power-fully, as though it streamed from his glorified Humanity, flows into the Soul like a River of Oyl mixed with Fire, which affords that unutterable Delight, which cannot be conceived by those that know it not experimentally.

Here Christ saith: Drink, yea, drink abundantly, O Beloved!… The Soul becomes filled, swallowed up, and transported into a kind of Rapture, not being able to express those Pleasures, Gusts, Imbraces, Love Extasies, which are then piercing through it.

And in this State, there is such holy Commerce in pure Love, betwixt God and the Soul, so there is between the Soul and other Saints; who cannot but wonderfully own and love one another, and delight in that Likeness of God, which they see in each other…. Here we bear one another's Burdens, and so fulfil the royal Law of Love; for we can keep nothing as our own, but what we heart-ily communicate and make our Brethren Partakers of, because they are Part of our selves: Here we come to practice that heav-enly Law of loving our Neighbours as our Selves, and of doing God's Will on Earth, as it is done in Heaven; for which End Man and the visible World were brought forth….

The Soul being brought thus far in the Heart-work by the Power of Jesus, through the Practice of the Cross in Self-denial and Resignation, lives in habitual springings up of the Love in the Centre of it's Spirit, where the Work is near finished; the Will being constantly drawn toward the Heart of God, in the Chariot of Love. And in this State the Soul is completely fitted for Ascen-sion, and the Opening of the eternal World, which is part of the Head-work; for in that the spiritual Eye is seated, which is ca-pable to see and to know the Wonders of Eternity.

And though some in Rapture may be taken up into that World, long before the Work in their Hearts, Wills, and Affections is fin-ished; yet such must afterward go through the work in Nature, of rectifying all their Properties, and of bringing their Wills into Death, and pure Resignation, that so they may be fitted for the Birth of the Love….

The Ascension, after this Work of Regeneration in the Heart, is more weighty, and more tending to Perfection, than any Rap-ture of Transportation before, can be; because by such a Work the

Will is brought up into a constant Union with Christ, which by Ascension is more confirmed and established, the Heart through that, being more raised above all mortal corruptible Objects, and more reduced to a passive silent Waiting for the Opening of the *eternal Temple*, whence the infallible Voice proceeds, and where the great High-Priest sparkles with the most bright Beams of divine Glory.

But the manner of the Soul's Ascending from the Internal to the Eternal World, is very remarkable and wonderful. It cannot of itself move one Degree upward: That same Hand of Power which carried it downward to see the Wonders of God in the Depths, must carry it upward to see his Wonders in the high Places above. So that in this, the Soul is meerly passive; The Spirit of Christ being the Agent which descending with an overshadowing Virtue upon it, wraps it up swiftly, and in a strong Force, (by which the Soul's Acts are for a while suspended) translates it, as it were, in a straight Line from the inward toward the Inmost.

In this Translation or Ascension, what Wonders are seen and felt, I shall not particularly express: But in general, this I must declare, that there is an unutterable Power transmuting the Soul in this Ascent, which first comes into the Womb of the invisible Worlds (out of which they issue) in which it finds a universal Silence or Stillness; and above which it discovers a great Glory, inhabited by glorified Spirits, who live there in perpetual Harmony and Joy…. To be taken into this, is a further Degree of Ascension, being the second Mansion in the eternal World; where Myriads of Angels attend those Commands, which come out of the most holy Place, which is the last and highest Mansion in that World, answering to *Love* as the second to *Life*, and the first to *Light*, corresponding with the threefold Manifestation of Father, Son, and Holy Ghost. But to speak much of the two last, requires greater Experience than I have yet enjoyed. Neither is it expedient to describe the first, nor those Wonders which are in it, in Regard of that Blindness and general Enmity which is in Men's Hearts against the deep Mysteries of God in invisible Nature.

But after Ascension into the first, the Soul becomes so much indued with the Sense and Apprehension of those spiritual Mysteries, it was there acquainted with and hath such a clear View of the outward World and of the misery that most there lye in, that it cannot but weep over the greatest Part of Men as Christ did over Jerusalem, as seeing them exceeding ignorant of Eternity, and so of their own everlasting Happiness; and involved in the Spirit of the outward World, where the Prince of the World holds them captive.... After this also the Soul begins to discover the evil Properties and Habits of Men's Spirits, very much portrayed in their Faces, discovering in their very Aspects and Signatures those bestial and devilish Passions by which they are swayed and captivated within; so that the Eye many times affects the Heart with Grief, in viewing the sad Estate of Souls estranged from the Life of Innocency, and pure Virginity, and imprisoned in the dark Chains of corrupt Flesh and Blood. Here likewise the Soul is exceeding passive, and much comprehended in deep abstract Silence, by which it much enjoys unutterable Pleasures, and Gusts from the inward Ground of Eternity, having much Sense of the Nearness of that Kingdom where the angelical Thrones sing Hallelujahs, and sport themselves in the innocent Delights of their eternal Spheres and luminous Mansions. And as the soul passeth from the first Mansion toward the second and third, Jesus of Nazareth (in his glorified Humanity) begins to give great Demonstrations of his Presence, and to visit the inward Man with frequent and very great Impressions; so that it cannot doubt but that he is sometimes personally present, infusing the Tincture of his glorified Body into the Heart, which is sweeter than Honey, and burns like Oil and Fire mixed together. And truly this Dispensation is exceeding comfortable and very weighty; for the Discovery of Christ's Presence sometimes swallows up the Soul in unspeakable Joy, being transmuted with the Breath of his Mouth, which is most odiferous; and quickened by the Touch of his Body, which is most delightful; and pierced through with the Sound of his Voice, which is most harmonious and powerful; causing the Soul deeply to admire the Grace of God, and to cry out with St. Thomas: My Lord and my God! In this Dispensation Christ shows very powerfully, the Necessity of his Mediation, as God-Man; and that whatever we receive, is through Him, who standing in the deepest Union with the Father, conveys all Light, Life, and Love from himself unto us, who at the Time of the Restitution of all Things, Acts 3:21, will again breath the holy Ghost on his chosen Vessels, of which those in the primitive Time received but the first Fruits. He also reveals in this state, how the Mystery of Iniquity (even the Spirit of Anti-Christ) works in most sects of Christians; carrying them either to deny or slight the great Mystery of his mediatory Office: Or by Misconceptions to cry up his Blood and Merits, to the Prejudice of Mortification, Self-denial, and the imitating of his most innocent Life as our Pattern to walk by in this World.

Moreover, in this Dispensation, the Soul enjoys very great Openings of Eternity in the Heart, which are different from Openings in the Head, where the inward senses of hearing and seeing are resident; for whatever in a divine Sight (Eternity opening in the Head) we clearly and distinctly view and behold, the same (in a Heart-Opening) we really feel and handle in a spiritual Way, for in it we come experimentally to know and perceive the Motions and administering Influences of Angels: the Virtue and Efficacy of Christ's universal and particular body: the Harmony, Love, and Enjoyment of the Spirits of just Men made perfect, with much of the glory and Majesty of that Kingdom prepared for us from the Beginning of the World, into which none can enter but those, who have forsaken all for Christ, and devested themselves of all the Vestments of Corruption, and have put on the Robe of Innocency, which is the Garment of true Virginity, in which they will not be ashamed to stand before the Son of Man, in his Kingdom.

> Then be ye wise Immortal Sparks of Fire
> And strive to get you Garments of pure Light
> In which you may from mortal Dregs retire
> Into that Glory, where's no Spot of Night.
> O do but weigh how swiftly Time goes by,
> And how all earthly Pleasures, rise and fall
> As soon as they a Being have, they die,
> And nothing can their hasty Joy recall.
> But when the outward Garment is withdrawn,
> Eternity presents its constant Face,
> In which all Actions clearly will be shown,
> Which ever have been wrought in Time's Short Race
> But such alone can there possessed be
> Of Happiness, that have been born again:
> Others will feel the Pangs of Misery,
> Who in their Wills Corruption still retain.
> Then die to Sin, while on the Earth you live,
> So after Death, true Life you shall receive.

V

John Pordage

Son of a London merchant, Dr. John Pordage was born in 1607, and entered Pembroke College, Oxford, in 1623. It is possible that he obtained a diploma of a doctor of medicine at Oxford in 1640, but some scholars doubt this.[18] Certainly it is true in any case that he was not destined to practice medicine, but to be a religious. For whatever his other schooling, Pordage entered into the order of the Anglican Church and was made vicar of the church of St. Lawrence's at Reading in 1644. Soon, under the auspices of Elias Ashmole, he was made rector of the rather wealthy parish at Bradfield, a position he held until 1654.

During his time at Bradfield, Pordage began to have unusual visionary experiences. At first those experiences came primarily to his wife, Mary Freeman, an especially pious and spiritual woman whom he married for that reason.[19] Richard Roach later wrote that the theosophers' group "had its rise...with a fresh conversance and Holy Gale of a Divine Life and Power opening first and principally in Mrs Pordage...[Dr. Pordage] married her for the excellent gift of God he found in her, which gift he also became in a high degree partaker of."[20] Soon Pordage himself was experiencing remarkable phenomena, including angelic apparitions, and these were witnessed too by others in a small group of theosophers who gathered around Pordage and his wife in a prayer group.

But although he was deprived of his livelihood, and although Dr. Pordage found himself in extremely difficult circumstances for the remainder of his life, these outward difficulties only served to intensify his, and his group's, convictions and inward life. Their persecution did mean that for some years they lived spiritually in the "outer darkness" surrounded by wrath, suffering something akin to what St. John of the Cross called the "dark night of the soul." Eventually they were restored to angelic communications and to the spiritual light, yet until his death, Dr. Pordage and his small group kept themselves out of public view and therefore censure.

From the early 1670's until his death in 1681, Dr. Pordage wrote most of his elaborate, lucid, and concisely expressed metaphysical treatises. All these treatises were based wholly and directly on his own spiritual experience, exemplary of which is the treatise *Sophia*, which consists of twenty-two daily journal entries dated from 21 June to 10 July, and which contains biographical data from the year 1675. Pordage's magnum opus, *Göttliche und Wahre Metaphysica* [Holy and True Metaphysics], was also written during this time, probably concluded in the year of his death, 1681.

But none of these works were published during his lifetime and, even more surprisingly, only two were published in English after his death. Although all his works had a wide private circulation, and were extremely influential in both England and the Continent, it remains a strange fact that Pordage's primary works—albeit written in English—were published only in German, and have been accessible only in that language to the present day. How is it that Pordage's writings have not been available in his own language, and that even in German editions his name was changed to Johannes Pordäschens?

There is one primary answer. Pordage and his colleagues, I believe, felt the necessity for his anonymity after the scandalous persecutions of the 1650's and the spiritual and financial difficulties through which they had passed. He earned his keep through later years, in part, as a medical doctor and herbalist in relative seclusion, and wanted to live an unhindered ascetic spiritual life of prayer. Theosophers, after all, are wholly uninterested in proselytizing, as Pordage pointed out to his persecutors years before; what matters to them is spiritual purity and experience, and since publicity hardly conduces to this, he preferred a public silence and withheld publication.

But this decision produced the anomalous situation in which we find ourselves now: in order to discuss Pordage's works, originally written in English, we must translate most of them back from their German editions. Although this is a somewhat unsatisfactory arrangement, for the present it will have to do. The works that follow include, first, an extremely compact, lucid letter on spiritual alchemy written by Pordage to a woman who had begun the spiritual life in earnest, and second, excerpts from his treatise *Sophia*, the first theosophic work devoted more or less exclusively to Wisdom. Not surprisingly, both reflect the practical concerns of this Sophianic school, the first being a letter of spiritual advice, the second a diary of spiritual experience and speculative insights. Without question, Pordage is one of the most rewarding authors in this tradition.

A Philosophical Epistle on the True Stone of Wisdom to One Who Is Earnestly Digging

Loveworthy Lady,

It has become known to me that you have found the material of the Stone, the right *materia* of the true Stone of Wisdom; so have I felt stirred and impelled within me to entrust and discharge these few lines to you. Now the *materia* is, as you know, the son of eternal Nature; it is the essence and Being of Godly love; it is the soul's paradise; it is the heavenly blood of the Virgin; it is the heavenly Tincture; it is the seed [Saame] or land of pure Nature, so it has life in itself; it is the impregnated body through which it becomes possible to sing praise and thank-songs of the holy Trinity in Unity. However, this is not enough, for you must not remain stuck here: because here there is still no peace for you; you must not here rejoice that you have the *materia* of the great wonder, namely the fat oil of the holy Tincture, of the holy Essence, so you are not also satisfied by your first fruit. But rather I want you to seek yet further, and direct you in the Art and Method so that you may form and fix the Stone, or should undergo water and fire which is the wonder of all wonders, or the mystery of all mysteries; wherein is found the true blessing and bliss of eternity. For you are inflamed, brimful in this love-fire, because you have found such a precious oil of life, such a precious discovery, and such a holy *materia*. And now you want to go further, and come to know the Art and Wisdom, how you make, form, signify the composition of the stone, wherein you attain knowledge of the eternal world's wonders.

Believe me, it is not an easy thing to make the holy stone of power, even if we have already attained the true *materia*. A. Pontanus practiced and sought it five hundred times after he already had the true *materia*, and before he could make it, but he did not cease testing and trying until he overcame. Likewise should your virginal heart do, and in seeking the Pearl not give up until you have found it.

The *materia* is, as you know, the red earth that is found alone in paradise; it is the red tincture, the purest sweetest blood of the eternal virginal humanity, so it is called the virginal Seed of virginal nature, where the virginal life of a virginal heart [Gemüt] flows out of its root.

The oven, namely the *philosophorum*, or your oven was, as you know, a great mystery, twofold, one in another. The outer oven is made of lime and tile; nonetheless, it is wonderfully made of the spirit of the greater world and its constellations or stars, and is no other than your outwardly visible body of the four elements together. But after you have found the *materia*, you have no hope of [making the stone] once the earthly outward oven is broken. [You cannot make the stone if beforehand you have broken the earthly oven, for then you would have no hope of making it.]

The inward oven, which the *philosophi* hold as a high secret mystery, was your *Balneum Mariæ*, a glassy phial, in which your *materia* is made a substance and essence more precious and worth more than all the world. This is locked and sealed with the *Sigillo Hermetis* under lock and key so that nothing of the power of the *materia* will evaporate, nor may some strange *materia* penetrate into it. This holy oven, this *Balneum Mariæ*, this glassy phial, this secret oven is the place, the matrix, or bearing-mother [Behrmutter] and the Centrum, wherein the holy Tincture wells forth, boils up, and has its origin.

The place or the state there where the Tincture has its dwelling I do not think it necessary to directly name, but rather exhort you only to knock on the ground. Solomon tells us in his Song that your inner dwelling is not far from the navel, and is like a round cup that is filled with the holy liquor of the pure Tincture. [Song 7.2]

The fire of the philosophers you should know; this is the key that remains secret: therefore you should believe and know that the understanding of this fire is the key to the mysteries, which unlocks all things, and makes the work itself possible; so that the artist is required to do nothing other than be diligent and watchful. The fire is the love-fire-life that flows out of the holy Venus or love of God; the Martial fire is too sharp and too fierce, so that it would dry and burn up the *materia*. Then here alone the love-fire of Venus has the qualities of the right, true fire.

This enlivens and pleases me that you would be an earnest seeker. Muster your virginal will so that you become a true, seeking artist; because now you will—after coming to recognize and know the three great matters or mysteries of the Stone, namely the true *materia*, the right oven and the true fire—need to guard your Talent or Pound in a shroud, and be a pure maiden. Do not let it get far from you! Hunt it much more after you come to know it, so that you become what you know, going forth and seeking it, so you become what you find, because it is the gift of God that he gives to the earnest seeker.

You see that the hardest and most tireless work is still to come, and this is the composition and fixing of the stone. The hidden treasure lies in the consummation and completion of the work. For the composition of this heavenly stone you must come to learn the heavenly or holy philosophy, which has its end in true theology: otherwise you may not bring the philosophical work in your oven at any time to an end. The true philosophy is not the trifling nonexistent philosophy learned in books and through art, against which Paul warned us, but rather it is coming to know God in the pure primordial nature; it is to know the art and method of how the Godhead is introduced and suffused in each quality of nature. And this true philosophy will encenter you in the knowledge of the holy trinity, which knowledge is sufficient for the true fixing of the stone, after which the wise of all times have sought.

In this true philosophy you will learn how you should know yourself aright, so you also come to know pure nature; then the pure nature is in you yourself. And when you have freed pure nature from all evil sinful selfhood, you come to know true selfhood, then you also know God, because the Godhead is hidden and develops in pure nature like a kernel in a nutshell. The true philosophy will teach you the right mixture, the right quantity in weight and mass, what you should place there, and what take away. The true philosophy will teach you what is meant by and how to understand descension and ascension, distillation, sublimation, and circulation of the *materia*, because the ancient philosophers expressed these mysteries through dark words and artistic speech. The true philosophy will teach you who is the father and who the mother of this magical child, as well as what the nourishment through which you may support it, no less also what the colors are that this noble stone must attract, and how it can be prepared and made. Here you see that the end of the work itself is crowning and glory: go forth therefore, and your heart bless the work that your soul has begun. And because you are a young artist in the work, I will describe for you a process, so that when you plough with my calf, you will understand my riddle, and nothing different.

The father of this child is Mars; he is the fire-life, and from Mars as the father comes his quality. His mother is Venus, the gentle love-fire, and from her goes the son's quality. Here you see the little man and little woman, man and woman, bride and bridegroom, the first wedding or marriage Galilean in the qualities and forms of nature; which come to pass between Mars and Venus when they return from their fallen condition. Mars, or the marriage-man, must become a holy man, so that he will not spoil the pure Venus when taken into the holy marriage-bed. Venus must become a pure Virgin, a pure virginal woman; otherwise she will not marry the angry, jealous Mars in the anger-fire, nor live with you in union; rather, the state of unity and harmony are rent by the conflict, jealousy, disharmony, and enmity under the qualities of nature; so there can be no union between them, nor any true marriage; and so because there is no marriage, there is also no conception, hence no creation of life, and no birth of this magical child, no stone, and all the work is lost.

So you must as a learned Artist think and look earnestly after the union of your own Mars and Venus, in order that the marriage bond be rightly tied, and the wedding between them will be really be wholly consummated. You must well see that they lie closely together in bed, and live in sweet harmony because virginal Venus will in you give forth your pearl of the water-spirit, gentling the Martial wrath-fire and so the Martial wrath-fire will sink itself in love and gentleness, wholly willing in Venus' love-fire; and thus both qualities as fire and water will mix with one another and flow together, reconciled; out of which union and conjoining will be given the first conception of the magical birth, which one can call the tincture of the love-fire.

And although the tincture in the [Behrmutter: Bearing Mother or Mistress] of your humanity is conceived and awakened to live, so there is still thereby a great danger to be feared, that because it is still in the body or Behrmutter, it may not rightly ripen or be broken or may be prevented [aborted]. Then you must become a good nurse, taking good care during childhood, according to your own pure heart and virginal will.

Further, you must support the Tincture alone with a nutriment or nourishment and drink, so that your nature is temperate: therefore it must be nourished alone with the nutriment of its own mother, that is, with the water of life, with the milk, with the annointing Tincture, and with the heavenly blood that flows out of the breast of the virginal Venus: but you don't want Mars too near, for such nutriment is too bitter, sour, and sharp, and is for a delicate tincture of life like a poison and death; and the wrath-fire of Mars would suffocate and kill the tender child in the body of humanity; there the love-fire of Venus will powerfully strengthen and waken it. And so you must shelter and care for and nurse the delicate tincture of life, and give it nothing that goes against its nature, and only give it what nourishes it. So will the little child grow beautiful. But here you must see well to it that you don't excite the Tincture. Although the child may cause some trouble, go sweetly and be friendly with him; be tender and graceful, and above all do nothing that goes against his pure nature. Because if it takes another form, you will make much suffering, wherein would lie a great danger, and whereby you would suffocate the delicate child's life, or through negligence of the virginal seed, spoil again its reception, conception, and life-creation.

But after you have brought the virginal seed in Venus' quality through careful nourishment to its powers, and have nourished and supported him daily with the virginal milk and with the virginal blood, so that he is strong enough to take harder food, then you must test and prove the child of the tinctured life in the qualities of nature; because thereby again is great uneasiness and danger; consider that the body and bearing-mother may suffer injury in the testing, and thus also you, around the birth. Because here the delicate tincture, the delicate child of life must descend into the forms and qualities of nature; that is, suffer and endure the testing and stand it; it is necessary to descend into the holy darkness in the dark Saturn, wherein no light of life is visible: therein it must be held imprisoned, and bound with the deliverance of darkness, and must live on the food that the prickly light of Mercury will give him to eat; which to the holy life-tincture is nothing other than dust and ashes, or poison and gall, or fire and brimstone. It must go into the fierce wrath of Mars, from which it must (like Jonah in the belly of hell) be swallowed up and experience the curse of God's wrath; and also be tested by Lucifer and the millions of devils that dwell in the wrath-fire's quality. And here the holy artist sees the first color in this philosophical work, for here the tincture appears in its blackness; it is the blackest black; the learned *philosophi* name it the black crow or the black raven or also the blessed darkness, because in the darkness of this blackness is hidden in Saturn's quality, the light of lights; and in this poison and gall is hidden Mercury, the precious medicine against the poison, the life of life: and in the fierceness or wrath and Mars' curse is the blessed tincture hidden.

Here the artist thinks that all his work is lost. For what is now become of the tincture? Here is nothing appearing, nothing to see, to know, or to taste; nothing as darkness, as painful death, as a hellish anxious fire, nothing as wrath and curse of God; that is, in this putrefaction or dissolution or destruction of the tincture of life; but here in this darkness is light, in this death is life, in this fierceness and anger is love, and in this poison the highest and most precious medicine against all poison and sickness.

The ancient philosophers named this work your descension or cineration, pulverisation, death, putrefaction of the *materia* of the stone, corruption, *caput mortuum*. This blackness or black color now you must not despise, but rather have patience in suffering and sustain your penetration in the stillness until forty days of testing, until the days of your suffering are completed; then will the seed of life itself awaken, sublimate or be heartened, itself be transformed into white, itself be purified and made whole, give itself redness, that is, be clarified and fixed. From here on, if the work is brought this far, it is easier work: because the learned philosophers say that from here on, it would be woman's work and child's play. So that if the human will is permitted to become still and as a dead nothing, then the tincture will work and do everything in us; if we can stay still in thought, action, and imagination. But how hard and sour becomes the work of the human will until it has been brought to this form, that it thus may stay still when all fire will be visible, and all tempters storm in upon him.

Here is, as you see, great danger, and one can very easily despise the tincture of life and the fruit in the mother's body will be ruined, when you thus are ringed and besieged on all sides by so many devils and so many tempting or testing essences. But so you endure this fire-test and difficult tempting, and bring it to victory: for then you will be at the beginning of your ascent out of hell, sin, death, and out of the grave of mortality, and indeed see first appear the quality of Venus: because then will the tincture of life be out of danger of the dark Saturn, through the hell of the poisonous Mercury, and through the curse and painful death of Mars, the burning and flaming wrath of God himself, with might broken out, so the gentle love-fire in Venus's quality has the upper hand, and the love-fire tincture has governance. And then here governs the gentle courage and the love-fire of the holy Venus as the heart and queen in and above all qualities. Nonetheless, there is here still the danger that the work of the stone may still go astray. Therefore must the artist still wait, until the tincture changes with the white color, and is wholly clothed in white, which he must wait to see after long patience and being-still; [the whiteness] really appears when the tincture flows roused into the lunar quality: then one sees the Luna of the tincture, a beautiful white, the brightly lit splendour of the fully consummated white color. And here is the darkness in the light, and death changed into life. And this bright and splendid white nourishes joy in the heart of the artist, and gives hope because the work is going so well. Because now is revealed the white color of the illuminated Soul-eye of purity, innocence, holiness, one-ness of the will-unity, heavenly mindedness, sanctification, and righteousness, which the tincture is clothed with over and over: it is bright like the world, beautiful as the dawn's aurora. Now appears the holy Virginity of the tincturing life in which is no fleck or wrinkle, nor blemishes more to be seen.

Through this work the ancients nourished the white Swan, called albification, or white-making, sublimation, distillation, circulation, purification, separation, healing, and arising; because the tincture is made like a shimmering silver; it is, through frequent subjection in Saturn, Mercury, and Mars, and through the frequent resubjection in Venus and Luna, sublimated or raised up and clarified. This is the distillation, or *Balneum Mariæ*: because through frequent distillation of the water, blood, and heavenly dew of the holy Virgin Sophia is the tincture in the qualities of nature purified, and through the manifold circulation, that is, the in, out, and through-going of the qualities and forms of nature, it is made as bright and pure and polished silver. And here are all impurities of the blackness, all death, hell, curse, wrath and all poison that flow from the qualities of Saturn, Mercury, and Mars, separated and hence is this named the separation; and if the tincture in Venus and Luna reaches its whiteness and brilliance, such is named its sanctification, its purification, and its white-making. This is also called its arising, because the whiteness arises out of the blackness, and the holy Virginity and purity out of the poison of Mercury, and out of the red fiery fierceness and wrath of Mars. Now here is fear and hope mingled in the heart of the artist. Meanwhile he still is surrounded by fear, because he still might make a mistake or let his hand slip; but soon as he clings again to courage and hope, [error] does not come to pass, but rather his work has a happy outcome if he pays attention with all care and assiduity, so that the yellow color may arise and be seen in Jove's quality; and in Jove will Luna's white color be changed into a glittering yellow. Luna in the whiteness gave the tincture life's essence and a white body; but the yellow exaltation in Jove signifies that one has been restored with a new soul and that in the body and Bearing-mother [Behrmutter] of eternal nature a new life has come about. This the artist inwardly will become: so that the blind see; the deaf hear, the mute speak, the dead come to life, and joy arises out of sadness.

Now after the tincture of life is impregnated in Luna's quality with a body, and with a living soul in Jove's quality is restored, so the artist rejoices, because a jovial, holy joyous kingdom of the tinctured life appears; but still the artist still has something to fear: because the birth of the tincture is still not yet completed and still lacks something. Because if God has been in the qualities of nature as well as man, so is man nonetheless still not God or become divinized. The tincture of life still lacks the spirit of the Holy Ghost; such must travel on her wagon. This works in oneself as fixation in the solar quality: because Sol gives the tincture spirit; it gives the tincture color, fixation, and consummation. The color that Sol gives is a carmine scarlet color, a deep red or bright, splendid, shimmering gold, or a clear brilliance of the sun, or a rose-colored blood. This is the fast and enduring color of the tincture, which

Sol gives; it is the majestic brilliance and bright-illumining color of the sun's appearance or pure burnished gold. And here are all colors changed into this one, because it is the unchanging, permanent color.

Now is the stone fixed, the elixir of life prepared, the love child or the child of love born, the new birth completed, and the work wholly and completely done. Gone are hell, the curse, death, the dragon, the animal and the serpent, night, mortality, fear, sadness and misery. Because now is the resolution and the home-bringing of all that was lost, both inwardly and outwardly found again; because now you have the great secret and mystery of the whole world; you have the pearl of love; you have the unchanging permanent essence of the holy joy wherein all healing virtue is and out of which all increasing powers come; where emanates the effective power of the Holy Spirit. You have the woman-seed which has trod upon the head of the serpent; you have the seed of the Virgin, the white and red, the milk of the Virgin and the blood of the Virgin in an essence and quality.

O wonder of all wonders! You have the tincturing tincture, the pearl of the Virgin which has three-in-one essence or quality; you have the body, soul, and spirit; you have fire, light, and joy; you have the quality of the Father and that of the Son; and also of the Holy Spirit; and these three fixed in one permanent essence and being. This is the Son of the Virgin; this is your first-born; this is the noble hero, the serpent-treader and he who throws the dragon under his feet and treads upon it. The ancient philosophers name him the red and white Lion. The Scriptures call Him the Lion of the House of Israel or Judah and David.

And thus you see where the true *philosophia* is conveyed; namely in a holy body wherein you will find the life of the Godhead in pure nature, wherein you come to know God in nature. Now is paradise in nature again found, the six days' work in the soul has reached its end and is now gone into the peace of the completed consummation: then because the Fixation is born, so is a consummated life without any shadows of change; it is a ever-lasting day without night, an everlasting joy without sadness, an eternal life without death: because here now is the paradisal man clear as the brilliant shining forth of the holy Sun through and through, like gold that is throughout bright, pure, and clear; also without any blemish or fleck. The soul is now an enduring seraphimic Angel, and may make itself into a physician, theologian, astrologer, into a holy Magus; it may also make what it will; it may do and have what it will; because all qualities have only one will in unity and harmony. And the same one will is God's eternal unmistaking will: and now is the holy man in his own nature become one with God.

But therefore do not misunderstand me nor judge what you do not understand. Judge nothing before the time when the Judge stands before the gate. For me it is enough if you fully understand and recognize that what I have written to you here comes from a pure love to you. At least you can recognize and judge so much as you have tasted of the tincture that reveals itself and changes you; and what is more, have found and have completed the tincture in your work in every and each quality of nature. Such will with my love for you remain:

Your co-artist in seeking the true stone of the holy Wisdom

J.P

From
Sophia: The Graceful Eternal Virgin of Holy Wisdom, or Wonderful Spiritual Discoveries and Revelations That the Precious Wisdom Has Given to a Holy Soul
(London: 1675)

General Content of This Tractate
Every soul that thinks to attain Holy Wisdom must first have a strong desire for her, and unceasingly persevere in prayer, whereby one will be moved and stirred through the contemplation of her high excellencies and wonderful beauty and especially through remembering her as a true knower of the mysteries of the knowledge of God both in and outside nature and a lover of all His works. Hereby in the Ground of the Soul will awake a strong and sharp desire [for] this spirit of Wisdom with all earnest investigation and seeking, whereby if he wants to do only

one, he nonetheless accomplishes everything, and can make what is old new again.

This hardness and sharpness of the soul's desire in her fiery ground will be named in this tractate a hunger and thirst: And souls awaken that which they love and seek after (as has come to pass with our Author): Thus She will come with her Holy *Principio* and Light-world herebelow according to her promise to satisfy and to still the anxious hunger and thirsty desire that She feels in the souls. Nevertheless, this may take a long time, indeed, continuing so for twenty and more years (in some cases), persevering and proposing marriage to this heavenly Virgin of holy Wisdom before she really appears and reveals herself to the soul-spirit in stillness and peace to quiet, to entrust, and to strengthen, and to still the strong impulse of its consuming hunger.

Because thereafter [nachdem] the soul seeks many ways, for it would like to seek out and find Her in various ways, but in its strong seeking and hunting after Her, it had often been misled, and had lost hope, finally becoming wholly tired and exhausted. And when then neither an earnest prayer nor spiritual contemplation could do anything adequate, neither pleas nor imploring for the least of her influence, that she would come herebelow and would dwell in the soul, so the soul in itself becomes satisfactorily convinced that in the power of its own active or effective spirit through the working of faith, hope, and the like (as in which it had labored a long time) indeed would have no possibility of breaking through the wall separating it from the heavenly principle. And because it thereupon finds that through *ascending* out it had been constantly misled and had missed its goal, that it is not on the right path ([even] if it were privy to revelations and glimpses of the heavenly countenance). It realizes there is no other way that the Wisdom of God and Her *principio* can be attained than through *descending* and sinking into one's own inward ground, and no longer seeking to rise out of oneself.[21]

Whereupon it now thus sinks into itself and before it the gate of Wisdom's depths is opened directly and in the blink of an eye, and it is led into the holy eternal *principium* of the lightworld in the wine-celler of the New Lebanon, in the new magical Earth wherein the Virgin Sophia or the Virgin of God's Wisdom appears and announces her message. This is the content of the other

chapters, which [reveal what] is kept in the deep teachings of the
passive or enduring stillness or peace of the soul. Because with a
praise-song [this] will be resolved: Wisdom will teach her apprentice to sing of this great revelation of the new creation and planting of another paradise.

But there [if] the soul is not vigilant and wakeful enough, always contemplating in the *Centrum Naturae*, through this passive,
enduring stillness, in the *Abgrund* or Chaos, out of which this new
paradise must be created and formed herebelow, so that the soul
does not again fly out and into the heights, then is the soul in
great danger from an uncountable horde of evil spirits from the
dark world as out of the elementary and astral principles, to be
gruesomely experienced. But the holy Protector appears again in
the direst emergency, and if the soul stands firm in the middle of
these inner wars, and these her powers weaken, and her courage
is knocked down, and the evil spirits ring around the exhausted,
courageless soul-spirit, then one is empowered as in the foregoing section, as had been given to learn. There goes forth a new
suppression [of evil], and the disciple in Her holy art and science
opens a fresh section wherein the soul learns how earth stands in
harmony with heaven, or how the lower part of the new creation
stands in lovely harmony with the upper: which comes to pass in
the third chapter.

The third section treats of the true, inner, and essential purification and of the secret fire and oven of Wisdom's true apprentice and further in the fourth chapter.

Now after this work must the spiritual artist follow the whole
Process of the holy Mysteries and not wait any more. And so he
must first discover the creation or production of the new magical
earth, and how within is the living working of the secret fire and
hidden ovens of the wise in the manifold powers of the Vegetation or vegetabilistic life, wherefore it may be called the planting
of the inward Garden of Eden. And in this paradise the soul-spirit
receives the chalice of Wisdom wherein is the Elixir of life and the
vegetabilistic quintessence. This is the content of the fifth chapter.

And after this comes to pass the first forming and planting of
this paradisiacal earth in the mystical ground of the soul, discovering and revealing something new, namely the melting and dis-
solving of the former heaven, through which it may be renewed.

This is discussed in the sixth chapter.

Now these are the prerequisites or necessities that are required in a true philosopher whereupon [alsdenn] Wisdom travels forth under the following particular conditions further to be taught, in that She teaches that a philosopher or lover of the Holy Wisdom 1) must come to know himself and his own nature as it exists in heaven and earth, 2) must know God and Wisdom in himself, 3) must know Wisdom's great depth or Abgrund, and 4) must come to know the key to such great depths as well as to open all mysteries and wonders that lie hidden in Her fiery region, and how to lock them. Such things are treated in the seventh chapter.

Hereafter does the soul-spirit induce an exact contemplation of its self-knowledge, and imagine Wisdom in the form of a sphere, and recognize also the harmony of the microcosm or the small world with the macrocosm, or great world. And so for the eighth chapter. These parallels are further explained in comparison with the visible heaven and its lights in the ninth chapter, and with the visible earth in the tenth chapter. Then in the eleventh chapter is presented an image or pattern 1) in the vegetable 2) in the animal and further in the twelfth chapter in the mineral kingdoms. Which is very strange.

Hereafter and in the thirteenth chapter follows a rather extensive description of the human little world-sphere and its fallen and broken conditions; and in the first place the earth-sphere, and then in the fourteenth chapter also the heavenly eye. Wherein many prophetic words in scripture especially out of the Revelation of John are explained.

In the following chapter the spirit of Wisdom leads her apprentice to her different gates or doors, stands him before them, and gives him the key in his hand, with which he can open them.

The first door, to which she brings him, will be called the door of conviction. Which is to be differentiated from the previous conviction under the dispensation of the Father and Son or servants. This door opens in the seventeenth chapter. Wherein by such suggestions will it also be indicated what the condition and dwelling of the soul will be when it separates from this life, because it will either be under the first dispensation and the service of the Father, or under the other, as the Son's service; for this third and last service has not yet arrived.

Herein Wisdom in the eighteenth chapter opens the other door, which will be named the door of the destroyer or the purification, which is the first door of the renewing, nearby which She also teaches wherein stands the service of John the Baptist and Eliæ [Elijah].

Wisdom's third door is the door of dissolution, which follows next upon the preceding. Because thereby the hieroglyphic or secret sense or images and aphorisms of the ancient wise, directly in this magical door, will be explained. And firstly in the nineteenth chapter, the interpretive teachings of the ancient prophets, and then the teaching of Christ and his Apostle in the twentieth.

Hereafter and following the twenty-first chapter will the apprentice of Wisdom be led forth to the fourth door, the door of the new creation. Which is the other door of the renewing and in the twenty-second or last chapter in different circumstances instructions with examples of the new magical heaven and the new magical earth in men will be set forth, together with a clear teaching of the different qualities in this last chapter; whereby finally and fundamentally will also be investigated and clearly discussed where evil originated. And how infinitely needful [unumgänglich nötig] it is to want to go through this door.

The First Chapter

21 June

As I lay in my spirit in great hunger and painful thirst, surrounded with a fierce thorny anxiety in which I could find no peace, struggling with doubt and unbelief, I was filled with mistrust and suspiciousness [Eysersucht] and with hard and gruesome thoughts against Sophia, or the essential Wisdom, She came and permitted her healing power to descend into my spirit herebelow, soothed my bloodthirsty wounds, stilled my fierce hunger, assuaged my strong thirst and fearful desire and made my spirit purely gentle and mild, annointed me with her holy oil, which gave me inward peace and [so] I sat in a gracious passive stillness. Hereupon She convinced my spirit that She would come herebelow to heal my hope- and helpless spirit and to bestow her general and highest, purest Balsam and medicine on my painful wounds: then I would feel truly annointed with her wonder-oil or Balsam which gave me instantaneous relief; nevertheless I still lay between hope and fear, and I knew neither hand nor medicine through which I would experience such comfort and restoration.

The Second Chapter

22 June

I felt and experienced this precious oil and Balsam mix with my spirit and this gentled, restored, and softened me with stillness and peace. Thereby She convinced my spirit that I was still outside the way that I in my own ability worked for through night and day, that I in my own power anxiously sought, and earnestly in my own might had struggled for. But meanwhile, I in my own working in all eternity was not able to prevail, and She came to teach me that I in my own power and ability remain stagnant, and that I must wait in suffering stillness; And to this end would will the holy oil and Balsam to flow in me, so that it should still and gentle my all too heated and seeking and struggling spirit's sharp and hungry fire: since such would not [be] the right way to the gate of her depths. Because individual working and seeking in one's own power and might could not reach her Centrum. And although I had well sought many ways to reach her eternal *Principium*, also in hope, in faith, in patience, in mildness and humility, and through all pleading and imploring, through strong crying and earnest calling, still all this remained the way to reach neither her nor her *Principium*. Because I wholly sought outside myself and gladly ascended outside myself, and in the power and capacity of my own working spirit wanted to break through the separating wall of her heavenly principle, partake and nourish myself in her; but which could not be: [I had to recognize] her principle is in myself and not truly to be found or sought outside me. Which was very hard for my spirit to believe and to accept, to me a wholly new teaching and a new direction. Because although I already sank down in myself in gentleness, humility, patience, and calmness [Gelassenheit] with my will-spirit to the spirit of God the Father and to the holy will of Wisdom, so I saw always outwards with the eye of my will-spirit, and saw outside myself, meaning that I enjoyed the principle of Wisdom without me and therefore too with earnest desire struggled and worked through

the way of ascent, but in such ways one could not attain. Then
Wisdom permitted Herself to descend herebelow in my spirit,
and the eye of my spirit turned inward, so that it saw inward in
itself and through the way of descent finds Her and Her *principium*
for which my spirit longed, and to find Her and Her *principium*, I
may turn the eye of my understanding inward in my self. Now
after my eternal will-spirit with the eye of my heart was turned
inward, I really experienced in me the reigning power that my
spirit sought. Because I felt a mighty-working power that made
all my working powers and qualities mighty and my spirit earnestly was impelled to seek; also, words and material lay in the
mouth and all my wheels [Räder] or soul-powers were salved
with a precious oil which made them peaceful and gentle. But
who this was that I sought I knew not, who this Driver was I
understood not. I felt well an oil-light power of a penetrating
power, a circulating or up-and down-moving power, an animating impulse in and through all powers and qualities in my inward and eternal man. The name and nature of such power, however, was unbeknownst to me. I knew not what name I should
give Her, nor how I should name it. Still I felt it as a moving impulse. I felt a moving power, that gently and lovingly worked in
me and stilled the fierceness of my hunger and the gruesomeness
of my thirst assuaged; also She taught and assured me that She
would advance her work and won't fail to bring her plans with
all delight and joy into the day. This sudden change astonished
my eternal spirit so much I wondered if I was dreaming, and still
I waited between hope and fear. I hoped in myself the work would
go forth and stood also in fear that it would rekindle my former
hunger and painful thirst and also that it would diminish or dry
up my precious oil that salved my inner spheres, and that my
hungry and thirsty anxiety in my spirit would return.

23 June
    As I in the eye of my understanding still always held on this
loving-gentle oil-annointing which moved so gracefully in the
qualities or Forms of my soul and spirit, the unbelief, doubt, mistrust and all previously perceived suspicious thoughts were made
to fly out of my spirit; courage cast forth all fearfulness from me,
and I was by this impelled to wait in my moving spirit or power

(which I, because my inward man to this time was still unknown
and invisible, felt stir only as a thin, subtile, pure penetrating working and circulating or ascending and descending power in and
through all sensible powers and abilities of my spirit and through
all working qualities and forms of my soul) and this invisible spirit
in prayer thus said to me: I am in you here descending: I am come
in your nature; I penetrated through your brass gate and have
broken through all your iron bolts; and you are come upon my
power, my wholesome oil, such flowing into your eternal sensible and understanding powers and capacities, forms, and qualities therein to mix. I am come to manifest my new creation in you,
to make a new heaven and earth in you, in which nothing other
than righteousness, namely, the right nature of myself, should
dwell. Thus the word of Peter instructed: We but wait on a new
heaven and a new earth; in which righteousness dwells. She led
forth and said further: I am come to make such in you yourself
and this new invisible creation, inwardly in you, and not con-
structed outside you. I am come to make a new philosopher out
of you and to teach you the true *fundamentale* and hidden *principia*
of the holy and heavenly philosophy. You should listen to me
and learn how I will form this new creation in you yourself. Your
eternal spirit should stand by me and you should see this with
your eyes. Because I am come not to advance in an apparition nor
to make known in a revelation but rather through my creating
word actually work it and bring it forth. Because I am come to
really manifest it through my creating Fiat and you should see
the art and way, how I through my magical art will accomplish
this in you. And you should see it done with your own eyes. Thus
began this speaking power in this way to form the new creation:

Firstly, She showed me inwardly Her holy Chaos in myself,
which was like a round circle, a deep Unground, a sphere, wherein
one could see or hear nothing, but rather was a profound Nothing without ground, the immeasurable, wherein from the eye of
my eternal spirit was a visible nothing to be seen, and also all
things were invisibly hidden. This holy Chaos revealed itself to
be a great immeasurable space or place, the nothing as a pure
working power in itself; it revealed itself to the eye of my spirit as
an unformed clump and as a complicated [verwirzte] mass. It was
a great depth without form, and empty of all Ideas. This I saw

(after I with my understanding-eye of my spirit well had observed) the fundament and the ground of the new creation, that should thereof become formed in me.

Thus was it shown to me, secondly, that in this profound Unground was a wise, clever and understanding spirit, which in and through this wove and was suspended and was the working agent in himself. And I saw that it was a quick, fine, subtile and penetrating spirit, a through-weaving spirit, a in- and forth-driving spirit. Then was it given to me to know that this mighty-working spirit could be no other than the spirit of Wisdom itself. Thereby observed my eternal spirit what might be the nature of the spirit of Wisdom: there I saw that Her spirit is an invisible power, a fine power, indeed, nothing other than pure power, a pure Act or working, a weaving motion or impulsion, a sharp, quick, penetrating, circulating, working power, an active, working and mighty power. This I saw to be in holy Chaos, and this working power I felt to be in the sensible and understanding power and ability of my eternal spirit and in the qualities and forms of my eternal soul.

Further, and thirdly, She showed me how She through the holy art made the four eternal elements go forth out of Chaos, and how She raised them out of the mixed Mass, and as thin vapour impelled them upward; there She mixed them one with another and so were the four eternal elements mingled with one another and coagulated together or through Her, confirmed and made essentially by Wisdom's art, and given number, weight and mass to one like temperature free from all excess and strife, so that all were united in unanimous likeness and harmony. Wisdom said to me that this happened through her working power in me, the mingling and essence making (coagulation) of the four elements as changed a unified eternal element into a new Earth, Her dry or fast land, and her holy and fast ground whereupon She wanders and cares to dwell. And this new earth She has planted in my soul, that my spirit in such may live, wander, and dwell in the innermost center of my heart's formed and planted earth. Here Wisdom said of the new earth that I will dwell in your spirit and with you wander and speak and nowhere else will I permit you to find me.

The speaking Word said further: See the centrum of nature, the centrum of your new earth, and there has Wisdom in the heart and midst of this new earth planted a central fire to kindle and to warm, to fix and germinate, to make what through her hand in this new earth should be sown. Without which central-fire the new earth would be raw and coarse [ungeschlacht] and would prove an unfruitful earthly kingdom or ground and foundation. Because there I really feel that She planted this center of her gentle warmth of a fixing fire to be fruitful in the midst of this my new earth.

Further, I really felt that She poured forth a precious fieriness or sap like a powerful living-oil, and mixed it with the central-fire, where it was gently and lovingly made to burn and might be kept from going out. The other form of the central fire you may let be stifled or muffled and put out; but make this oil so that the central-fire burns lively and joyously and maintain the burning flame of this central fire: And it is like the nourishment and food where upon the central-fire feeds and also eternally is maintained, so that there is nothing to provide for, and the holy fire may continue so long as it is maintained and fed by this oil. Thus the holy Wisdom mixes, through Her magical art, the oil and fire in Unity and Harmony, in the heart and center of the new earth, in order to make this newly formed and created earth fruitful and that it may bring forth rich fruit.

Further, and fourth, Wisdom brought forth from the new earth a pure clear crystalline water of life, like a stream out of the newly formed and created earth, and this brought about so that it might be a fruitful earth and ground where the water came forth; because the Water makes it fruitful, there where before it had been without this water of life, so through the vein and course in this new earth [renewing] what previously had been an unfruitful kingdom, a wasteland. For which reason Wisdom wishes to bring forth the stream of water of life in this new earth.

After this Wisdom sows, in this new earth, this heavenly land, the eternal undying and unchangeable seeds of life with living seeds with Her own hand, and thus it is filled with herbs and may garner a rich harvest. Because out of this earth grows all trees of life, whose limbs and branches are so richly laden with fruits that they bend down. All plants are of good-spirited savor and are delightful to the eye, herbs growing instantly up there, those that were strewn with the seed of life, that the first Adam grew for food and nourishment. Thus appears paradise in an instant in the heart and center of this new earth, and thus is found the lost garden of Eden, this delight-garden with all trees, plants, and herbs out of the seeds of life, which they had in themselves, without tilling, ploughing, or sowing this new earth in itself is brought forth in all fruifulness again only out of Wisdom's tincturing oil and Her powerful sap and penetrating power, which makes this delight-garden come forth in all fruitfulness without work. Because in you yourself is the circulating oil, the penetrating tincture, the working power, the living life and movement in and through everything in Paradise. Here I saw the fruits and herbs of paradise, that my eternal man eats and from which he should live, such were peace, love, gentleness, humility, unity, harmony, patience, brotherly love, purity, innocence, sincerity, steadfastness, truth, hope, faith, constancy, and similar heavenly herbs that are filled with the holy power and oil, so with the marrow and fat of the beloved oil that flow through them.

Here said the speaking Word further: Behold now your new earth, that inwardly is formed in you and observe the paradise and the garden of Eden and see how this goes out of your new ground and forming earth, sprouting and blooming without trouble or work in the power of my penetrating tincture and my circulating oil which is the sap of your fruitfulness. Recognize this your paradise and your garden of Eden that now in you yourself is formed and planted, after which you have longed and have worked to nourish. See that there is no other way than that paradise arises in you yourself, and the garden of Eden is again renewed in the self, so that it is formed through my creating power and Fiat in myself in you again created, and thus to a plant of my own planting and to a garden of my delight and joy, to the works my own hands would make. So know that I in my garden in you mingle my wine, my oil, my heavenly power and sap with the herbs, plants, and fruits, that have the seeds of life in themselves, wherewith they are fruitful and multiply, and thus you are the Garden of God and in you yourself may become fruitful soil and no desert or unfruitfulness in you will be found: because the garden of all fulness and overflowing is planted in the middle of your new earth. This new earth is holy earth: this new ground is holy ground; and it is your holy land; wherein no other than my pure virginity and right nature dwells. Nothing grows in this new earth but good seed; no evil seed is sown by me; nothing other than the seeds of eternal life; no evil seeds of eternal death, no other seeds than those of immortality and incorruptibility; no seeds of mortality; no perishable seeds are sown in this newly formed ground and earth-kingdom; no strange seeds, no seeds of other ways or qualities than those of my own holy nature; the seeds of my Godhead and my eternity; no serpent-seeds; no poisonous seeds are sown in this new earth; no seeds of enmity and contrariness is sown by my hand; no thistles or thorns and no roots of bitterness; no anxiety-herbs; no fierceness; no anger; no envy; no negativity, no hate, no grudging or jealousy; no strife grows in my paradisal garden; no weeds; but rather all herbs and plants are for your sustenance and good to eat. This paradisiacal garden formed in the midst of your new earth has a perpetual spring and summer, which bring forth rich flowers and comely colors. It is a rich country full of overflowing harvest. Therein is no winter nor fall; no unfruitfulness is found there. So see now your new-formed earth, which is made living and nourished by my oil's power and sap, and see how your newborn paradise and newly created garden of Eden and delightfulness therein arises: for through my creating power and Fiat of the Almighty is it formed and planted in your heart. Turn your eyes inwards and see it there; because I have planted it in my newly-formed paradisiacal garden in your heart or bosom, watered with my Water of life, my oil and power with my seeds, herbs, plants, and flowers mixed, and my blossoming lilies and roses. Therein will I wander and talk with you; therein will I truly have communion with you; therein will I be your truest friend; therein will I reveal myself to you and my love make real. Outside this holy ground and this my paradisiacal garden I will not permit myself to be found; you may outside it seek but never find; because in your holy land alone will I wander with you. In this your paradisiacal ground or garden grow no forbidden fruit; no seeds of mortality; but rather trees, plants, and herbs through which flow eternal life and immortality.

Further this power of Wisdom gracefully made known to me the progress of future things: in that She prophesied to me that just as she had formed and created in me my new earth and the garden of Eden and had established the paradise in the midst of my new earth; thus would She also make for me a new Heaven in the spirit of my soul, planted in the sensible and understanding powers and capacities of my inward eternal man. Yes, in my heart and in my will and in my senses would She plant this. And after She had completed this Her new creation [or rebirth:] in me and had made a new heaven and earth and paradise in both, would She also create a new Adam, another Adam (by which She meant my own eternal spirit) and that She would place me therein with might and mastery as a master and king to reign; thereby I might be tested, tried, and proven. But She warned me that I must stand my forty-day trial and not, like the first Adam, fall from paradise, but rather She turned my eyes to Jesus Christ, so that the other Adam would stand a right test in truth, constancy, love and faith, and would make [these qualities] into a household over God's treasure chest. This (She said) would be now my model and image and thus must I follow His example.

Herein would She give me a spirit of prayer that I might earnestly pray that the fear of the heart in the days and hours of my test be verified with me and that I would be made true and steadfast as Wisdom's true hero, whereby I would fight Her fight, and through the Seeds of Virginal Wisdom might bruise the head of the serpent and overcome it.

Then was it further given to me to know that Wisdom's Might could create Her new Creation in an instant, bringing forth a new heaven and earth; but She must bring forth her new creation in me little by little or in degrees so that my inner spirit might with her hear, see, know and understand how She brings forth and creates the new heaven and earth out of Her own unformed Chaos in order and with differentiation; how She brings an order out of disorder; and a differentiation out of confusion; how the new heaven and earth would be brought forth out of Her eternal Chaos. Also how the subtile, penetrating, working and weaving spirit of the Wisdom of God suspended over the deep ungrounded Chaos of the four eternal elements and through their mixing-together brought forth the new earth, and out of the new earth formed paradise, and how the spirit of Wisdom in the paradisiacal earth might bring forth plants, herbs, trees, fruits and flowers, that have in themselves Her Seeds of life.

Now accordingly Wisdom brought forth before the eyes of

my understanding this newly created earth and planted paradise in the midst, the right true delight-garden, through Wisdom's power and order, and in my heart or bosom was planted, hidden and enclosed in the newly created earth or paradisiacal garden, and [accordingly She] gave my eternal spirit time to observe this through Her magical art and understanding, this wonderful forming of my new earth; and all this in the midst of my heart's ordered locality. And thus ends my first *lection* of the holy Philosophy, that my understanding capacity (which belongs to the eternal spirit of my inward and eternal man) through the holy Wisdom would learn. After this Wisdom gave me a praise song, that I might Sing her praises because She has formed this new earth and renewed paradise, and that this really was inwardly born in me and planted through Wisdom's creating power.

> Come, most beautiful Love and eternal Bride to test the Soul's Root
> Ray forth out of your beauty and let your sweet light illumine us!
> The wild primal dispersal and the coal-black night
> The old earth in me that She will again bring
> To primal purity. Create again anew
> My outward-turned heart, let it rejoice in you.
> Melt all selfhood and make it sinfree
> So that it is eternally devoted to you alone.
> The heavenly-seeds now really She brings;
> The other Eden so joyfully upward springs.
> The beautiful Sharon-Rose and Lily there rises
> In the midst of a great mass
> Of beautiful flowers and heavenly graces
> Because there no rebel worm is, so little harm
> May come by. In the *centrum* goes forth
> Wisdom's power, and paradise flies forth.
> Let my love then come into Her garden
> That freshly blooms; permit me all Her profits
> There She accompanies me; there She offers her fruits
> (With their lovely scents) and presses Her nectar
> That there so richly flows; and sunken
> In Her spiritual properties, one becomes drunken.
> May She remain here by Her shimmering follower,
> And eternally may the banner of Her love fly over me.

Twenty-Second Chapter

10 July

This day Wisdom visited me and said: I have brought you to my other gate of renewal and restoration where all things are made new. Such is my lovely and graceful gate; it is the day of my lily; there my lily on the peak of the mountain should sprout forth and rise, after the prophesies of former days, and ancient prophets, to which I would have you investigate and seek after. I want to show to you the new creation, the new world in you yourself, the microcosm, or the little world, the new *globum* or world-sphere in you yourself that exists out of heaven and earth: because the ancients are lost and gone, and their state should no more be found. Know therefore that I could destroy the old world in an instant and erect a new world and my new heaven and earth in you; but after your wish I must change it in degrees and accomplish it bit by bit in order that you become a wise philosopher and may see, know, and learn the art and ways of how I raise up a new creation in you, and that you on this my day may come to understand the aphorisms of the ancient patriarchs and the dark speech and prophecies of the prophets and the explanation of the words of the wise, namely the teaching of Christ and the Apostle in the holy scripture, which until the appearance of my morning-star have been swallowed up, as in the sealed books. In the beginning God the Father first created heaven, and later the earth. But I will in my work of Creation in you begin first with your new earth, and then continue to your new heaven, and then further to the new Adam.

Here Wisdom led me further, and said: See your new earth, as the first part of your new *globum*, or world-sphere, in you yourself: referred to in 2 Peter 3.13. But we await according to His promise a new heaven and a new earth, that is, nothing less, and regardless the old heaven and earth will be dissolved or disappear, so we await a new heaven and earth. Now I say to your spirit: see this new earth, your new earth, the promised earth, the earth of which so much is prophesied, this new earth (that you with your eyes of the heart or spirit before you see) is the new earth according to the promise of God to Abraham and his seed, also to Isaac and Jacob, as you may read in Gen. 12.7: And the

Lord appeared to Abraham and said: To your seed will I give this land or earth, this land of Canaan, and this was a figure of this new land or earth which I now point out to you. Is this not a dark word and speech? Who would understand it? Gen. 15.7: I am the Lord; I have led you out of Ur of Chaldea that I gave you possession of and as inheritance. What kind of land? The land Canaan, a figural land. But I say to you: See your new land, according to the promise that God made to Abraham and his seed. These were dark proverbs in the days of the Father and of the Son, that I now come to open to you, that is namely what my forthcoming day will mean. This new earth is even the earth of which the prophets knew, as you may read in Isaiah 65.17: See I create a new heaven and a new earth…. [skip 176-7]

This awoke my spirit as from a deep sleep (because I was astonished over the view of this new earth) and drove me with my questioning spirit to observe what the nature of this new earth was. What were its qualities and characteristics?

Now after my spirit so often had called for a vision, Wisdom began to show me in their essence and independence, what namely this new earth in its original essence and being was, according to Her promise, so that one might make a wise and understanding *philosophus*.

This new earth I saw in myself a true, essential, independent, firm, and constant earth in its essence and independence; it was a deep ground; it was firm like a dry land and earthly kingdom upon which to wander: as deep as the visible earth of this outward birth is. Only it is of another nature. It is to the outward eye still invisible; it is not coarsely visible or conceivable, nor is it such a coarse, fat, graspable earth as the visible, four-elementary earth of this visible creation; rather, it is a visible, spiritual, essential, independent, firm earth of itself, spiritually, magically, and philosophically to be understood; that is, this new earth is a spiritual earth, far higher and more united, sublimated, or heartened and spiritualized than the dense, coarse, visible and graspable earth of this visible creation. Here is the philosophical earth, that is, the earth of the philosophers; which is a kind of spiritual, invisible, and supernatural earth that cannot be seen by the common eye or spirit, nor can it by dense reasoning-man be understood nor known: for him it is truly invisible and inconceivable. But to the illuminated eye and the spirit of the inward man, of the wise philosopher, is it a visible and graspable or conceivable earth. This new earth is a magical earth; that is, it is a coagulated, joined-together, or essentially created earth, new-made through my own holy *magiam*, and this coagulated earth is made out of the four eternal elements, namely formed out of fire, air, earth, and water. Yet it is not formed out of fire, air, water or earth, but rather out of a quintessential *materia*, substance, and being, and out of the mixing and coagulation of the four eternal elements, that exist in number, weight, and mass in a similar temperature. There also will the quintessential earth be formed, which out of a very deep understanding may be named the magical earth as that which through the holy *magiam* forms in an instant. This magical earth is the authentic, visible, material, essential, independent earth, although against the coarse, visible, and material earth of this outward birth it may be named an invisible, unmaterial and spiritual earth.

Don't imagine that this is some imaginary earth, an idealized earth, a mere shadow: it is a real land, a real ground, an essential, independent earth, into which one goes and can wander. This is called a magical earth; because it is an essential, true, and independent earth, hence its spirituality or subtile essentiality only appears as an invisible, immaterial earth. Yet this magical earth is for its dwellers, for whoso should dwell in it, most comfortable, and filled with their nature; Because no one other than eternal spirits, no one other than the inward eternal man with his heart, will, and mind, and with his soul and affects can dwell therein; but all of these are invisible powers and thus is this magical created earth a comfortable earth for them. Because just as the outward visible world is created for outwardly visible men; so is the inward new earth created for the inward invisible man, that he might there live and wander. This new earth is even so comfortable for the inward eternal man as the outward world is for the outward man.

This new earth, to the eye of my heart, would be the underpart of the world-sphere and in the likeness of a central-earth, imagined to be like this outward earth of visible creation, only that it is different in its spirituality or spiritual subtile essentiality, rareness, and clarity, and was but a fixed *centrum*. It appeared to be both within and without me; and can both move and remain still, and also in the power of its subtilty and spirituality spreads through this whole visible earth, so that it is closed out of no place, nor held to any one place; where also my spirit was, there I was in this new central-earth, and it penetrated everywhere in this whole visible earth. It was an inwardness in this newly created earth; so that in this visible earth no one went nor could be in some place; it was my newly created earth in me, and thus also present with me; and if I with the spirit of my heart was really to turn inward in it, then "it" was in all places and through all places in this visible earth; and was simply invisible to the reasoning man, immaterial and inconceivable; but in the spirit of the inward eternal man was a visible, material, corporeal, essential, independent and conceivable magical earth.

And there so universal and omnipresent [is it] that wherever the outward man turns, to which places or in what land in this outward birth, the spirit-man has no need to be outside this new earth; because it was everywhere and closed nowhere. It is present in and through all places of this visible earth, if he would only turn his heart, will, and mind inward in himself, and permit it not outside his own earth in himself; because it turns on the act of his spirit through his own free will itself and would lead him outward like his brother Esau, the outward reason-man, in his land and kingdom; but otherwise the inward man has so great and wide a kingdom in his own earth as the outward man always has in his.

Now after the nature and being of this newly created earth was really and livingly revealed to me, so that it was not alone in me, but rather where I was, it also was, and my spirit needed nothing outside it to live, I observed Wisdom open further in me her great, wide, and broad outward borders and reveal the nature of this newly created earth in me with its implanted qualities and characteristics.

1. The first quality of this new earth was that it was an eternal, unaltering, indestructible earth, because it was made out of eternal material, namely out of the mixture, coagulation, and compaction of the four eternal elements. And this earth was an immediate effect and consequence out of the similar mixing and temperature of the four eternal elements, and so is named the quint-

essential earth; because it is made of one essence, not fire, air, earth, and water, but rather quintessence or the fifth element, that out of the four is arisen. For which reason one may well speak of the one-elementary earth, so called because it is made out of the one eternal elementary earth. Because even though it is created out of all four eternal elements, it is not an air-earth, or a water-earth; but rather it is a one earth made out of the mixture of four elements, and thus a one-elementary earth. Because it is also an imperishable, eternal, and unchanging earth, and has an un-changeable nature in it; and can undergo no change nor dissolu-tion or destruction. Because of this eternal material is it known as an eternal earth.

2. The other quality of this earth was, that it is an essential independent earth. It is a fast, independent earth; because it is created out of essential independence, namely out of the four eter-nal elements of eternal nature; but these are eternal essences, im-mediately generated in themselves out of God's eternal Chaos; because this one-elementary earth as immediately out of the same mixture, must be necessarily a one true essential and indepen-dent essence in itself. And hence is it necessarily a true, essential, and independent earth.... Hence must it be either an *ens*, or a non-ens in itself: but it is no non-ens in itself, because it is generated out of an eternal immediate essence....

3. The third quality is that it is a material and consequently an essential earth. And so it is in its essence a material earth, so it can be no unmaterial earth; but so is it a material essence, a material earth. And such it is in truth; however, its material essence is highly pure, subtilized, sublimated or enheartened and spiritualized, so that we have no words to express its likeness: because we can liken it to the air, fire, or light and clouds of this visible creation, which are the subtlest or rarest bodies and the highest corporeal being that we have; and the most spiritual material essences and independent entities with which we can compare it: so are all still too gross, fat, and too heavy material being to describe or express the spiritualized materialized being of this eternal earth. Hence we have a lack of adequate words and likenesses to describe the unmaterial earth. Certainly it is not that it is not without material being and corporeality, but rather because the material of this earth is unified, subtile or rare and spiritualized, so that one cannot

conceive it with thought or imagination. But now in the appearance of Wisdom's days She names it the magical earth: and because She best knows the nature of this earth, so also she knows what names best to give it. Accordingly, She names it according to its rare subtileness her *materia*, and according to its subtilety, her part, and also according to its flowingness, her magical earth, because it is a flowing *materia* and a penetrating *materia*, that penetrates and flows through all things: thus what material essences belong to this earth, She names essential qualities of the magical earth. But you must not here understand with your dark reason and imagine with mere imagination only a clear idea or image of the earth, and a mere shadow of the earth, without an essential, independent being; no way; for then you would see no true earth, but rather a clear non-*ens*, a mere appearance without an essential *materia*. The word "magic" but gives one to understand a hidden, essential, independent earth; that is however so subtilized and spiritualized that dumb and blind reason (however sharp it otherwise is in its own *centrum*) remains nonetheless unable to conceive it. But you may look inward and say: Who should then participate in this magical earth, whether it is unmaterial or material? What matter whether it is true, essential, independent or a false, fabricated mere imagination of an existing earth, if the reason should not be able to participate in it? Answer—the spirit of the inward eternal man in union with the spirit of faith; that is, if he is illuminated with the light of faith and consequently sees with the eye and sense of faith, which alone on this earth can truly partake of the magical earth; he alone may see it: because the eternal spirit of the eternal heart is alone given an eye to see; the stumplike reason-eye is unfit for true participation in such things.

4. The fourth characteristic: Fourth is that the earth of which I write is a visible earth, and so it is also a material and essential and independent earth. It is a visible, palpable, and comprehensible earth, a subtilized earth that belongs to the sense of inward eternal spirit-man; so is it also comfortable through being known through his heart and seen through his eyes. Yes, it is also a fast and virgin earth, a heavy ground, whereon the inward man can go and wander. And so it is a visible, tangible and comprehensible earth whereon man can step and wander.... But one can here ask: why then is this inward magical earth named an invisible

earth, since it is in its essence a visible earth? Answer: the holy scriptures name this magical earth an invisible earth, and this inward creation an invisible creation (Col. I.16): Through Him are all things created, that are in heaven and on earth, both visible and invisible, that is, all things are in the invisible heaven or in the visible heaven, are in the invisible earth or in the visible earth of this outward birth. Here we see that this inward earth is named an invisible earth; because its nature is subtilized, so flowing or flows in all its weaving motions....

Another reason why this inward earth is named an invisible earth is because this inward new creation is hidden in this visible creation; this inward magical earth is in this visible earth hidden and cannot be seen, and therefore rightfully may be named an invisible earth....

The third reason why this inward magical earth is an invisible earth is because the outward reasoning-man and rational spirit in outward man cannot see it: because this magical earth is in all places and like water its kingdom flows everywhere, and in all districts, so this invisible earth may be neither seen nor known by an outward man of flesh and blood nor through reasoning (even if he knew all arts and sciences of all the schools of the earth). Unobserved, it is present through the whole visible earth of this world, yet cannot be see by outward man or by reasoning-man. Therefore one may well call it an invisible magical earth.

The fourth reason why this magical earth is in its essence adequately visible and yet is named invisible is because the spirit of inward man, which was in the beginning created for this invisible earth, cannot see it, even though it is in him. Because although it is already before his eyes and in all places in this visible world present, so he can not see, feel, or know it; because he is so enraptured and blended with the spirit of this world and with the sensual life of this present outward world that this inward visible earth is become invisible.... [But] this invisible magical earth may be seen by a true Christian philosopher; and it may also be seen by the children of Wisdom, for Wisdom opens it for them, and allows them to see and know this invisible magical earth. All truly faithful to the spirit of faith have the gift of God the Father and their eyes are illuminated with the light of faith, which makes this invisible earth visible, and all else invisible.

Finally, this earth in its essence or being is a visible earth, so it is no invisible earth, even when considered in the delicate onefoldedness of its being. This is it a visible, tangible, and conceivable earth, hence also an independent and essential earth.... But to whom is it conceivable, and by whom is it comprehended? Answer: this earth-*principium* is comprehended by the inward man (when his eye is opened); it is conceived or better, seized by the eternal spirit of the eternal heart. The eternal heart of the eternal spirit is the eye that in union with the light of faith grasps this earth; thus alone can the inward eternal man seize and comprehend in its measure [Maaß] and not by outward reason-man; because it is another *principium*, globe, or earth from the sphere of this outward birth. What is comprehended or grasped of the inward magical earth through the opened eye of the spirit of the inward man? Answer: this *principium* of the inward earth whereof we speak; it is a universal *principium*, and is stretched out over the whole visible world.

It is closed out of no place, but rather is in and through all and every place; so that the spirit of the heart clearly comprehends and understands its width, breath, and length, for it is so wide and broad as the visible creation is; and clearly understand that the end of this outward principle marks the inner principle's border, so that the inner complement of the outward principle is the same; and in its border enclosed.... But you must know that this inner earth-*principium* cannot be extended to infinity: because the circumference is not without its own aim and border, but rather God the Creator has set this principle its own aim and border, so that you should go so far and not further. God alone knows the border of his circumference, and to Him is it not immeasurable or unlimited. To the spirit of this inward eternal man and his understanding and comprehension is it an unending circumference, apparently without end or border....

And do not raise this matter before the schools and academies of this outward visible world so that they in all their grades and dignities with their caps and gowns, all based in reason, might be driven to laugh at and mock at these two different worlds or principles that are hidden, the inner in the outer, and the invisible in the visible; but rather let them know that near their reason-spirit they also have an eternal spirit which is capable of knowing and comprehending the inward magical, essential, independent world. Thus you see that the inward world in its essentiality is a comprehensible world....

5. The fifth characteristic of this inward magical earth is that this inner earth is a created earth, Isa 65.17: See, I create a new heaven and a new earth. Now therefore is a created earth in its essence a created earth-*principium*, so is it an essential and independent earth in its eternal essential independence. Now it is a created *principium* or earth: because it must be either created or uncreated; but the text says created and I have pointed out to you the material or generation-reason whereof it is created, namely out of the mixture of the four eternal elements in number, weight, and measure, through the understanding, science, and art of holy Wisdom, and the ground, whereof these four eternal elements are made, and by which God himself created, was through the eternal chaos. Thus you see the ground whereof this inward, eternal, magical *principium*, world, or earth is created, namely out of the mixing and conjoining of the four eternal elements, and out of this one eternal element, out of the union and harmony of the four, springs up this one-elementary *principium* or earth. Now is it one essential, independent *materia* of created essence, so must it be in itself necessarily an essentially independent earth....

Further I say that this means that God the Father, who is the Creater of this new earth, has created in union with Sophia, His own Wisdom: for the Holy Trinity works and creates nothing without eternal Wisdom; and so also can Wisdom do nothing without the eternal Holy Trinity. Thus God does and creates nothing without Wisdom; and because Wisdom with the Godhead is joined and unified in invisible ways, one always is together with the other in union. The Holy Trinity works in and through Wisdom and Wisdom in and with the Holy Trinity. Here is the Holy Trinity the foremost creative-origin, and Sophia or Wisdom is the secondary instrumental origin of this inner creative *principium*....

Here you see the art and was of her creating or birth: that the eternal Holy Trinity is the foremost origin and the Holy Wisdom the secondary instrument; and the instrument in Her hand, the creating Word in creating *Fiat* of the Almighty, the bringing-forth of this inward world or *principium*. It goes forth according to Her magical understanding and art in herself, because She alone knows how fire, air, and water are weighed in weight, number, and measure; and also She knows how to coagulate or make together, and how all is joined in an eternal harmony and uniting-together. And after She through the art of Her holy *magia* has formed and brought all together in an eternal element, she creates this inward *globum* or earth-sphere. And from this composition or bringing-together art through the art of Wisdom and Her magical ways is it rightly named the inward, eternal, magical world or *Principium*.... Now which eternal searching spirit would namely in this ground and forming or creating-art of this magical earth not be peaceful and satisfied, but rather with words darken oneself and sink into a labyrinth and bewildering error-garden?

It is important, finally, to recognize the end-purpose of this creation of the inward, eternal, magical earth, for such a wide, broad, and spacious place was not created without reason. Because [otherwise] that would be as if God and Wisdom had created it in vain. But in fact it was created to an end and purpose; and certainly (as no one may doubt) for a dweller to dwell therein. One may ask, though: who is this dweller for which it has been created? Answer: it is permitted to no one to doubt that it is this inner world of God and Wisdom created for the first Adamic men and those who came after. This was the purpose and aim of the creator, that the first man Adam in his Angelic form with all his seed and kingly descendents in their first-created form might be dwellers in this magical world, and live in this magical earth and ground, and should wander therein. Because the dweller in such a world should be the inner man, the eternal man, the spirit-man with his eternal powers and possibilities, namely with his heart, will, and mind, so also his soul or heart and its affects or desires. For the outward man is created this outward coarse visible *principium* and *centrum*. The inward eternal invisible spirit-man is born to possess the inward, eternal, invisible world and to be nourished therein. The outward visible mortal reason-man is but born to dwell in the outward, visible, temporal world.

Thus you see who are the dwellers that belong to each world or *principium*; and also that the aim of its creation is that some dwell in each; and that each belongs to its own *principium*. For the inward spiritual-men belong to the inward *principium*, that with its spiritualized and subtle or pure created nature is joined with fruits, trees, herbs and plants...just as the outward world has its trees, herbs, plants, flowers, and fruits.... O wonder over the art and the understanding of holy Wisdom! Each world comes with nature, characteristics, and qualities that correspond to the dwellers therein; the inward with the inward eternal men, and the outward with the outward reason-men....

But you will ask me: when was this inward world created, where does it lie, and where is its place that we might find it?.... So I answer: that time and place are two undifferentiated conditions that arise together with all created essences and being; because the inward world is a created realm and so must have a time [of its own] and a beginning to its existence and a place wherein it exists.... [As to the question of where this inward world is]: The spirit of eternity has many mansions or dwellings whose effective characteristics in eternal nature are brought forth in the house of immeasurable eternity; which Christ Jesus well understood and gave us to understand in John 14.2, when he tells us that "in my Father's house are many dwellings." By God the Father is to be understood the spirit of eternity, the true eternal God the creater and maker of all worlds and principles: by the Father's house understand eternal nature, with all its effective qualities, which is the great immeasurable and inconceivable eternity. And in this *principium* of the immeasurable eternity are many dwellings, that is, there are many different dwellings, different principles, different world-spheres and circumferences, without confusion and mixing with one another, so that all are in the inner half of this unending, inconceivable circle of eternity, in which each innerhalf remains in its own enclosed circumference, and none is mixed with another, nor overflows, but rather each independent world remains in its own sphere.

These many different and particular dwellings of eternity in the immeasurable eternity are not observed by men. For these many dwellings have been enclosed only in two, namely in hell and heaven, in the dark world and in the light world, in which it is said that all eternal spirits that are separated out of love and this visible world, necessarily must go either in hell or in heaven and nowhere else stay than these two *principia*, namely the dark and the light world. All sinners caught in unholiness and wickedness and who die without penitence and faith, go immediately to hell, and the faithful and penitent sinner goes out of the outward principle immediately to heaven and thus they make out of these many dwellings only two, and would neither hear nor accept that one might go to any other waystation. Such speak of a dwelling or waiting room wherein eternal spirits may go, as if one after death could go alone either to hell or heaven. And they stop their ears against all who would speak of some other dwellings, and to those who would say more than two, they cry "heretic" and "blasphemer" and pay no attention to Christ's own words, which expressly and without doubt speak of more than two. And they do not observe that none of the spirits, when they are separated from the body, can travel immediately to the condition of salvation, save if they have completely been purified and freed of all sins and selfhood and without a fleck or stain. And they do not think of the fact that no one in this life, in this fleshly life, goes without sin and can be free from all earthly sins, and thus in a mixt state must die, in a condition outside good and evil, outside light and dark, outside flesh and spirit, thus in a condition of weakness and incompletion: because the completed condition in this world (according to its fundamental laws) cannot be attained in this world. And the holy Scriptures are clear and unambiguous that no impure spirit nor anyone unclean can enter into the condition of the New Jerusalem (Rev. 21.27). The Scriptures tell us: "Err not, nor lead into error." (Eph. 5.5) Because no whores nor impure nor misers nor idolators can enter into the kingdom of God and Christ, nor understand their spiritual ways. Who save the fully completed can say that his spirit, heart, will, and mind and heart and affection are not born after the creaturely and are not subject to it? And thus all who die in such an impure condition do not partake in the kingdom of Christ and God, but rather after Rev. 22.15 are outside it or shut out from it. But where must all these eternal spirits go, who die in a condition of impurity, weakness, and incompletion? The Holy Scriptures say, some claim, that the heart-awakened [verherzlichten] state is limited to the heavenly kingdom, and because there are no other dwellings permitted for purification, all must go damned to hell. O gruesome sect! This is their teaching of grace, and predestination, and their condemnation. But Christ was a good Samaritan, a gentle, warm-hearted latitudinarian and taught that in the house of immeasurable eternity of God the Father are many mansions.

To come to an answer to the question, however, permit us to observe how many dwellings are created, before the dwelling of this inward eternal world, or how many more were generated. We read of the high eternity and of the highest eternity, which is the eternal world, and that which differentiates them is named the still eternity. Before and above this is the unknown eternity, the unknowable Godhead, which no one other than Itself, knows what it is. But out of this unknown *principium* of the highest eternity is the still eternity immediately outside Him, through the power of Him, and He generates it. The still eternity is immediately outside His holy essence or being, so is it generated by Him. And this is over the eternal nature, and was created before the eternal nature. And such is the first or foremost *principium* and the first dwelling whereof we read. The other dwelling or eternal *principium* generated out of this eternal world, was God's eternal chaos, the deep ground of this eternal nothing, whereof the eternal nature with all its seven working qualities was created. This is the other eternal *principium* or eternal dwelling and is called the immeasurable, inconceivable and endless eternity. Out of this unfathomable deep and immeasurable circumference or periphery were created many eternal dwellings in this house of God the Father. And the other eternal world is generated out of God's eternal nature and out of its working qualities. Out of this immeasurable eternity were many different dwellings created under which was the first dwelling-house and differentiated world of the angelic world-circle, the angelic *principium* or circumference of the angelic world: in which the angel in his heart-awakened [verherzlichten] condition of God's angel in the glory of his majesty showed (Job 38.7): There the morning stars sing praises with one another to Me, and all the children of God jubilate. All understand this of the angelic hierarchy, that there thank God with praise and singing and jubilation and serve Him in harmony and unity of love. And...so God had held within here with his work, his creation, and created no more *principium*, but rather God and the angels in holy joy and play of holy love and in the highest communion in all eternity have lived with one another. The Fall of Lucifer and his angelic thrones out of his state or house, which broke asunder the eternal unity and the one-holy bond of the triumphant love under the high angelic thrones, further brought about God's Work in his creation. Because in his Fall and damnation Lucifer formed his own hell, which became the dark world and the darkfire world, and this is his own eternal *principium* of eternal darkness; this his groundless pit or abgrund, his fire-and sulphurous hell-fire: which his own hand has formed and made. Because the warmhearted, high-praised, and merciful God had not created the dark, anxious, fire-world to pain the eternal spirits. The Devil has made this in his own fall, for he broke in his fall the bond of eternal nature and he formed in himself a *principium* of dark anxious fire....

Now after the Fall had happened, and its world-circle stood independently, and a dark world, the source of pain and anxiety, was evident, God moved in the far creation, to create out of the working qualities of his eternal nature a light-*principium*, a light world, a love world, wherein God would reveal to all men His Good, His love, and His compassion. To which end He placed the paradisiacal *principium*, a light-dwelling, directly opposite to the hellish and devilish world. Likewise Satan had formed a hellish world and *principium* of darkness; thus formed God a light-*principium*. And likewise as Satan's dark world stood in wrath and anguish; so stood this [other] in love and joy, and it is called paradise, and the paradisiacal world.

And here you see how many dwellings were created. But the time and the begining of their creation was immediately after the Fall of the angel from light, and after he had become a devil: so that their birth and creation was immediately after the formation of the dark world; then the Holy Trinity in union with Holy Wisdom, truly revealed and brought to light this inward light and paradise world *centrum* or *principium*. Whether this is seen in the eye of eternity as an Idea, or like a reflection in a mirror, or as a potential, but not actual world, this truly lies in the eye of eternity, and has been brought into being through the art of its creation. From this time onward appeared the light or paradisal creation and not before. Now this *principium* of light, love, and joy, was really created, essentially made and was revealed, and so was its time and beginning created with it, along with its created circumstances and consequences. The Holy Scriptures call it paradise or the paradisiacal world, the paradisiacal *principium* or dwelling. Here God through Wisdom created the first Adamic man in in him all that came after, that should be the inheritance of this new-created *principium,* world, or dwelling, and fixed it as a Garden of Eden or delight and joy. And thus was created the inward created paradisal world (as no one may doubt), and has its beginning before the outward visible world became revealed....

And where is the wise and book-learned and disputer of this world who can say to us how many created dwellings God in His infinite Wisdom and good in his immeasurable eternity has created for poor, lost, and incompleted sinners, that they might go therein when they are separated from this outward fallen *principium,* whereof Christ spoke and pointed out? Oh! What should we then think of eternal spirits with eternal souls that died under the day of the Father's Purification, and of all our ancestors that died during the Son's days in mixed conditions, and consequently can come neither in the inward paradisiacal condition nor in the clarified condition of Mount Zion? Where are they all gone? Have they all immediately gone into the dark world, wherein the devil and his angels under the dragon's mastery and violence tortures them? What sort of God would this be? So this is why Christ, the true latitudinarian, would entrust us with these words, that in his Father's House, that is, in immeasurable eternity, are many created dwellings: in which many eternal dwellings, when we are separated from our bodies and this outward world, our eternal spirits together with our eternal souls go, and in which eternal spirits according to their grades of purification dwell; thus they may come to and may enjoy the peace of paradise....

God is mighty enough out of His warmhearted nature to forgive all sins, and to lift all punishments for sins, and it is His delight to forgive sins; for he has delight in compassion; it is His delight and it goes more with His holy essence to forgive and to be merciful, than to send His hand's work through the way of the vengeful punishment of the dragon in the dark world, which would go against His Majesty to want to cause suffering. But where remains God's all sufficiency? And where is His almightiness, that He cannot Himself punish, but rather must send to another power to be punished? I say again that God did not create hell, nor did He create some eternal spirits that should be eternal dwellers in such a hellish *principium*: also he sends no eternal spirit there, nor is it the kingly prerogative of His own eternal will that has sent anyone there.

But here you will turn and say: how then came so many eternal spirits of sinners to hell, if God did not send them there, and give them over to Satan and the dragon to be tortured? Whereupon I answer: that it is certainly true that a crowd has gone there, yet God has neither created such a place nor has He sent anyone there. The question then is: how came such great crowd there? Such you must know, have themselves made their angel into a devil, and the dragon has formed his own anxious *principium* and *centrum* in them, in what was a vast and empty space and place without dwellers in it: because no other dwellers dwell there than the fallen angel himself, so you can see that God has not created it nor sent someone there: because they were God's enemy and stood in enmity against Him.... Because in the dark world is the *centrum* of a dark magical fire, is an almost irresistable might, through which the eternal spirits (who give up their will to it), are entangled and overcome, so that in their eternal nature they become it: so then such that thus permit themselves to be sucked in and to really become a hellish *principium*, they become then dwellers therein, and otherwise no one goes there. And without this inward strong magical fire that the spirits sucked into themselves would there be eternally in itself no dwellers in hell, and no one remaining there. So that this dark magical *centrum* has not one single dweller other than those that thus sucked it into themselves. And so the devil knows all too well, that his dark *principium* would remain without dwellers: thus he…goes about and in and out like so many roaring lions, to seek if he can bring them as a theft to hell, and entangle them. What is it then, that he as a theft seeks to bring there? Answer: He afflicts not the mortal spirit of outward men, but rather he seeks after their eternal immortal spirits. Why and to what end? Merely and only this: he seeks to make them dwellers with and near himself in his anxious *principium*. Through what means does he seek to do this? Through incessant going in and out and around that he might seduce and prostitute them, that he might turn them to him with their free will and heart, spirit and will, that they become with him, and thus his evil nature dwells in them, inwardly, so that their nature is impregnated with his evil seed, and man in this way in his spirit becomes an incarnated devil, and so himself becomes a comfortable dweller with and in the anxious source. And in this way the dark world comes to have a unnumbered crowd of dwellers....

Thus you see how many eternal spirits through abuse of their own wills make themselves dwellers in the suffering *principium*, in that they themselves transform themselves into the devilish nature, and thus become one will and nature with the devil, and not that God has ordered them there, or that He wants them there, or that they are fated to go there. Why would we make of God the source of man's eternal suffering and damnation? Why do we need to? Why not far more the dragon and devil and the act of our own free will that turns itself from God's will and to the dragon's and devil's will? Because this is consistent with the teaching of the Old and New Testaments, of that I am absolutely certain.

VI

Gottfried Arnold

Gottfried Arnold, born in 1666 in Annaberg, Saxony, was one of theosophy's greatest scholars. Arnold was influential above all for pointing out with enormous erudition how the theosophical doctrines of the Böhmean school are in fact found also in the writings of the early Church fathers and mystics. In his book *Das Geheimnis der Göttlichen Sophia* [*The Mystery of the Holy Sophia*], Arnold scarcely mentions Böhme, relying almost totally on quotations from early Christian writers, and Pordage, whose work undoubtedly inspired Arnold, is not mentioned at all. After Pordage's *Sophia*, Arnold's work is perhaps the most influential of the works devoted solely to Wisdom.

During his productive life, Arnold wrote many influential books, including extensive Christian histories, in particular his *Unparteiische Kirchen- und Ketzerhistorie* [*Impartial Church and Heretic History*](1699), the first modern theological history to take some forms of early Christian Gnosticism—particularly Valentinian Gnosticism—seriously. For Arnold, as one might expect, what mattered in theological history was whether a given writer manifested correspondences with the theosophic views we have been elaborating in this work. The true history of the Church was that of the *wiedergeborene*, those who are spiritually reborn through gnostic experience, a concept that includes and transcends phenomena connected with being "born again" in contemporary Protestantism. The titles of his later works are indicative of the same perspective: *Historie und Beschreibung der Mystischen Theologie* (1703), and *Theologia Experimentalis* (1714). Much more a scholar than a gnostic like Pordage, Arnold's treatise shows a different side of theosophy, one rooted in works like the Book of Wisdom.

The Mystery of Holy Sophia
Das Geheimnis der Göttlichen Sophia
(Leipzig: 1700)

Description of Holy Sophiae or Wisdom
From the Holy Scriptures and Ancient Teachings

I. How and Why the Holy Wisdom Appears Unknown and Despised by Men, As Well As the Consequences Thereof

1. It is unfortunate! Every day before our eyes we see how the eternal origin of all good, the holy Wisdom, is unknown to natural men, and despised and held as little by most, but also inexactly observed and understood differently.

2. Because also by otherwise goodwilled men by nature, she and many other holy things are unknown, and even the ancients realized only a part of this, as the Book of Wisdom (7/12) has it: "Wisdom went before me (in all things) but I did not know that she was their mother."

3. And in the Book of Job he testifies the same of her (28/21) "One cannot find her (Wisdom) in the land of the living; because she is hidden from the eyes of all living beings, and is unknown by the birds of heaven." As also in Sirach 6/22: "She is not known by many, in that all holy wonder and mystery is for most scandalous and null."

4. The principal reason for this dreadful ignorance of such men is the deep apostasy[22] from all holy understanding [Sinn] and the veritable invasion of false life, which derives from either dwelling in earthly and sensual things or in pride and scorning all things that come from God. Hence the pure and clear being of eternal Wisdom can find no place in such souls and hence she must withdraw back into her pure holy element and conceal [verbergen] herself.

5. The ancient [uralte] secret God-learned Dionysius offers still another reason why God dwells in an inaccessible light and can be seen by no one: Div. Nomine Cap. VII, no. i: "God is not only transcendent Wisdom and his understanding has no number, but rather is above all reason, understanding, and Wisdom."

6. From this ignorance of Wisdom derives their disgraceful

scorn, which grieves her friends, who have specially testified and lamented of this in their writing, some of whom I'll now name.

7. In the holy scripture she speaks thusly: Prov. 1/24, 25: "I invite you (natural and unconverted man) and consider you; I reach out my hand and no one pays attention: rather, you withdraw yourselves from my counsel and rest not in my reprimand" or according to the Septuagint, "You make yourselves unfit for counsel," that is: you deaden the abiding inward discipline and admonitions of the Holy Ghost (which is the Spirit of Wisdom) and do not follow it. 1 Thess. 5/19; Acts 7/51

8. Another way to describe this scorning is that one sins (Prov. 8/35), that one goes by Her (Wisdom 10/8), that one secedes from her (10/3), that one goes astray (Sirach 4/20). Likewise that some, who have heart, do not persist in her (6/20) or do not pray to God for grace and courage to withstand the testing and remain true, as it says in verse 21: "She will be a stronger stone of testing and he will not hesitate to throw her away."

9. But this scorning of heavenly Wisdom is also close to the human blindness as the third reason—guilt of the false Wisdom which serpent is loosed in the World and has invaded the hearts of men. Because one's heart always fastens itself to things and wants to have and to hold them, hence seeking to asess and judge them: so the fiend throws uncountable kinds of falsely renowned arts and sciences in his way, seeking to make him forget the true eternal good, or again, that he might lose what he has found.

10. Over this the holy lament and too in the scriptures are warnings (how this precious name is misused) named earthly, soulish, or devilish (James 3/15) yea, it really is a pure folly and foolishness, as Paul details and gloriously leads forth from (I Cor. 1/19, 20, 22, 26, and 2/1, 4, 6).

11. Now I have myself many years lived under the same appearance of Wisdom and the same folly, led there by common school-learning and a real natural curiousity; and also by my secret emotions and enticements, yea, testimonies reveal whence all this came: so that I by some measure of communicated light might truly know her—after all sorts of dangerous enticements and by anxious prayer and searching. Afterward, she with long diligence abstains and cares for a soul through the testing, until she will know it in real union.

12. Therefore have I through and according to Wisdom's own counsel wanted—which is necessary—to be led by the hand to this most precious communication, and certainly was guided in part by the clear words of the holy scripture and by the most ancient Christian teaching. But these [words] are not meant for those who are really friends of Wisdom, who already recognizes and satisfies them, nor is this written to the mockers and would-be wise: [but to] he [who] would like to serve God's blessing, for there is a good desire there, but even with so many scruples and reasons he cannot help himself.

13. But it is to me very serious, and none other than about the glorification of this precious name and the guilty praise-knowledge of her unspeakable majesty, as also for my own benefit and that of others. Therefore I will demonstrate in this whole description of these mysteries clearly and through the unanimous testimony of so many unassailable sources and undeniable images, some taken from the mystics and others unacceptable to the reason, which on account of its darkness, neither knows nor has received them; thus neither the mocker nor the borderline holy and burdened hearts may have any excuse, as if they didn't know.

14. I want to comply with the earnest warning in the scriptures, which concerns those forementioned who would mock or ignore or toss off the outward testimonies of her and her glory. For perhaps many still self-assured and naturally impudent hearts may be struck by this and go after its traces and accustom themselves to obedience.

15. Wherefore no one is permitted to look at these as mere empty words, like the world does, which commonly despises the pure teaching of the written word, because they harden their hearts and hold her as unpowerful.

16. But rather the authentic lover and children of eternal Wisdom are given her essential power and experience it for themselves without any doubt whatever: Thus this concerns not less, in the long and the short of it, all disobedient and inverted hearts that are threatened in the holy scriptures.

17. I also most freely admit that I have felt her disciplining rod through sharp punishment, shame, and uncovering of my suffering in my soul, that I must experience with the least unfaithfulness and disobedience. If I in this way do not have to ex-

perience even the outwardly hard forcing methods and burdens, afterward her love has supported always exactly in the narrow and simple way [so] that she would not be forced to leave me at all.

18. But the aforementioned threat reads as follows: In Proverbs 1/26 ff: "Because you did not rest in my correction: so I will also laugh at your accident and your disgrace when that comes which you fear. When what you fear comes over you like a storm, and your anxiety and need come over you like weather, then you will call me but I will not answer: they will seek me early and not find me. Thus you will eat of the fruit of your ways and be bloated with your evil counsel's blows."

19. In the eighth chapter, v. 35: "Whoever sins against me (Wisdom) does violence to his soul," according to the Septuagint, "makes godless his soul." "All who hate me love death." And 9/12: "If you are a mocker, you will bear it alone."

20. In the Book of Wisdom 1/4, 5, 6: "Wisdom will not enter a soul around whom evil malice swirls, and will not dwell in one subject to love of sin. Because the Holy Ghost will fly from one who practices deceit and he will be overcome when the sins come upon him. For Wisdom will not permit the guilty slanderer from his lips; Before God is his inward testimony; an authentic witness of his heart and a hearer of his tongue."

21. In 6/24: "Of poisonous envy Wisdom will have none." And 10/8: "And whoever neglects Wisdom suffers not only the loss of not knowing the good, he even leaves a monument to his ignorance, so that it may not remain hidden, wherein he has gone astray."

22. In Sirach 15/7, 8: "The ignorant men certainly will not attain Wisdom, nor will the sinner see her: She is far from high appearance and the liar will not think of her."

23. But is it not true, O soul, you who still do not want to know the discipline and unceasingness of Wisdom in your heart even when you had looked precisely at it? Don't you hear, often, your strange emotions, impressions, and thoughts, which scold and intimidate you over all bad intentions or works and warn you with all strictness of injury, so that your heart sometimes becomes tight and you feel inward anxiety and worry, not knowing whence it comes?

24. Is it further not clear that such thoughts don't agree with

your impure heart but rather are directly opposed and contrary
and, exactly like a disobedient student under a master's discipline,
strike you sharply and earnestly?

25. Think then of such an inward discipline, whether or not
an even harder, even unbearable strictness would from outside
come over you, where you did not follow it? And whether, if you
aren't convinced in your conscience, that now a commanding
threat like a testimonial to the discipline that you experience, must
be fulfilled, as far as you scorn it?

26. All this should undoubtedly convince you that something
true and holy within you is emerging, of which you with all good
speed could have taken notice, seeing what should be recognized
therein. Here I will not draw on the many similar warnings in the
New Testament, wherein all unbelief and disobedience of the
Evangelium of Jesus Christ is extensively discusssed, but rather
would like to draw on still further expressions of the ancient teachers as testimony.

27. Augustine warns thus: "The beauty of Wisdom reminds
us outwardly and teaches us inwardly; all that sees her are transformed to good, but it is permitted of no one to turn her to bad:
No one can judge her; no one judges rightly without her." And
elsewhere: "[If] one still jeers at her admonitions, remember: one
makes the deepest wounds with the instrument of the wound-
doctor." [Lib. 2 de Lib. Arbitr. c. 14, and Serm. 146 de Temp. To.
10. p. 352]

28. Isidorus Pelusiota holds this as the reason Wisdom is despised: "Why do most people lust after all things but not after
Wisdom? In part because they judge according to appearances
and not the essential; in part because they look for what brings
immediate profit rather than what they should need for the future; and in part also because they have a perverted judgement,
indeed, because many think not at all on the future life." [Lib. 3,
Epistle ep. 251]

29. Still another reason: "Wisdom is despised 1. because one
does not recognise her majesty, like the swine treading precious
stones underfoot; because they do not know her power; and also
they do not care about precious spices, but rather seek acorns and
slops. Thus whoever does not know precious wisdom, scorns her.
2. Because they already think themselves wise. Someone who is

puffed up balks before lovely food. Likewise they who are puffed up with the wisdom of this world throw aside holy Wisdom. 3. Because the heart is laden with the sickness of sin, to whose unhealthy mouth the true bread is a veritable burden. [Humbertus de Roman. Lib 6. Spec. Relig. c. 16]

30. "But it is no wonder," (to continue) "that the folly of men is so opposed to Wisdom. And it is a sign of folly when one scorns Wisdom: likewise is it a sign that a light is watery when it won't burn. Wisdom is bitter to fools because She punishes what they love and praises what they hate. 4. Finally, because the fool's heart is elsewhere, and not his own, but rather is dependent upon richness or lust. Therefore is her body there, where Wisdom teaches something; but the heart [Gemüt] is with other things, and therefore what should be collected is separated.

31. Once more, beloved soul, request truly that your heart not be closed or hardened against the love-rich enticements of holy Love which she so gladly offers to you. Yet do not discard the following message with your ignorant reason, but rather take it into your soft and supple heart and with earnest obedience really strive to experience all this blessedness. You will inwardly transform so that you will not feel all this as outer appearance but rather as an authentic being and life of Wisdom that her friends have so praised.

Chapter VI
Of the Eternal Sophia's Gender and Virginity

1. Here is opened in the soul a truly important mystery—the blessed restoration of the lost paradisal purity and completeness. Whereof I must only announce part of this in letters [words] and leave the rest for real experience. But I do earnestly testify that this mystery of faith is to be received in the purified mind and conscience, and that the Holy Spirit allows only the pure to view it: Therefore the gross earthly insensible animal-men can do nothing here.

2. So is it certain what Hieronymous reminds us: "That in the Godhead is no gender." [Lib. XI in Esa. c. 40; as also in Basilius Seleuciensis, Orat. VI in Noam]: "The invisible nature is not separated into man and woman and is also not subject to birth or

propogation. Because a being that has no flesh has nothing in common with the bodily." Thus all impure fleshly senses of this subject we here cover should be carefully removed from it.

3. We know that the Son of the Father revealed himself as a man and in his incarnation performed "a manly God-work," as also said in Maximus Schol. in Diony. Areop. c. 4, Coel. Hierarch. p. 21. Therefore if he is and remains unified in his one and holy nature, and has not the least human characteristic: so is he in a strange economy herebelow allowing us humans to cultivate and replace the lost blessedness.

4. Next, we may now see how through a similar economy, we find described in the Scriptures holy Wisdom in the images of a woman, a virgin, a bride, a mother, a nursemother, a teacheress. And this is meant not merely as an outer comparison, or flowery speech, but as her being itself: in that she is sought and found, really and personally, in the eye of the heart. Wherefore one may confidently refer to the experiences of her lovers and friends, as one of the greatest mysteries of the Lord that alone they who fear him find.

5. But this is also not seen by the ancient Fathers as error or fiction, as they have known it through the letters of the Scripture and their own experiences, as Hieronymous thus strongly affirms [To. V. Oper. p. 129], namely the feminine gender names.

6. The Hebrews say expressly and without hesitation that the Holy Spirit in their language is described *in foemininae* or in feminine gender. They understand also the words: "How the eyes of the maid are in the hands of her Lady," thus: that they understand through the maid, the soul, but through the Lady, the Holy Ghost. Indeed, also in the Evangelio, which is written according to the Hebrew, read the Nazarenes: The Lord speaks: "Now is my mother brought forth of the Holy Spirit."

7. It is impossible to deny that the Holy Ghost in Hebrew is described in the feminine gender, in Latin as male, and in Greek, *in neutro*, because in the Godhead is no gender.

8. We can remark further from what was written above Christ's cross [John 19/30], in three main languages, that three different genders were named: Hence one knows that they have no gender who are truly separated from all sensual things. Thus one receives faith under each image of the holy being which the spirit and the

Scriptures offer.

9. Another teacher has in his thought compared Psalm 128/3 with Proverbs 30/10, particularly the "masculine woman" after the Septuagint. "We must come to know this masculine woman (or mann-weib), namely she whom Solomon sought to 'take as his bride,' whereof he himself said: 'I well know that she leads me, that she holds me, and I am become a lover of her beauty. Wisdom has received me like a married husband.' Now this is the masculine which completes everything and in the performance of her healing work is strong." [Zeno Veronensis Sermon de Ps. CXXVII fin]

10. This the ancients also knew in some measure, and expressed in dark aphorisms what should be seen and experienced in much greater clarity. Namely, that eternal Wisdom certainly ought not be condensed into a male or female gender, as is the case with inept, corrupt, disgraceful works, but rather is [to be seen] in the heavenly pure understanding of a completed pure virgin.

11. That she consequently is revealed in and can and wants to work in such a likeness, as it befits each soul, that it should be brought back to its lost glory through the new holy birth. And that she gives herself to holy souls herebelow, revealing herself in such necessary forms of the work of holy completion as a virgin, as a fiancée, or as a mother, and so forth.

12. The ground of these deep mysteries lies hidden herein. As Adam in his desire turned out of God and sought to love outside him and his indwelling holy Virgin of Wisdom: he lost this his secret bride, as also elsewhere, according to the expression of the ancients, can be proved before the eyes.

13. Now here was the heavenly Sophia separated from him and (because he had become earthly-sensual and had need of a woman) so was woman built out of his rib, according to Scripture, so thus he lost his feminine characteristic and kept only the masculine. Now if man wants to return to his former paradisal completion: So he must bring back the given-away woman-seed, and make the woman in the man a blessed bond.

14. Now to that end was the Messiah in the feminine gender in Mary certainly a man, and introduced the masculine part again into the body of the virginal woman, just as he carried in himself

the virginal image. Whereby the ground was laid that the masculine and feminine powers could be together again in one image
and being, and the new creature as a masculine virgin could be
completed after [according to] the rebirth before God. In which
then the masculine fire-quality governs, but through the light-
power of the woman must be gentled and tempered just as the
Son through love tempers the Father's wrath there, where the first
complete image of Adam and not Eve remains and is glorified.

15. So many ought babble not from the reason's quarreling
and controversy of this wonder of holy Wisdom, but rather, desiring hearts should seek and hunger further after God, who will
give them more in the spirit than a man can disclose. Because
from here to the end is touched upon somewhat the earnest war
that is after this treasure excited: But the mocker and slanderer
will meet his judgement and painful harm.

16. I know very well what was known by the Valentinians,
and what fables they proposed, although I also do not have space
nor time to devote to it. They had namely said: Christ is of a twofold gender. [Cyrillus Hierosolymitanus Catech. VI de Monarch.
Dei circa med.] "Sophia or Wisdom was born out of herself without a man; Christus taught the thirty aeons or worlds of knowledge of the Father." [Tertullian Lib. adv. Valent. c. 10, 11]

17. Likewise they had named Sophia a mother and also the
Holy Spirit and Jerusalem, and she is described as a woman that
the Enthymesin has borne. [Tert. c. 21, 23; de Praesc. adv. Haer. c.
7 Iraneus passim; Clement Alexandr. annexae, p. 729].

18. But now is it clear that the ground of our former thought is
to be found in the holy Scripture and among the ancient teachers:
thus is it further revealed that this eternal Virgin is described as
an unstained Virgin and a pure Bride. She, says Solomon, pervades everything with her purity and nothing stained can approach her. [Wisdom 7/24, 25] And James: "The Wisdom from
above is before us the first immaculate or pure." [James 3/17]

19. Thus is she the holy purity and discipline itself, and "an
unstained mirror of holy power" [Wisdom 7/26] in which the
Father in himself through his holy power bespeaks everything
and the Holy Ghost engenders everything (so far as it is considered in eternity as in God himself). But she engenders nothing in
her own desire, movement, or will, (as the God-learned express

it) but rather only reveals what is born. She is and remains without any stain or admixture; thus she wills or seeks nothing but what the will of the Godhead generates in her. And thus is she called a Virgin and Bride or God's mate, words that by Augustine were very well expressed [§9.10, cap. 7, after Rev. 21/2 and Wisdom 8/3].

20. Therefore is she moved alone by the eternal Spirit of God whose body (to speak in pure understanding) she is; but she in herself is eternally peaceful and still as a suffering ray of the majesty and glory of God. This appears to go alone and eternally one in the centrum of the holy love, and goes not the least bit elsewhere. He permits nothing else to penetrate into him than this heart of the eternal Godhead, namely the highest love-being of God.

21. Consequently is she an unchanging eternal reflection of this love of God which she mirrors and in which she has her joy; also she is loved and held in turn by the Godhead on account of her purity and beauty eternally. Also is she therefore infinitely separated from all individuality and single and free of all that is not of the essence of God's love itself, which calls as the eternal word in the heart of the Godhead.

22. But no one should wonder how this purest Virgin, indeed, this eternal and highest holiness, can be introduced to and unite with a human spirit. For we will below describe how to know this union, how she really goes into holy and pure souls and spirits, and how she thereby completes and purifies them and unites [them] with the Godhead.

23. O all-blessed treasure: when will you reveal these all together with us as virgins of spirit, soul, and body, and your purest, tenderest Lamb (whose Bride you are) bringing us clear-headed disciplines where you go with him? But you go nowhere back—other than to the Father's love—not back into the Fire, nor below you in the creatures: Ah, testify for us in your completed purification and thus forth in the heart of the highest Trinity that you alone essentially reveal!

Chapt. XIV
On Wisdom's Secret Teachings

1. Now Sophia sends the soul, after all necessary discipline and first milk-nourishment, also stronger food, so that it may be nourished and wander in the new life. Because after the inward ear is opened through so many knockings within, and is made ready to receive, the heart [Gemüt] is also humbled, and the will bound: she willingly lays out her treasures in a unified heart even more, and entrusts even more important things than one might have hoped.

2. Because then is revealed that this heavenly visitor, in everything true and concealed in silence and highly esteemed, reveals all further graces of obedience, unmediately uncovering a good part of the secret counsels of God. And this all the more, because it is not mere speculation or empty of meaning, but rather such delicate material that it is among men the eternal and highest good to encounter it; thus such a one (who encounters it) must himself learn to be true and consonant therein.

3. Therefore she calls not only to those who are fools and that "the intelligent or crafty should notice," [Prov. 8/5] but rather she really demonstrates to her children with her teaching that she "has been present with her good counsel and knowledge," that she permits her teaching to be still more luminous, and makes it shine like the distant morning light, and distributes this as wise sayings. [Sirach 24/32, 33]

4. No one is to doubt this who thinks he knows something better or perceives this only at a distance, as this visible world-being offers and shows. One can easily be convinced of the highest necessity of the instruction of Wisdom, if one only experiences what is expressed in the Book of Wisdom 9/16, 17, 18.

5. "People hardly can make out things upon earth, so how much less can one search out what is in heaven or know God's counsel? Where God has himself given holy Wisdom and sent the Holy Ghost from on high: there it is that those on earth are set on the right path, and men taught what pleases God and become learned in it."

6. But we must remark on some necessary conditions for the teaching of the allknowing Sophia, in order that we may view

these her highest, important works more exactly.

7. Now she offers next her curative teachings or news of holy things, given also as conscientious advice and counsel in the heart, as peculiar profit, ways, and means of overcoming evil, and ways to be nourished upon the best.

8. Then she thus witnesses of herself in Prov. 8/12: "I, Wisdom, dwell with prudence, and find the knowledge of wise inventions." And v. 14: "Mine is counsel, and sound wisdom, and all that is, I understand and strengthen." For Solomon also praises her, "That she knows and understands all, and points the way carefully, and guards in her glory that the work of God be done." [Wisdom 9/11, 12]

9. The nature and ways of such secret instruction is not expresed with words and this above all because it is a mysterious secret work. Likewise David himself expressed it: "God gives in secret his Wisdom to know." [Ps. 51/7] This also the ancients have reminded us: "The word of Wisdom is [a] secret (mysterium) which is beyond the powers of human speech." [Hermes ap. Lactantius Lib. 4, c. 7]

10. This is because all things are described in likenesses, and Wisdom herself is described as an inextinguishable light from which a ray goes out to people. [Wisdom 7/10] She is like the sun, which is above all stars and of all lights the greatest. [Wisdom 9/29]

11. This her light one must want to enjoy himself, as in Solomon 7/10; this light which she herself then "through her teaching makes to shine like the dawn, so it illuminates from afar." [Sirach 24/32] That is: the spiritual power of her hidden teaching goes into the soul in secret ways and causes in the necessary places a transformation and bettering.

12. Thus have the ancients out of their experience put it: the soul as a spirit becomes enlightened by the spiritual light of the pure Wisdom of God, just as the essence of the air is illuminated by the corporeal light. [Aug., Lib. ii de Civ. Dei c. 10] Wisdom is an unstained light like the clarity of the sun; thus she appears to human hearts like the sun to the eyes. [Lact. Lib. 2, c. 8]

13. Here it indeed follows that all this comes to pass inwardly in the soul, and one must not posit this outwardly, like the poor people who dwell in blindness and even lead others still further into blindness. For she offers herself or guides in the holy souls,

in order that she herself might be received in them, as in Wisdom
7/27, 8/17 and thus she explains her works without noise, as
Augustinus explains [Lib. ii de Civ. Dei c. 4] and she transforms
[the wise] through communication of this light [Aug. Lib. 14 de
Trin. c. 12].

14. Thus eager lovers [of Wisdom] seek inwardly in their hearts
[Gemüte] where alone the source of understanding is opened and
where what is holy and blessed should be revealed. For her spirit
alone is deep-grounded and investigates everything not only for
herself alone, but rather also guides the new creatures of man and
teaches through her own inner and blended power and clarity.

15. Thus thereby the hearts [Gemüte] visited by her may know
everything that is unfalsified, clear, and distinct and in her mirror
find everything revealed, whereof one would not know from outside himself. And thus we know whereof we have accepted all
inward, salutory remembrances, rewards, and "inspired good
thoughts" (as a teacher called them) [Basilius M. Homil. in Prov.
init.], namely from the brilliantly shining light of our mistress
Sophia.

16. But the more one follows this light, and awakens in the
new birth, the more one takes it into oneself. "Through all holy
powers the newly created heart views in itself the character of the
images of the holy Form and recognises the secret and intelligible
beauty of the likeness of the Lord, attaining also the treasures of
the inward laws and the wisdom that is taught by herself." [Marcus
Eremita in Præceptis salut. ad Nicolaum, circa med.]

17. This is certainly a high grade of the new birth that we speak
of, if the new light-body of the spirit Jesu or Wisdom in man is
cultivated and revealed as a fire-flaming illuminating being,
whence comes all heartfeltness [herzlichkeit] and further illumination. But it depends upon the same spirit of Wisdom as the
spirit of prophesying [Rev. 19/10] to proclaim what is necessary
to those in a state of weakness, and to reveal mysteries, as it expressly states in the writings of the ancients. [Vide vel
Chysostomus homil. 28 in Matth. c. ii., Lactant. Liv. 2.c.3, Isidorus
Lib. 7, Orig. c. 2 &c.]

18. But that material or subjects which this spirit is engaged in
opening in us should soon become known in us by the contemplation of Wisdom's fruits. Now this instruction of her teaching

must move us toward trueness [fidelity] and wakefulness to wait and to observe inwardly in stillness and gentle spirits, as the unavoidable ground of all following heartfeltness of which we here only will find a silhouette. The body or essential body of Christ and Wisdom must each seek and take from God himself.

Chapt. XVII
On the Spiritual Marriage with Sophia

1. I come now to a subject so important, certain, and essential, but also my idea and feeling is too great for the tongue to express. However, it suffices to not address those who already possess this, which would make this description too long and unworthwhile, but rather [address it] to those good-willed souls that might be drawn to it.

2. Also what I say here has nothing to do with contemptuous reason, which would plague us with a heap of contentious afterthoughts: how Wisdom can be at once Virgin and bearer, mother and bride. All such impudent spirits will be wholly repelled from the border of this simple blessed love-kingdom, until they turn back from their arrogant bullheadedness and receive their kingdom as little children, which is much to be wished for.

3. We find good grounds in the Scriptures where Wisdom is addressed not only as mother, but also as virgin, bride, mate, and playmate. Here the well-experienced Solomon certifies this: He desires to take her as his bride and is resolved to be guided by her (as betrothed) that he may live with her Wisdom 8/1, 8]. Likewise also his whole song speaks of this love of the soul-spirit with Sophia, as in the preface to this poem ought to be pointed out.

4. Another faithworthy lover speaks out of experience: "They [the Godfearing] consider her like a mother and take her like a virginal wife." [Sirach 15/2] In which words a remarkable mystery lies hidden, which must repeatedly be confirmed by living experience.

5. Namely in the beginning (if the powers of the soul still are entangled [or confused] and the good has not yet broken through and had victory [Sirach 4/18]) will Sophia know the soul inwardly under the image and qualities of a noble and earnest love-rich mother so long as she has to bind, break, punish, and reform the

fallen nature of man, as in the aforementioned reports.

6. When the soul is faithful, respectful, and obedient in everything, and the sincerity of its love has been tested and proven
legitimate through many haard struggles against sins as through
so many authentic tests: then she changes her earnest form gracefully and takes on another as "a virginal woman." [Sirach 15/2]

7. Because thus must she exactly and in full awareness proceed, after being affected by the unfaithfulness of the first men,
which grieved her. Then only will she permit some secret love-
glances, kisses, and other quickening indications offered to such
proven friends and pure virginal love-spirits as certain pledges.
But the complete wedding day and the open completion of such a
union she withholds until man's total perfection.

8. And from this first taste or pledge of the future complete
wedding is here alone the talk by which she ever more takes the
place of a caring and disciplining mother, in that she if and when
necessity requires it, mingles earnest instructions with her caresses.
But the last wedding-festival belongs only to angelic tongues to
describe and to the spirits of completed righteousness to enjoy. In
this are the sweet rays of her love and her kisses so delicate and
penetrating that the soul-spirit finds them wholly indescribable.

9. In truth all the lust of youth and supposed pleasures of those
in love are less than nothing next to these heavenly delights. It is
an authentic power out of paradise, when a spirit anticipates this
most beautiful of all brides. It is a sweet rapture and overtaking
of all the soul's powers and a sinking of all senses in this love's
flow.

10. When this dove is taken into her lap [womb] this brings it
an olive branch of untainted joy and the certain hope of all cer-
tainties. In the kisses of her mouth she permits him to enjoy all
freedom and salves him with life-balsam as much as one wants.
One is then allowed to lay upon her breast and suck to satiation,
and all her pure powers stand open in paradisiacal love-play.

11. In her whole vicinity is pure delight [wollust]. Never will
a man receive an earthly bride more tasteful, chaster, more modest, and lovelier (more gracefuly) than this highly praised virgin.
Indeed, there is not the slightest comparison between them in this
case. It is also only a shadow of what one otherwise can say, and
of what the Song of Solomon reveals in poetic thought, and of

what (after the actual enjoyment of it) may be sketched.

12. O pure delight [wollust] come and visit yours still oftener and don't let your love's attractions be lacking! For we otherwise in ourselves neither desire nor are able to speak out: So you see yourself, oh you most beautiful of women, by our fallen nature in this troubled valley of our pilgrimage. We long therefore to be immediately and henceforth at your secret side, my one and pure turtledove!

13. You know indeed she whom you must seven and again seven years serve; and may become like Jacob, walking in the right way, or if it is still not completed, then your flesh is an unpleasant Leah, until the time comes for your loveworthy Rachel, that you may with joy bear in your arms.

14. Only you don't want to omit in the house of our Father to also now and then greet love-attractions and also those who have to serve: so they aren't dismayed by difficulties and listless after your fatherland or despair of the fulfillment of your promises. But let her every instant be prepared to embrace you, and if you are carefully attentive and pay attention to her love-counsel, it will be revealed to you.

15. But again to come to the subject itself, it will suffice to devote some attention to the ancient holy ones. From these other Christian teachers can we further see that this is undoubtedly no empty fantasy or dream search but rather a subject that to noble hearts more essential and true may be consummated as much as a bodily wedding, and realized by those who have found as much as the least something of the pearl.

16. Above all, a holy teacher writes: "We must recognize the manly consort, namely she whom Solomon sought to take for a bride, and would be a lover of her beauty, namely Wisdom, whom he took as a mate. This is masculine completion and subjection of everything, and strength in the execution of this holy work pleases God; she delights him through her teaching and completes through the science of present and future things."

17. This consort of a Godfearing one spreads herself around his whole house, penetrating everywhere through all his works like a fruitful vineyard. But the house is the dwelling of our souls with which each one through the fear of God and walking in his ways, will unite with the dwelling of Wisdom. [Zeno Veronensis

Serm. in Ps. 128 med Tomo 3 biblioth. Pat. Lugd. p. 375, and
Hilarius in hunc Psalm 556]

18. Referred to here is the masculine virgin and companion of
Proverbs 30/20, also to be seen above in Ch. 5, n. 9 [in this work].
This is she whom Adam lost in paradise and in Christ must be
found. Thus the soul-spirit of a man abstains from all other things
and loves and clings to the heavenly alone in itself and through
his faith and new will really seeks and finds his rightful virgin
and spouse, helpmeet and playmate, beauty, and is friendly with
her and inwardly with her remains intimately united.

19. Again [he] finds a Virgin and Widow [and] then her new
paradisiacal treasure and bridegroom again as a light and a love-
tincture, with which they unite and are satiated in her love, so
they no longer hunger after anything outside. For previously the
poor spirit in his blindness had always lusted and hungered; but
because he meant to still only a fleshly earthly lust he had instead
of the true helpmeet found only flesh and blood. By contrast, when
the will goes beyond all other trust and bondage, this is called
also holiness and innocence—then he meets Wisdom.

20. Then she permits the man a proper union with this treasure, so that he may enjoy what belongs to him in eternity,—so
that he forgets his earthly help. Then she gives of her pure love-
essence in a complete spiritual marriage with the spirit and offers
herself to him and helps him in everything, in a purer delight
[wollust], approaches nearby and nurtures him, indeed, so he lacks
nothing. Whoever experiences this can confidently testify to and
trust in this. But because it is so inward, and one must pass through
[deny] so much, only a few are able to have faith.

21. Nevertheless, the ancients testify of the holy condition of
this high holy marriage, whose sweetness and merit far surpasses
what in the world may be called beautiful and good. There they
speak of her qualities and of the company and communion with
Sophia. "I have anticipated taking her as a bride, and am become
a lustful lover of her beauty." (There you have [1] a beautiful bride!)
"She makes their nobility glorious." ([2] a noble). "She is the native counsel of the knowledge of God." ([3] a sage). "What is richer
than Wisdom, who accomplishes everything?" ([4] rich). "Her
works are virtuous" ([5] a virtuous companion).

22. "I have decided to bring her home, that I might live with

her.—I will find peace by her. Because her company has no bitterness and her companionship no pain, but rather joy and good. In her friendship is great satisfaction; in the practice of her company is sagacity, and great glory in her conversation."

23. Accordingly, this belongs to one who longs to partake in this incomparable treasure, so that one renounces all other things for her alone and gives up all will and mind to her, and holds to her. So one will bye and bye come to take her sweet protest into his heart, speak with her intimately, reveal all his laments to her, deliver up all her orders, and thus wholly dwell with her blessed speech, counsel, answers, and guidance.

24. And therefore heavenly Wisdom is without many lovers, since [following] the flesh spoils their way, and they follow after strange paths: so will the righteous souls long all the more lustfully, and hold to her all the faster, for she gives them all delight, and all her graces and niceties, all her treasures and adornments, yea, her whole glory she grants them. Therefore her surpassing excellence which has overtaken one and taken one prisoner, must break out:

25. "You call my heart, my sister, beloved bride, with one of your eyes, and with one (shimmering and alluring) necklace from your throat! How beautiful are your love slopes, my sister, dear bride! Honey flows from your lips." [Song of Sol. 4/9]

26. So in love and caught, Solomon testified in his whole song, and such counsel he also gave to others, that they should keep company with Wisdom as with their nearest relation: "Call Wisdom," he said, "your sister and the sagacity of your friend." [Proverbs 7/4] Because in kinship with Wisdom is immortality. [Wisdom 8/16]

27. Permit us to see yet closer this communion of the soulspirit with Wisdom, and with disciplined, purified, eyes of the heart, as they do not know how to imaginatively understand the ancients inwardly and essentially. "The ancients held it as indisputably necessary that one above all things should transcend the shame and impurity of this life through the vehicle of the body before one can be joined with the beauty of Wisdom." And then further, that a soul "seeks in humility that it may unite with her eternally in a chaste companionship." [Diodachus de Perfect. Spirit. Ch. 52, p. 890; Joh. Climacus in Scala Paradisi Gradu 7, fine]

28. Thus a person who wants to enjoy this high wedding must be wholly dead to all fleshly lusts as was discussed in chapters eleven to fifteen: because the animal man does not attain this jewel, and a swine will not find this pearl. But rather this gloriousness is alone in the eternal spirit and the eternal soul wherein the image of God is found and in this is the newborn and formed Jesus, although the outward part of man also participates in this joy and bliss.

29. But of the inward, eternal man was it said by the ancients that one ought to look to the all-sufficing marriage with Sophia and in such understanding certainly may be neither indecency nor reduction. Thus one finds this explanation:

30. "The soul has a conscious feeling in which it touches Wisdom and embraces her like a lustful lover. As Solomon says: 'Love her, that she might embrace you.' The body becomes debased through an impure embrace: but if the soul wholly embraces Wisdom, and is truly united and admixed with her: so it will be filled and impregnated with holiness and purity." [Basilius Magnus Homil. in init. Prov.]

31. "Wisdom gives herself to all. But she is unstained and chaste and people are through her transformed into Wisdom. No earthly or heavenly beauty, no embrace can compare with the beauty, sweetness, and satiation of Wisdom. Now whoever wants to love, why not love her?—wooing her in order that she might come to him. Because just as a lover's eye always longs after the delights of the body, so she seeks a beautiful heart." [August. Enarr. in Ps. 33 and Serm. 146 de Temp.]

32. So delightfully can some of her loveliness be spoken of, but these are only some glances and allurements from her after one's first penitence. Who can express what she daily confides in her paramour's inwardness out of her light and love-realm? It is neither advisable nor possible for anyone to inconsiderately reveal or gossip out of her most secret love-cabinet: there not once can an earthly bridegroom reveal the hidden secrets of his companion.

33. But so much more will a gallant and desiring spirit further [be] encouraged if he is convinced by experience that the testimony and praise of this graceful blessed princess transcends all comparisons or art. She is complete in all aspects and makes the

spirit who approaches her enkindled and wounded with her hot love-arrow in the innermost depths: in order that to him all other loves will disappear, and he will seek to nurture her love alone.

34. It is better to be silent and only think about what follows upon such noble communion. "Wisdom" (say the ancients) "dwelling by a faithful one" (like a wife in a man's house) "is not always unfruitful and without children, in order that she should bear the man something virtuous." [Clemens Alexandrinus Lib. 1 Strom. p. 284]

35. She dwells in the soul's house and from her come forth children, who are like oil-lamps around our table, namely the Lord's table, whereon we may take sustenance, as the living bread, which to take there, enlivens us. And now just as from a wife, children will be born, so out of Wisdom comes the works of a good will. These ring the table and overshadow the knowledge of our Wisdom with the fruits of the best of all work. Thus may each Godfearing one be blessed." [Zeno Veron. and Hilarius II.cc]

36. O if all noble hearts would permit their minds to turn into this source alone: how they would so easily forget the vile foolishness of this past [temporal] world!—how they should race and run after positions and marriage—and the anxious suffering life under the earthly flood [would] fall away and a gentle peace in the womb of this love-rich mother and spouse enter into the heart!

37. One would not bear burdens [worries] which the world breeds, or hold this or that false view. How one would leave behind [the notion of leaving] remainders to youth [children] or the continuation of his name through sexual propagation. Because Wisdom would bring an undying remembrance, kingdom, and marriage, for the bridal treasure [dowry] and innumerable holy births of virtues as the fruit of her marriage and love's-cultivation.

38. "You long so after children" (speaks one) "and want not to be seen unfruitful: you can indeed have children, but those who are generated out of Wisdom as a mother through spiritual seeds. There you can engender God's children, through God's Word—but not such a father as the world, of which comparison Paul spoke: 'I have generated you through the gospel. Permit it to be fulfilled what is written: Blessed is he who has seeds there in Zion, and friends in Jerusalem, not in Babel.'" [Sixtus Calius Auc-

tor Lib. de Castitate ad quendam vere Christianum. To. 7 Biblioth.
PP. p. 842]

39. Of these fruits and spiritual children is it good to say something in particular, inasmuch as human hearts are moved toward understanding the immense profit in this topic. [But] everything remaining is best left to the delight which is permitted in this wedding and purest of all wedding prayers. They will well experience that the subject here so weakly expressed is but a silhouette of that which comes to pass for Wisdom's lovers.

FIN

VII

Johann Georg Gichtel

To write about the life of Johann Georg Gichtel (1638-1710), after Böhme among the most authoritative of our theosophers, is also to write about his works, for the two are very nearly inseparable. Indeed, the bulk of our information concerning Gichtel comes directly from his own hand, or from the hand of someone very close to him. For Gichtel was author of *Theosophia Practica*, an enormous seven volume collection of his letters along with his biography—838 letters dated from 1668 (when the author was thirty) to 1710, the year of his death, comprising some 4000 pages. If this source of biographical information is somewhat limited and slanted—Gichtel was nothing if not an irascible and polemical writer—its limitations are counterbalanced by the unparalleled glimpse they offer into the life of this theosopher, the "Hermit of Amsterdam."

Gichtel's life began in Ratisbon, Germany, in March, 1638, and can be divided into three parts: from 1638 to 1664, when he began to encounter difficulties with the clerical authorities in Ratisbon; from 1665 through 1667, when he moved about, staying for a time with Friedrich Breckling (1629-1711); and from 1668 to his death in 1710, the time during which he lived, wrote, and taught in Amsterdam. Naturally, most of our information about Gichtel (often hagiographical) comes from this last period, during which he established his community of the "Brethren of the Angelic Life," the *Engelsbrüder*, or the "Angelic Brethren," and become more generally known as a theosopher.

Gichtel's death is forecast at the end of *Theosophia Practica* by reference to archetypal cycles of time. Sophia appeared to Gichtel in definite temporal cycles during his life, and these cycles culminated forty days before his death, when "the heavenly mother of wisdom revealed herself anew in 1709, December 13." This time of revelation was the greatest, Gichtel said, since early in the founding of the Angelic Brethren, and reached its zenith after Gichtel's death early in 1710.[23] The cycle of revelation was renewed in subsequent years among the remaining Angelic community.

Gichtel's primary written work, as we have seen, was his voluminous collection of letters, but he left several other major works behind as well. Among these is a treatise, dated 1696, entitled *Eine kurze Eröffnung und Anweisung der dreyen Principien und Welten im Menschen*, or, *A Brief Revelation and Instruction on the Three Principles and Worlds in Man*, attributed to Gichtel and Johann Georg Graber and published in 1723. This work—which to this day is in print under the erroneous title *Theosophia Practica*—includes some very important illustrations on planetary symbolism and the human microcosm, detailing the process of theosophical illumination that is discussed at length in the text.

Gichtel also edited the first major collection of Böhme's writings, entitled *Theosophia Revelata*, published in three successive editions: 1682, 1715, and 1730. Between 1680 and 1682, Gichtel and his colleagues accomplished this remarkable project of collating disparate texts and producing a single, fourteen volume edition in octavo. This was in fact the primary German edition of Böhme until the work of Werner Buddecke in the twentieth century.[24] These two multivolume series—Böhme's work in *Theosophia Revelata*, and Gichtel's own letters in *Theosophia Practica*—were deliberately complementary, Böhme offering the primary revelational paradigm of theosophy, and Gichtel concentrating on its practical implications through guiding letters. What follows includes Johann Ueberfeld's hierohistory of Gichtel's Sophianic revelations, and selections from Gichtel's letters, mainly those directly concerning Sophia.

From
Theosophia Practica

Johann Georg Gichtel, Leyden, 1722
From the *Introduction* by Johann Wolfgang Ueberfeld

The first marriage-feast of the first marriage took place at the end of the year 1673, and at the beginning of the year 1674 (when the divine talent had now gained ten of them) whereof mention is made in the letters. This is the only one of which we have no creaturely knowledge, and which has remained hidden from us in the spirit of God, in those then very evil years of my youth. The second, however, was the more glorious and took place in 1683, and lasted until 1685, almost three years, in which the most friendly and merciful God wished to double what we missed in the first.

At this high wedding in which the heavenly virgin appeared in the *ternarius sanctus*, gloriously transfigured, it was that she married us two brethren in one spirit, and called my brother by name, and went back with us to the year 1668, and informed me, that it was that very brother J.G. Gichtel, whose pilgrim spirit she had allowed me to see after the baptism of the holy ghost.

What joy this awakened in the spirit to find ourselves in spirit and nature in God, no tongue can express, and a lasting eternal joy which made us forget all succeeding sorrow and which cannot be taken out of our hearts. God be ever praised, who hath changed all our tribulation, sorrow and death into our eternal well-doing, and still doth do.

The heavenly first wedding feast of the second marriage took place in the year 1690, in the midst yet of the ingenerating of the divine love, whereby our dearest savior Jesus Christ clothed himself entirely into our inward and outward form, with all the substance of the creature, thereby indicating that he had now become unto us, what we are, and thus acccordingly both bridegroom and bride, both tinctures one substance, and yet in a twofold personal distinction in the mirror of wisdom.

In this manner bridegroom and bride were without divine form and clearness, and Sophia had become to the soul a Leah...but her love in our spirit went as deep into the ground of the souls, as deep as the divine love had concealed itself. This love embraced our spirit in the most friendly manner, and spoke itself in an eternal bond into our hearts with the words: I am eternally thine, and thou art mine; the enemy shall not part us!

[But thereafter Gichtel's group suffered a serious schism.] Our persecutors were our own dear brethren in Christ, and other people considered pious; wherefore the first envy struck the deeper into our hearts, the deeper we were united to them in love. And though they had indeed changed their love into wrath, they were purely stripes of love, that we received from them. Yea, whenever they placed the knife against our throats, we would but love them, knowing that they were innocent of what they did, and that it was only for the sake of Christ, in whose process we stood, that the judgement was over us.

But they had no outward power in the land, whence they could only kill us with their tongues....

What the father is in the fire, that the son is in the light, and in the heavenly humanity of Jesus fire and light are one divine being, which is called *Sophia*, which is treated of throughout this book. This glorious wedding took place in the years 1705-1706, and by God's goodness lasted a year.

The first wedding feast of the third marriage took place at the end of the year 1709, and the beginning of 1710, shortly before the author's departure from this world…. On that occasion the virgin appeared in the same form as in 1683, when she made us brethren acquainted with one another, and welcomed us, now our parting, where, according to the outward man, we were to lose one another, was to be the same. God be praised! The second wedding (which took place after the author's death) was in the year 1716, which God in his mercy reneweth unto us every year.

Your fellow combatant in Christ, JWU, 1721

Letters of Gichtel: Selections

3 September 1697

Our heavenly Virgin is so enamoured of our *limbus*, that no man can believe it; but our fickle mind and inconstant will and heart prevent her influence. And if you are minded to woo her, as indeed I perceive the tinder to be kindled in you, earnestly seize in prayer, praying for a steadfast mind and will, and for the teaching and guidance of the Holy Spirit, because wonderful incidents open themselves, surpassing all reason; never shrink back, though body and soul languish, but let God's word be your comfort and inheritance.

For the Virgin desires to have body, soul, and spirit for her own, to nourish and provide for it herself, as a faithful consort for *his other half*; we must also ever follow the lamb.

12 March 1696

…Nor should I have discovered our…mode of worshipping God, if God had not, out of his great love, opened my eyes and allowed me to be ejected from the synod, and forever banished me from my native country, with the confiscation of all my property. Which was a cause of my illumination…. Wherefore I greatly pity our young people, for giving too much time to books, gathering much reason-knowledge, as I also did, and never approach God; and if God's mericful love had not …banished me from the world, I should never have come near unto Christ.

3 November 1696

So the heavenly Sophia plays with all her wooers, and tries them, whether they are serious, for where there is no honest earnestness, the marriage is long delayed, which is well to be noticed.

9 September 1698

We have again received a medicine in the inward man, viz. Christ's substantiality, which Böhme calls Sophia, wherein we can set our imagination…. [and] we can in ourselves comprehend ourselves in Sophia and drive away the devil's poison in body and soul.

As soon as in our soul or body the devil moves himself or assails the inward man, the imagination runs to the most sensible place, searching out what the enemy intends, calling on the virgin in the heart for assistance.

That takes place either by the evil conjuration and influences of the constellation, or the strife of the elements in the body, in the stomach or other members…or by false images or thoughts in the soul or mind.

As soon as we feel this, we curse it, draw our imagination inwards, and set it on Sophia, who immediately enters into the imagination, tinctures the painful spot in the body, and casteth out the devil's poison.

[Though the devil opposes the tincture-fire of the virgin] we do not allow the imagination to go out of Sophia, until the enemy is put to flight and the pains have disappeared.

And if the imagination become too weak, we add prayer and sighs, so that the devil may be arrested, but we must be in earnest. With this sword we have hitherto, by the strength of Jesus, barely resisted and driven away many an evil influence.

7 June 1698

True knowledge must go through many a fire before it is fixed and can be brought into the sidereal mind; otherwise it is only a dead letter.

Although it is not believed now, experience will prove that in paradise [will dwell] those who have been like him [Christ] in this world.

2 August 1698

Now as no birth can come forth from the man without the woman, nor from the woman without the man, so without Sophia or Christ we cannot do or bring forth anything good. This mystery God hath opened to me, that thereby I have been led not to attach myself to any woman, nor do I repent of it, for she has given me a chaste mind, and preserved me from Venus.

1 September 1698

...There is no other God besides love, and is nothing that can quench the wrath but love.... In which strife only Sophia and the priesthood of Melchizadek are fundamentally known. For what I here mention is only the husk; the soulish taste cannot be described, and the world could not comprehend it.

13 March 1696

For the life of eternity is nothing but love, and if we wish to enter into that paradisic life, we must also be nothing else but love, so that one equality may comprehend and hold the other and since you are inwardly apprehended by God you have the true teacher in yourself, who shall instruct your soulish spirit, and teach you how to pray aright...

10 July 1696

And assuredly we should require no teacher without us, if we are attended by this teacher within us. But since we are not all masters in one day, and many trials assail a pilgrim in the wilderness, an exercised mind can often give useful instruction to the unenlightened.

15 January 1698

O the great blindness! We look without ourselves and seek God above the constellation, whereas heaven is in us.... the heavenly wisdom is in us; she teacheth, guideth, and leadeth our hearts, minds, souls and senses, and therein dwells the holy trinity.

He that has experience can testify to it—historical faith is but a knowledge of the letter,—.... unto [those without experience] the Son shall one day say: I know you not.

11 January 1691

I have been obliged to wrestle with the hellish spirits as man with man; the blessed angels have played with me during the day like children; but all this is but a paradisal prelude, and whoso would seek for it, would be deceived.

May 1694

Imagination will not do it: there must be faith and power in mouth and heart, not empty words which will not overcome the devil or the world.... If the creaturely wrath is to be overcome, it cannot be done without love...now if a powerful true love is to arise, there must be a true faith and root.... The devil is more learned than we.... our learned men are more blind than moles, and know nothing of the soul's condition.... But if the soul is become entirely a devil, and wishes to remain a devil, who can change it? I have experience; ...I have learnt neither from Luther's catechism, nor from universities, [but from] the Pentecost school of the holy spirit, who leadeth into heaven and hell, so that we see with our own eyes, and need no telescope.

28 July 1699

It is more pleasing to enjoy conjugally the love of a virgin, than merely to kiss her; understand me spiritually, for she helpeth us in the conjugal union of our will to bring forth Father, Son, Holy Spirit and Wisdom, which effect a kiss has not, whence it is called to be born again of water and of spirit.

The virgin of God worketh in the soul, again to behold her bridegroom, whom she lost in Adam, wherefore she desires to have us entirely in her arms, and is jealous of our earthly loves.

It is no self-imagined thing—what I write is pure experience and intuition; the sufferings are the pangs of labour, at which nature is terrified, and thinks of all kinds of means to protect herself, which gives the *spiritus mundi* opportunities to try us.

The virgin brings the first forming and creating powers as a dowry into the soul, clothes it herewith, and surrounds it with her powers, viz., a body of power, wherein the soul becometh God's servant and priest, and also can step before God and take what it asketh for, as much as it requires for its bodily necessities.

This magic forming in faith the devil has proclaimed to be necromancy, etc. I pity the poor people who think erroneously of us, when yet they do not know us fundamentally, persecute us, and yet want to be our followers. May the Lord have mercy upon us all…

13 March 1700

But when Adam broke off from the unity, viz, from the heavenly Sophia, and …wanted himself to do and create as his astral reason and *ratiocinatio* understood it, he lost the power of the light, and the darkness obtained government in him.

Which is indeed the origin of sin, in which we are now born and brought up, that we no longer know God's light, viz, Sophia, our heavenly flesh and blood, but look after the light of reasons, which can do no more than the other animals, feed and multiply us.

And when we have gratified this wish, we consider ourselves happy, go to church and the Lord's Supper, let the parsons take care of our souls; Christ has done everything for us; we stand in the historical clown's faith, and do not want to know anything of the cross of Christ, self-denial.…

1 June 1700

What should I, poor worm, have done these thirty-six years without Sophia, if God had not opened to me this mother of his divine powers? And how badly fared our apostate branches, when not one stood in the truth, and at last missed the narrow gate.

13 October 1700

Dearest brother K.,

The reason why prayer will not make satisfactory progress with you, is because you are still rich and well off; were you poor and feeble, need would drive you to prayer; he that falleth into the crater cries for help, as we see every day here with the children.

I tell you the truth, dear brother, praying is talking and eating and herein consisteth our growth of the inward man.…

Where now there is a great and fiery hunger after Sophia or Jesus, there prayer will not be wanting; but by prayer I understand not making many words, which I myself do not do—nay, I cannot even outwardly say the Lord's prayer. I need not trouble myself about words; the spirit of God seeth in my will, what I am anxious about, before I express it.

I hope you will in time be delivered from your reason, which lies in your way, and be introduced deeper into the innermost ground; this I fervently pray for you.

1 December 1699

When God in 1668 appeared to me a second time, and showed me the sufferings, I resisted for nearly six years and would not enter into the strife.... then my playmate appeared in 1673-4 a third time, putting faith, love and hope into my heart, assuring me mouth to mouth, as one friend to another, of her fidelity and poured such fire into my heart that I surrendered my own will and laid down my life for my brethren. I followed the spirit in the mind; as that went, I worked, so I did, and enjoyed the sweet love milk in pure joy; all wonder-mirrors opened themselves; what I prayed for often in thought only, stood there; until in 1685 the sweet love-play was turned into mourning, and the soul had to be weaned.

Then all was contrary; the working powers of God stood still, all prayers were fruitless, heaven like steel and iron, and God's heart itself closed, and there was no other means nor escape, but with Christ to go to the Mount of Olives and at last the Cross.

I cried for fifteen years: My God, my God, why hast thou forsaken me! But no help was to be seen. I was so beaten and pierced through with slanders that I no longer resembled a human being....

We must only pray: Father, forgive them, for they know not what they do!

24 February 1703

[In reference to the breakup of the Angelic Brethren]

I have not desired it; how could I have wished for such a dispersion and brought such indescribable anguish and sharp fire upon myself?

They fell in love with Sophia, but in none did she mirror herself. I myself did not understand it, and only saw it after their secession, seeing they went into the wrath, and introduced the principle into strife, and if we had not wrestled earnestly, we ourselves should have lost the pearl. For everyone fancied he had the virgin and yet was deceived, and when they discovered their error, they wanted with wrath to force the virgin, who however withdrew into her ether and left the young minds to their hunger, so that they could nowhere find the virgin but in her ground where she revealeth herself. Which ground was opened to me in the center of the soul....

And I am still in hopes that the love will finally triumph and tincture the wrath.

From
The Wonderful and Holy Life of the Chosen Champion and Blessed Man of God Johann Georg Gichtel
Anonymous

"The heavenly mother of wisdom revealed herself anew in 1709, December 13, in the same form in the holy ternary; and just forty days before she called home the blessed soldier she smiled very brightly upon the yet living theosopher U. [Uberfeld], pointing with her finger to the divine light pearl, that in the faithful and deep process in Christ of the true brethren, had become so transparent, and grown to such a degree of strength, that so small a spark had become so great a light, resembling Adam.

At one and the same moment the heavenly virgin appeared also to Gichtel's spirit in the greatest brightness with the divine jewel in the mind. All the powers of God in spirit, soul, and body, one power, concerning which he wrote thus to his brother U. on 17 December 1709: "You will feel powers which since Raadt's apostasy have lain hidden, and now again sensibly open themselves in the will spirit with a pleasant relish for which I have ever dug and searched in the soul, but could not apprehend them until the hour of God did strike."

On the nineteenth again he wrote: "I do not at all remember

Raadt: the virgin is so disgusted with this son of falsehood, that I dare not stir up his spirit with one thought"...God hath anew brought forth the virgin out of his majesty in the holy ternary, and turned two lives again into one with him in Christ Jesus, wherein dwelleth the trinity, working and creating, which powers God shall manifest in wonders.

This then is the virgin's dowry, which she receiveth from them, because God hath preserved the pearl in hell, wrath, tribulation and death, and put it on the virgin, four years ago, for a bridal ornament; it was on 20 January 1706 when God Father and Son embraced himself in the spirits of both, and comprised himself in a mirror of her divine wisdom.

From which time the light-pearl had again to pass through the degrees of the most holy fire out of the holy ternary, and be polished. Whereof with the divine permission we will show in the appendix the flower with the power in which it showed itself the first four years. The virgin kept it secret, until she had perfected herself through all the ten forms, and not only this, but there the holy spirit renewed the virginal growth every year, and Jesus, the virgin's son, now for the fifth time brought forth a God-man, which is God, praised for ever and ever!

But when she had just therewith absolved the fourth form of fire, and God had opened the fifth form of the virgin's substantiality, the heavenly bride led her bridegroom Gichtel home on the succeeding day, 21 January 1710.

VIII

Jane Leade

Jane Leade (1623-1704) was born—according to her own account—to a reasonably wealthy upper-class family in Norfolk, England. She and her family lived a good life, and she received a fine education. When she was fifteen, on a Christmas eve, she was dancing and celebrating with her family and friends, but heard a voice that told her, "Cease from this, I have another Dance to lead thee in, for this is Vanity." For three years she lived in melancholy isolation, occasionally reading books and almost always staying apart from people; despite the counsel of her father, Schildknapp Ward, and a chaplain, she felt the sins of the world upon her, and believed that because she had once told a lie, she would stay without the New Jerusalem. But at the age of eighteen, she "was so richly favoured by her dear and blessed Mediator, as to receive at that time the Seal of her Absolution and Assurance, in a manner very special, there being presented to her in a Vision, the form of a Pardon with a Seal to it."

When she became interested in marrying one of her religiously inclined friends in London, who apparently was not of her social class, her parents brought her back to Norfolk in an attempt to marry her off properly, which she refused, since she did not want to marry merely for earthly reasons. Eventually she married William Leade, a merchant, when she was twenty, with whom she lived happily for twenty-seven more years. With him she had four daughters, two of whom died, and two of whom reached maturity and themselves were married. Apparently she and her husband shared spiritual concerns.

But in February, 1670, her husband died, and the man to whom his money was entrusted absconded with it, leaving Mrs. Leade destitute. What could have been a catastrophe, however, she regarded as in another sense her good fortune, for like Gichtel and many other theosophers, she took this as a sign that she should throw herself wholly on the mercy of God. Thus she began to live wholly as a member of Pordage's theosophic circle, and slowly assumed leadership of the group, eventually coming to live with the widower Pordage in his house, so that the circle became a true community.

Leade had first met Pordage in 1663, a meeting about which she wrote in her preface to his *Theologia Mystica*. She soon became a member of his circle, but it was not until after her husband's death that she was able to devote herself wholly to theosophy. She and Pordage eventually lived in the same house, along with several others, the better to devote themselves to prayer and mutual religious understanding. During this time Dr. Pordage wrote his most important works.

After Pordage's death in 1681, the responsibility for continuing their theosophical work fell to Mrs. Leade. By 1683, she had had one of his more important treatises published, as well as some of her own, including "The Heavenly Cloud Now Breaking," (1681) and "The Revelation of Revelations" (1683). Upon reading the latter book, a wealthy widow offered Mrs. Leade and her group the use of her home for their meetings, an arrangement that lasted until her death, at which the group was forced to find another place to meet nearer London. Leade's group began to call itself the "Philadelphian Society," and even sought to proselytize, attempts which mostly failed. Because of this, and because of Leade's visionary mysticism, some other theosophers, including Gichtel, denigrated her, but her works are important for their visionary luminosity and for their championing of universal restoration, testimony to her gentle spirituality that would not brook the doctrine of eternal damnation. Leade often experienced direct visions of Sophia, and the following writings are based upon some of these.

The Laws of Paradise Given Forth by Wisdom to a Translated Spirit

The Law shall go forth of Zion (Mic. 4.2)
London: T. Sowle, 1695
Wisdom I have sought, and
    Wisdom I have found:
And now I wear her as
    My Garland and Crown.

Preface

To a certain person, that for many years had been led wonderfully in the ways of God, it came to pass that one day, upon a deep contemplation of the Paradisiacal World, there appear'd in the midst of a most bright Cloud, a Woman of a most sweet and majestic countenance, her face shining as the Sun, and her vesture of transparent gold, who said, "Behold! I am God's Eternal Virgin *Wisdom*, whom thou hast been enquiring after: I am to unseal the treasures of God's deep Wisdom unto thee, and will be, as Rebecca was to Jacob, a true natural mother; for out of my womb thou shalt be brought forth after the manner of a spirit, being conceived and born again: This thou shalt know by a new motion of life stirring and giving a restlessness, till Wisdom be born within the inmost parts of thy soul. Now consider of my sayings, till I shall return to thee again." Then after three days the same Figure appear'd in greater lustre and glory to this person, bearing a crown on her head, and spake to this effect. "Behold thy Mother, and know that thou art to enter into covenant with me, to Obey the Laws of the new creation which shall be revealed." And upon this a golden book being seal'd with three seals, was by her presented to the said person, declaring that in it were declar'd the deep mysteries of the Divine Wisdom, which had been sealed up from the past ages, and were now to be opened and manifested to her children that should be found willing to receive and to observe such LAWS as she should deliver forth in the New heart, and in the New spirit. After six days the vision again returned, and the Virgin Queen shew'd herself in most mighty majesty, being attended with a numberless train of virgin spirits, and with a very great army of angels; and this person was call'd by name to come and view Her, with her first-born children, and invited to join with them. To which there being a ready and hearty consent given, the said person was immediately admitted into their number. Then said the Divine Virgin, "I shall cease to appear in a visible Figure to thee, but I will not fail to Transfigure myself in thy mind: and there open the spring of wisdom and understanding." She also promis'd that by the opening of this spring there should be revealed great and wonderful things, that were to be made public in the appointed day: and so exhorting to vigilance and obedience to those counsels and laws which should be given out from her, she disappear'd, having first receiv'd such an answer as the blessed Virgin Mary gave to the message of the angel Gabriel, from this person who was encompassed about with the Heavenly host, and made a spirit of light. And as the law was given to Moses of old, being taken up to Mount Sinai to converse with God, so in the like manner it hath pleas'd the same God our Father to give forth in these last days the Law of Paradise to this spirit, who was some years after this caught upon on purpose into Mount Sion to receive it. There is no doubt to be made, but that these holy commandments so receiv'd will carry along with them to many awaken'd souls, the evidence of their Divine original: and as for such as from the many horrid abuses that have been made through pretensions to the Holy Spirit, cannot believe that there either is, or can be any true inspiration at this day in the world; I doubt not to convince the sober amongst them, and all such as are willing to humble themselves before the Truth, of the possibility, expediency, and necessity of Revelation to be again restor'd, in a particular discourse which is design'd to come forth very shortly. As for any particular objections against either the manner or the matter of these Laws, then, when they shall be proposed, it will be time to consider them. Now let us, who know that *the Law is spiritual* (Rom. 7.14) be altogether spiritually-minded, and worship Him who is Spirit, in spirit and truth.

I. The Delivery of the Law in Ten Particulars, Given Forth by Wisdom to a Translated Spirit.

These are the Laws of Paradise, which must be observed by all who set footing there, according as they were declared and given forth by *Wisdom*, as I was in the spirit. Who thus spoke unto me:

"Having cautioned thee that thou mayest not be secure, telling thee that the tempter and the tree are both here, I *Wisdom* bid thee take good heed, considering thou art yet but a stranger, and know not the constitutions, orders, and worships required by the King of this holy land. Lest therefore thou should'st miscarry here, as did the first Adam, and many more since, who have come thus far, after the similitude of the second, whom the dragon hath plucked down again, awakening in them the essence which were slain by the death: I do now present to thee out of my peculiar love, CHRIST thy looking-glass. In Him behold thyself, who was thy dying pattern, and now must be thy Living spirit; to act answerably to Him, bodily and spiritually. And as He was in Paradise invisible, and in this world visible, in like manner as now thou art; so the same law which was enjoined by the Father to Him, is expressly to be observed by thee: not one jot or tittle is to be abated therein. For here the New Covenant is to be reëstablished, in which the laws of pure and uncorrupted nature are again revived, which were engraven upon the heart before Sin entered to obliterate them. And as this internal law of liberty was lost in Paradise, so in all ages it could never be found by any till they returned thither again, to fulfill the whole righteousness hereof, through the birth, power, and spirit of JESUS, that hath imprinted the law of eternal nature upon the fleshly table of a pure heart, which becometh a law of life unto itself, that none need to say, Know the Lord from henceforth, if once come to know themselves after the law of this Paradisiacal life: which I will give thee out as GOD gave to Moses in ten particulars, that what is given thee may answer to the out-spoken Word from ME: who for a general benefit do require thee to record these following precepts, purely as they flow from my unknown deep.

II. The opposition Which This Translated Spirit Met with, during the Delivery of These Laws.

As I as strictly engaged to attend the giving out of *Wisdom*'s paradisiacal laws, that opened in me like a flaming shower, which drowned the old world, that a new world might in the room of it spring up, my whole new man walking up and down therein, and drinking of that pleasant river Pison, which waters this new-entered land, into which no earthly stuff must be admitted; I could not yet be free from molestation. For though sin, that strange deformed monster, must look for no welcome here, being forever banished from this holy place, yet after death in several shapes he threatens still to haunt me, often saying he will be avenged of me, for that I have exposed him to a violent death, for the making my way into paradisiacal freedom. Therefore he transforms himself now into a spirit, and pursues me, and would bring all my dead works after me; that so I might be restless even here, where according to the eternal law of liberty, I should rest from all fear and care.

This occasioned somewhat of complaint, which I brought be-

fore my mother *Wisdom*, telling her, that after death I did hope I
should have been freed, and that all wars should have ceased,
when I was once got in within this gate. But, replied her witness—
the spirit of prophesy in me,—I never said death would acquit
thee so as that no temptation at all should molest thee through
the subtlety of the serpent, who hath liberty to prove thee Here,
in like manner as he had liberty to prove thy dear JESUS; who for
this end suffered him, that he might give proof of an unconquer-
able stedfastness, during the appointed time that he was in Paradise to abide. So must thou here expect, that the man of sin may
by the angel of the bottomless pit be, though dead, again assumed;
and may make war against the Angel of the Covenant: as it is
said, *There was war in heaven*, as of old, so now again in thee. Therefore to the law and to the testimony, which within thy heavens do
open, do thou give good heed; that thou mayest prevail, and come
off a conqueror, by the keeping of the commandments, and the
faith of JESUS.

The last battle which is to be fought is in this Paradisiacal field:
thou art now to engage in a single combat. Therefore to thee I
bring my flaming armour, which is love and faith, by which only
thou wilt an overcomer be. Remember that charge of honouring
thy Father and Mother, and do not thou them disgrace. For now
thou art upon the public stage, where the whole hierarchy of
throne-powers do thee view, to behold how thy *Michael* in thee
will fight against the dragon, with his fiery might. The honour of
thy God is much herein concerned, that thou do over the beast
and the false prophet prevail, defying the number, and renounc-
ing the mark of his name, that nothing any more he may be ever
able to claim in thee. For through victorious faith holding out,
thou wilt see him cowardly sneak out of Paradise.

Since he will not care to abide there, if he see thee resolutely
fixed in the spirit of My might, who foreseeth all his cunning
slights, by which he would pluck thee down out of Paradise. Then,
saith he, my design would take place, and I should have Wisdom
in derision, that hath no better provided for her children, but left
them thus to be foiled by the dragon. See now how this evil one
will, if thou shouldest fall, reflect upon God thy Father, and Me
thy Mother: Therefore, dear child, for our honor stand; that so thy
days may not be short in the promised land. To which thou wilt

surely come, if thou canst hold out all the appointed time of temptation: then another remove thou shalt see where no more shalt
thou to the dragon's fury be exposed, but shalt the long and everlasting day inherit, and keep this sabbath without end rejoicing,
according as thou shalt here meritoriously vindicate that name of
Mine, which to the world is an unknown secret.

I was also further encouraged by *Wisdom* against the great
opposition which I felt, when waiting for the opening of the *Sixth
Commandment*, there appear'd to me all on a sudden, while She
was giving her counsel and charge, a glorious circle with all flaming colours: upon which I looked very stedfastly. It continued a
good space, as well as I might guess, near upon half a quarter of
an hour, before it vanish'd. This circle consisted of various and
wonderful colors, the inmost part of it was all clear and bright, as
the air without a cloud. Then spake *Wisdom*'s spirit in me, What
hast thou seen here but the *Magical Eye*, which is an all-seeing
globe, that includeth all light, power and might within its circle,
so that there is no need to go out for any supply, for that all lieth
within the compass of this all generating eye: and like as thou
didst see it rise in a *moment*, so shall it give new existences from
its own in the *twinkling* of an eye. This is the manner of *Paradisiacal* living, quite different from the way of the inhabitants of the
outward world, who live upon the mouldy bread of sense, upon
whose breast they hang, and cannot endure to be plucked from it;
though they suck in thence the curse and poison of God's anger,
which came in when the Paradisiacal life ceased.

But to thee that art come out and separated from these, my
counsel is, that thou entirely rest and depend upon this Divine
Magical Eye, and never wander out from it; so will it become to
thee thy basket and thy store: so will it be to thee thy fountain-
blessing, and thou shalt need to know no more, and to take care
of no more, than what this will give forth to thee. For it is an endless procreating source, that still puts forth new births altogether
supernatural, to which belongs a pure, sublime, organical body,
having highly irradiated senses, with uncorrupted and divine ra-
tionality, such as is grounded upon what is seen and known by
this eye. Hence may be demonstrated the singularity of those holy
beings which are generated from this source and origin. Here also
may be added the perfect animal and vegetable life, with the sen-

sitive and rational, they all making up the new creature or Paradisiacal man; but after a much different manner than that after which they are in the *degenerated,* or those that are *departed from the faith.* Which *faith* is here again to be restored, through a magical operative life that maintains its own being after a wonderful manner, cutting off all occasions of contracting more with a sinful state. For there is here no coveting any mortal or perishing things, which the low rational life stood in need of: but thou being born into this *seraphical* nature, which looks only in to God, whose eternal stores stand open and free for thee to come and take of, as thy proper right, hast no need to go to any other fountain.

Now as Christ said all that the Father had was his, so is it thine by virtue of the same Spirit of Christ in thee, who never crouch'd to this world for any of its unrighteous mammon, and who would not disparage his Father's house-keeping to seek any benevolences from creatures that lived upon self-propriety. Him therefore herein I present to be thy example; who had a body terrestrial as thou hast, but his Celestial Paradisiacal man had keys to open all the treasures either in Heaven above, or in the earth beneath. But I know thou wilt say, This is too wonderful for me to aspire to or to expect. Nay, not so: for whatever thy JESUS acted here and did, thou mayest not fear to imitate: that which is formed in thee, will certainly drive thee to this, if thou dost not check it by unbelief. The nature of that holy thing which is coagulated within, will contend for this its high prerogative, and not always, as if it were ass-ridden, be subject to bestial properties, and earthly spirits. Who must all to that new name written within vail themselves and bow: and that so it may accordingly be, I will not fail to aid thee with my *Magical Eye.*

Which shall give skill in this for thee to try
How good it is to live by Faith's *supply.*

IX

Ann Bathurst

Little is known of Ann Bathurst's life other than the sketchy description that follows as part of her spiritual diaries. When she began these journals, in 1678, she was forty years old, so we can from this project her as born around 1638; her journals ceased on 21 October, 1696, when she was "aged and sickly." We know that she, like her friend and colleague Joanna Openbridge, was fairly well to do, and that the Philadelphian Society met sometimes at her house; we know that she was an extremely inward-looking woman whose social contacts were fairly limited, and who spent much of her time in prayer. But the absence of most biographical data from her journals is perhaps not unexpected, since these are spiritual diaries, and the most important events in her life were spiritual events, whose dates and times she meticulously records, just as Gichtel and his colleagues did.

We begin with her description of her youth and maturity, followed by some of her dazzling visionary experiences. Bathurst here records in immense detail her spiritual life, which was clearly very rich. She was a visionary, in that she saw images visible to her inner eye, but she also chronicles her emotional life, and the feelings that accompanied these images. If some of the male theosophers, particularly Baader and Ziegler, tended toward extremely intellectual forms of theosophy, Bathurst and Leade tended much more toward the experiential and visionary, and to chronicling the emotional import of their visionary experiences. To our knowledge, this is the first publication of her work ever, and there remains much more such material, showing a woman's first-hand view of the Sophianic visionary path.

From the
Journals

I was taught as I've said when I was young. The boughs when young and tender will yield easily, so it is with ye tender soul before it grows old in Sin. And surely as the first fruits and first-lings of the flock God required should be offer'd and sacrificed to Him, so is the first of our age: as it is the most acceptable to God, so it is the most easy to Man; not having then such loads of guilt, if the Accuser should attempt to awaken.

It is I say much easier, yet not altogether easy: for about the tenth year of my age, I found the Accuser awaken in me a sence of Sin, yet not of any one particular sin, for I could remember none, but as if all my life had been a continued act of sin, which caused in me such great horrour and anguish, as even to despair of mercey, or at least to question whither I could expect mercy: but I was soon stayed with David's praising God in the 30th Psalm (hearing a sermon on it) I will extoll thee O Lord: for Thou hast lifted me up, and hast not made my foes to rejoyce over me: & c. So that my sorrow ecchoed joy. And in another Sermon I learned watchfullness of all times, lest Sathan should gett advantage over me, even to watch the use of things lawfull, or any appearance of evil. All which I still acknowledge I owe first to God, and second-arily much was suck'd in from pious parents & religious educa-tion, whereby both by precept and example I was accustomed to pray.

And about the fifteenth year of my age for my encourage-ment thereunto, I obtain'd a promise in Prayer, that the same should be answered; declaring to me how, & by what sign I should know that that prayer was answered. Which was accordingly ful-filled at its appointed season. And having had such experience how God heard, & in hearing answered, it did for the future en-courage me in all the pressures of my soul, to pour out my re-quests unto Him, who has required that we should call upon Him in the day of trouble, and hath also promised he will deliver us; and then we must glorfie Him and we do best glorifie Him by believing and Obedience.

About the Eighteenth year of my age, seeing the strict practice of some about me, it awakened in me a serious search how it was with my soul, to what end I was born, and to what end I ought to live; and finding little to accuse myself of, as to sins of Commission, I enquired into Sins of Ommission, and in Scripture record I found that Daniel prayed three times a day; and David said, seven times a day do I praise thee (which certain number may signifie many times, yet, I do think that David prayed seven times a day; for so He seems to insinuate when he says, "Evening and morning and at noon will I pray." I prevent the night watches. At midnight I will arise to give thanks unto thee. I prevented the dawning of the morning and cried & c. and ib. It is said; Rejoyce ever more, pray without ceasing. But I thought it only referred to set times, which accordingly with all privacy I began: but my mouth was stopped like one struck dumb; which caused great consternation & terrour, saying within my self; have I so many sins, and can I beg pardon for none? and so many graces do I stand in need of, and is there not any one Grace I can ask for. Yet still did I remain as one stupified and dumb, but filled with an awakened horrour & grief even to high despair; which soon was stilled with this inward reflection. I was nothing, & could do nothing, not think in my heart of God without Divine assistance: and His assistance makes our acceptance....

And in some few months I was seized with sickness, and that somewhat dangerous; as for my own part, being before a stranger to sickness I did not question but I should die; which caused me to mourn & weep to them that were with me, telling them, I had no assurance of a better Life, now that I fear'd I was to die, having lived a long time in sin, being now about eighteen years and an half old. Then some of them said to me, that I had been well educated & brought up in all sobriety, not knowing nor having so much as heard of the vanities that most then walked in. I answered, 'tis true I had been well instructed, & did practise what I was most capable of: when I was a Child I loved to pray with my sister & to hear her pray....A few days afterwards, all my sins were laid before me as they were also some years agoe, as I have already said, yet not one particular sin remembered, but that all my whole life was like one act of sin, and that Hell was to recive me; I said I had deserved the hottest place of it; and I saw Hell open to me, a great black dark pit; and I at the brink ready to go in.

And as the Lord taught me He was just and mercifull, so He made me to consider his power, whither He was not able to save me out of this horrible Pit, tho' I had deserved it. I did verily believe God was able to save me....

Thus for ten years & more, I was led as in a Land of Love, being much accompanied with joy & peace, and often in Meditation, as I was carried forth to various Subjects, sometimes of the Love of God, sometimes of the vanity of the Creature: other times I meditated of the unsuitableness of all things in the world, which can nowise be satisfying to an Heavenly Desyring Soul. But most most usual Meditations & admirations were of the Love, mercy, & pity of God to fallen Man; so that I was as one that could see nothing but Love, and in all could desire no thing but to be swallowed up in Him, & to be taken to Him, which earnest desyre was hard to be subdued, and to be contented to wait my appointed time till my change come. Many great and eminent answers of Prayer were given; scarce anything I ever askt in prayer, but was answered: He never gave me a desire to ask, but He allwise had a Hand to give and I did often know when I should not ask, by being straitned & could not; so that by freedom to prayer, or restraint not to pray I knew his will: and though I found it my duty to ask, yet offer'd up my desire allwise to his will, not daring to have any will, whither for my self or others. As for the things of the world, I willingly did not take thought for tomorrow. Of this much might be written, but I forbear.

At the end of these ten or eleven years (about the 30th year of my age) having some Difficulties to pass through I still bore up; but sometime after the sorrow prevailed: and not having skill to stand fast in the Christian armour, I was as one taken out of a Land of peace: I felt it at the same hour, even to a minute [April 3, 1667], how I was taken out of the Peace & Rest, and immediately putt into a wilderness to be tempted; where I was to fight my way through, & with the three great Enemies of Man, viz., the world, the Flesh, & the Devil. And as soon as by faith and prayer one seem'd to be weakned a second did rise up; and as soon as that Temptation seem'd to be overcome, a third arose up: so that I had not time to go off my watch, and even fainted—through long waiting. And when I did think & some times hope they were dead, then an unexpected one would awaken, so that at length when I found a sweet calm, I knew by experience it was a Cordial before some storm or Trial in the wilderness, where the world, the flesh, & the Devil maintained a continual war; yet did I never question my former Comforts, neither was I att this time without great Teaching and joy in God: in visions of the Night when asleep, and some few in the Day, which allwise taught and declared what I was to pass through.

Thus was I carried on about Ten years more; and near the end of those years I felt some great thing was to be known and enjoyed, but knew not what: and I had an hungering desire to know further of God, and how I might understand aright how to worship Him as He required; and that I might rightly apprehend the Intercession of Christ for us, how He was our Advocate with the Father, and how I should direct prayer to God through Christ, which I searched in the Scriptures, but could not understand it as I believed it might be knowen: I was extreme sensible of my own ignorance, how little I knew of God, and how ignorant of my Self, even as one knowing nothing. And as I had near ten years desyred a redemption from my former state, for though I was much stayed & comforted, yet I found there was a greater Interruption in my thoughts than I had had formerly; so I did greatly press for the days of old, saying: O that it were as in the days of old, when the Candle of the Lord did shine round about me; when I sat under his shadow with great delight! O when wilt Thou restore unto me the joys and stilness of thy Love?

After this for my support, on June 23rd, 1678, a year of Jubilee was proclaimed, & prophesied to me by an Angel or Spirit in a Dream or Vision; and after confirmed by another Angel in such a lyke dream; which was as they had said, and at the same time performed to me, to witt, at the end of six moneths, being December 23rd, 1678. But about a moneth or three weeks before, I was brought to that, as to be fully contented to take up my Cross dayly, if it was his will; being satisfied to wait the Good pleasure, not desiring deliverance of God as I often before had done. And I was no sooner contented, (as I have allwise found that Contented Resignation is the nearest way to Deliverance) but in three or four weeks at most, on Dec. 23rd aformementioned, I was taken out of this bewildred place and put in to such a Calm as is not to be express'd: that as the very Day, hour, & minute of my being set in the wilderness were so plainly felt and perceived, being so different an air; so the taking out of it was as sensible, leaving all storms behind me I was as set into a sweet still Heaven, and new senses given me as one not in a Body; so that I felt my self quite taken out of all disturbances of outward senses and sett in a new air or another Climate, and another Spirit given me that was accompanied with New understanding, being as one who had putt off an old garment, nay like one uncloathed of this mortal Body, and a new Body brought forth to manifestation; which caused great joy and admiration much more felt than can be expressed.

And in a few moneths after, there opened a view of the Heavenly Canaan as followeth, for which and for the many Manifestations of the Eternal Love of the Father, through His Son of Mercifull Love, communicated by his Holy and Blessed Spirit, I offer to God alone all the praise, honour, Glory, power, & dominion of things in Heaven, & things on Earth, and things under the Earth, as is most due: To whom be Eternal Praise. Amen!

A Transportation or Manifestation made to Me, whither in the Body or out of the Body (as S. Paul saith) I cannot tell; but I was often made sensible, where my Body lay, and that my Eyes did above open, by my spirit's return to it. *Which was on Monday night, March 17th, 1679.*

Being in Contemplation of Moun Zion, and earnestly longing to be in Mount-Zion state, and also to understand what that extreme Agony meant, which I had been in fourteen days before; that held me about half an hour when I was in bed. It was like a Dark flood cast forth from the Dragon, which was ready to swallow me up; but my alone Defence was Prayer, crying without ceasing, & saying nothing else for the greatness of my Anguish & fear, but O Jesus! O Jesus, hide me in thy wounds! Thus for the space of half an hour, till there became a most blessed and gracious Calm....

And being very sensible of the difficulty of overcoming the Beast & Great Dragon, and to gett out of the Babylonish Principle in our progress towards Heaven, my longing grew still stronger to be in Mount Zion. And as I was in these desires I thought, but what if God should come & appear to me at this instant? upon which the flesh seem'd to retreat, & recall her earnest suit, as framing to my self that the sight of God was terrible. But Faith soon check'd those fleshly-fears, by representing that this was the place which I did groan, thirst, & long for, and that till I was fitted and made meet for this Inheritance of the Saints in Light, I earnestly desired some comfortable Prospects and Visions of that Glory, as Others have had, to encourage me during my wandrings in this Howling wilderness. This I say, I had often press'd after, namely to have some tastes of the Heavenly, till I should arrive at the fruition of it, thereby to stay my holy impatience: yet at the same time I was afraid lest the Sight of such a Glory should make it more difficult for me, to be content to stay here in the Body, and should encrease my thirst, even to fainting for the Living God. These thoughts made me pour out my request crying out, O stay me with flagons, & comfort me with Apples, for I am sick with Love! And soon after, it being then near half an hour past eleven at night, as I lay looking up by the spiritual Eye of Faith, I saw Paradise with the Tree of Life in the midst of it, very pleasant & not to be compared to any thing here below: the fruits that grew upon it were of most beautifull and pleasant Colours, the leaves were of a most fresh and lively green, the grass under it was young & tender, & of a pleasant green Tincture. I could see no weeds, and all appeared as it had been newly watered.

Yet this did not fully satisfie me, except I might also see the Kingdom of Christ. Then was I caught up higher, where I saw Jesus in the appearance of a Man, all surrounded with a most glorious Light, which greatly transported me, for now I knew I was come to the place which I had so long desired to behold. Whilst I was here I appeared to my self (I mean my Angel appear'd to me, but I understood it not) at which being surprized, and the flesh shrinking at the greatness of the Glory, I perfectly felt a Touch on the top of my head, which drew my spirit out of Me, as you draw a knife or sword out of a Sheath, & it cut as it was drawn forth, I felt it cut like a two-edged sword. Thereafter I appeared as a spark of Light, and according to my desire I sometimes mounted up to see Jesus; and then descended again to Paradise: all which motions were very swift.

After this I desired to see the Father, and after a little stay in the Kingdom of Christ, I was had up to God the Father. But Oh! Oh! oh the Glory! the Splendor! the Brightness! the exceeding unexpressible Glory that was there! at the sight of which I threw my self down before Him, crying—continually for above a quarter of an hour; My God! My God! I'm now come to the place to which Thou hast called me; and which I so long desired to see. I am now come to enjoy Thee! Thee! being got above all those difficulties I have—been so long wandering through, to witt; the Kingdom of the Great Dragon & Beast with its Babylonish Principle. I can't express the delight I took to see my self redeem'd from all those burthens, letts, and hinderances I had so long groaned under! Then I saw the Dragon, the Beast, & Babylon lying on the Earth; the Dragon was of a long shape & of a green colour like a serpent: it had four short legs, the foremost the longest; It was terrible to behold, the very thoughts of it since made me almost to tremble: it appeared as if it had lost its prey, and given it over. The Beast appeared like a grey-lyon, & seem'd very eager & fierce to find what was become of his prey; but I feared him not,—being extremely pleased to see my self so safe. But soon after the Beast saw me & fixed his great Eyes upon me,—with his jaws wide open, as one watching for the Prey, which was in his Sight tho' out of his reach. The Babylonish Principle lay on the ground in the appearance of toys and trifles of several sorts, & of prospects for Children. They were represented to me as if they had been spued out, and therefore were not to be taken up again....

I desyred also to see Hell, which I saw at a distance, in the likeness of a dark Smoaking furnace; even a thick darkness which comprehended no light. Then my God told me (as I sat in a cloud of light & in the felt Embraces of God the Father his Divine Love, which I thought I was to abide in for ever.—never to go out) that I was not come up to abide there as yet, but that I was first to pass the briers & thorny way, Paradise being hedged about with thorns; and none can enter into it but by passing thro' the thorns and stones. Then I look't down to Paradise and saw such a thorny & stoney way as I had never seen before, being all stones, and no path-way to be seen, nor any body walking there; the stones were half as high as my self, sometimes it appeared all stones, sometimes all Thorns, and those the highest that ever I had seen, and very thick together; so as to sense it appeared impossible to pass. I endeavoured to go, but could not tell where to tread. I took care that no long Garment might hinder me. I thought I would enquire of Travellers that went that way to direct me (though I saw none) but presently I was check'd with a stay; they need a Guide themselves. I ecchoed back again, Lord, send thy Spirit Truth to guide me! I looked very earnestly to see whither I could see any one in the same way with Me; at length I saw one whom I knew, who came forward tho' the way was very bad & up-hill, and I saw that the higher she came, the faster she went; tho' the way seemed worse & worse! [The more we advance in our way to Heaven, tho' the Difficulties become greater; yet through Grace & Experience we are strengthened to go faster.] But at last the thorny way seem'd to hid away & disappear, and in stead thereof appeared a pleasant River of Glass, which compassed Paradise, and Paradise appeared much more beautifull & pleasant than before.... Then I desired to see God the Father again and the Elders in Heaven with their Gowns, and I desired also to sit with them with a Crown on my head, and I did so. And when they fell down & praised God I joyned with them, falling down before the Throne with great joy.

Then I desired to behold Christ again and to see his Heart, as some had seen, which I behld flaming with Love to the Saints. Then I desired to enter into the Heart of Christ, and so I did, entering in & coming forth again very swiftly, for several times. After this, I was desirous to enter into whole Christ; and presently I was in the Person of Christ, where I felt & saw my self: I saw my Eye in & through Christ's Eye; and I saw my head, neck, & breast, in Christ's, as through a Glass; So I was satisfied. Yet I desired also to see & feel, whither my hand was in Christ's hand, and I found it was; and I laid hold on the hand of Christ with my fingers, and it felt to the hand that touched, as if it touched another hand, but to the hand that was touched, as if the right hand took hold of the left; (upon which my Spirit returned to my body, and I was much amazed, for I did not think that I belonged to my body, or should ever have returned to it again: but soon was I caught out of my body again more swift than an arrow out of a bow:) yea I saw my whole Man in & thro' the Transparent Body of Christ, which Sight did cause unexpresssible joy in me, to see that Christ was one with me, and I one in Him; the blessed Union, which I had long desired clearly to understand.

After I desired to see God the Father sitting on his Throne of Glory with a Rainbow over his head: This was an unexpressible great Glory & Majesty, streaming forth Beams like a Glorious Sun; tho' infintely transcending that we see here in our Orb: in which Glory were most beautifull & lustrous colours, somewhat resembling the Colours & compass of a Rainbow, but far more beautifull, which I beheld with great admiration. I desired likewise to the Christ in his Vesture dipt in Blood: then was I immediately transported into his Glory, and saw his Majesty cloathed with a Loose Garment; the outside of which was of the colour of pure Blood, but the Inside was as lined with white, which white seem'd to spread it self over most of the red. I was taken up some times with the admiring Consideration of Christ's Love, whilst I saw his Love-flameing Heart, from which some Blood streamed forth, and also several silver Chrystaline streams. Thereafter I saw the Son of God in his Vesture of Glory appear at the right hand of the Father, who appeared as before, on His Throne surrounded with an unexpressible Brightness & Glory, and the Rainbow encompassing all.

I desired also to see the Holy Spirit, which I saw in the appearance of pure silver Chrystaline streams, on the left hand of the Father. Then again I saw the Three, Father, Son, & Spirit united into one great Glory, making one great Glorious Light: and I went into them with the Elders, and we were all one great Light: then again they appeared Three as befoe; and the Elders apart, and I apart: and I beheld their Glory. And again I was swallowed up, like a smaller Light of a greater, and changed into the same Glory several times. But none can expect expressions from me answerable to those wonders & Glory, which there I behold, they being indeed beyond all expression.

Still continuing to behold this Glory, I saw no Angels, and therefore desired to see them; and immediately there were several of them compassing part of the Throne: they were like unto transparent Gold, with faces like men, having two large golden Wings coming forth of each side of their faces, which was most glorious: After this, seeing the streams come forth from the Heart of Christ, as I had seen before, like to transparent Silver, I asked what it was? He said, it was the fire which was to purifie the Saints. Then I had a mind to see the wounds of Christ, and I looked on his hands, and the wounders there did glister like the purest part of the Light, which I saw in God the Father, comparing them together. Thus I abode in this Glory, and would often go into the purest part of the Light of God the Father, and be one with the Father, and then come out again, & return as often as I would.

I desired to have an Ancient Christian of my acquaintance there, (who I knew had for a long time desired to see this Glory) that she might come & enter into this Light, from whence God is called the Father of Lights, and a little after she came. Then I desired that one of my children might come up, & she came a little after: and then another of them; and so till all were come in: They came in the same order as I had desired it.—First of all my friend entered into the Pure Light; then all my Children, one after another: and as they came up, I remember two little Children, which died one at fourteen weeks, the other at fourteen days' end; and immediately as soon as I began to desire it, they came like to Bright Sparks, one after another, and entred into this great Light and became one with it; as a Spark is swallowed up of the flame; then they came forth again, to witt, my friend & children, which were then living in the same order as they went in, they first which went in first; all severally, yet all as one case of bodies, I seeing them all together; and yet severally through each other.

Then I desired to see all the saints come up to this Glory, and saw them come like a Glorious White Cloud, two and two together, thick & close, a little behind the right hand of Christ; they penetrated into Christ's Body, and through his heart, came forth again, and entred into the midst of the Glory of the Father, as we had done before: and so there passed an innumerable Company, and they still ascended without ceasing, till I ceased to behold, and then they came out of the Father again in the same order as they entred in; they first which went in first, all severally, yet coming all out thro' each other, which was wonderfull. All of them sat down round the Throne, which was then of a very vast largeness; the Elders & Saints sitting round it: I looked to see whither the Saints had Gowns like the Elders, and I saw they had; though I saw they had none, till they had gone thro' Christ into the Father, and were come forth again, and satt down about the Throne. Their Crowns, as I thought were all of a size, they sitting in great order: the Bottom of the Throne was like one smooth glass. There were many more Angels than I had seen before, all like the former compassing the Throne; on the back side, as 'twere of the Saints and

Elders, a little above their Crowns;—where they might be fully seen.

Then I thought what the Lamb was, which S. John speaks of, saying, *there stood a Lamb as — It had been slain.* And I looked, and by the midst of the Throne, near the left side, at the foot of the Father there stood a Lamb, with its right side towards me, having a bloody place in its neck; and some blood was upon the wool as if blood had run down from the wound: It was alive. Then I desired to hear the Saints sing. All honour and praise to Him that sitts on the Throne: Hallelujah! But fearing lest I should not be able to behold so glorious a Melody, I fainted, yet hearkened, and when I could not hear them sing, my Spirit sang praises to Him that sat on the Throne; but I cannot remember what I sung. I still beheld the Glory untill it began to descend nearer, and the nearer it came, the less was the Light & Splendour: I said, The Glory is the less the nearer the Earth it comes; or is it not because my Eye of Faith is somewhat dimmed? Then pressed I with a streacking forward, that Faith might not fail, but that I might see the Glory as bright as I had seen it: Then the Throne disappeared and was gone; and I saw the Glory of the Father of Lights, far exceeding any I had seen before, like to transparent Gold mingled with a firey Light, which shines down to the Kingdom of the Son. This Glorious Light shined in great beauty thro' the Kingdom of the Son into Paradise below it, as a Reflexion of the first pure Light, and it became more beautifull by far than before, shading an unexpressible beauty over all the Trees and flowers, which appeared all transparent. After this, there was a Sheet of Light drawn before this surpassing Glorious & beautifull Light, and another Little Sheet seem'd to descend from it like a Cloud of Light upon the thorny ground, and lay upon it; I saw it as long as I lookt after it, it being near two in the morning when this last appeared; the whole having lasted about two hours. And the idea or respresentation of all remained fresh with me, from the first to the last of it, for some days together thereafter.

One thing is observable; that nothing of all I desired was denied me, but the hearing of the Saints sing, which I desired with some fear; otherwise than I had done all the rest.

There was, towards the end of this vision as I came nearer the Earth, a Request put up by me (finding I had nothing denied me)

Lord what wilt Thou doe with this Nation? and Straight way there appeared an Hand & arm stretched out towards them, with a slight moving of the Hand twice, looking like the warning or putting by of my request, with these words; *Concern not your self with that*: Implying that I was to attend to my Inward Teachings, and not to look out after National Conceerns, or the publick affairs of the world: saluting nothing by the way. But Oh! the ravishing & unexpressible joys I felt, when I sat in the delightfull Embraces of the Divine Love! A joy, which as it could never be apprehended by me before, so neither can it in the least be express'd by me now. And 'tis very observable, when God told me I must go down again, because I was not as yet come up there to abide, and when I saw the Beast & Dragon ready to receive me, I was not in the least displeased, neither found of any desire to the contrary, nor any fear, but found my self wrapt up in a quiet stilness, acquiescing in the will of God, with a great Delight in the present Enjoyment, finding my self above the reach of evils for the present.

Severall things are here set down short of what they might have been expressed; but all infinitely beyond any thing that can be any wise declared of them.

June the 24th, 1682

I perceived great peace opening upon Mr B, who was above 100 miles distant from me, so that I plainly felt it, and myself also in much stillness and peace, my Spirit in me said, great peace have they who love thy Law; O the peacefull nature of God!...

Oct. the 5th, 1682

In the still waiting on the Eternal World, that opened to me a Globe of all Light, spreading bright and large: and another Globe appeared of the Deity at one and the same time: and I had his eyes given me by which I saw in both those Globes; and my seeing or sight was from a beam or stream of Light opening in and from the Soul's Essence, which see itself or rather is original geniture or fountain song, and by means of it I saw into the Deity through my right eye. I say through my right eye, for it was not with it I saw, but as before from a stream or spirit of mind, which streamed up from the Spirit of the Soul through the eye...By which Spirit the Deity opened itself unto me, showing him to be the only

MOVING Cause in all Motions, actions, Life, vigour, Sap, in all things that move upon the face of the Earth, whether spiritual or material; and that this Essential Being of the Godhead did move itself, in and by itself, and moved all things for itself, out of this Element the Angels were made, and they although they know him, yet in his Essence they cannot know the All mighty, which is only visible to itself and by itself.

Now what this Deity is, how shall I who am but a Child either know or be able to express...except I have my tongue brushed by the Holy Ghost, or that I be enabled to speak inward from or back again into eternal nature before eternal nature was known either to angels or men, tho' all was knowable in God.

But O the Deity! it is the spring, the Fountain, the Order of all Good which hath itself in God, and is God, from Eternity and to Eternity, when time was not, and while time is, and when time shall be no more.... And O how do the angels wander even now and since time began, to see the works of time, for they that be angels and consequently angelical powers and properties, and are the offspring of God, yet cannot they comprehend the wonders of time any further than it is manifested by its workings and efforts.

I turn now to mention that Globe of pure Light which was seen at one and the same time by my left eye, by such a Light ray angling out of the Light...of the Soul. And as the Deity was seen by the right eye (through the Spirit of the Deity in us) as through a glass; so through my left eye I saw into the Globe of Light, thus looking with my right eye into the Deity, and with my left into the Globe at one and the same time, becoming comprehended of the different Essences, viz of the Eternal Essence, and Eternal Natures....

Besides those angels must needs be very knowing, for as much as they always attend the throne of the majesty of God, where they perceive and understand the...mind and will of God, their Father and their Generator, they have [capacity] to understand the wonders of Eternity, but their knowledge is chiefly attained by their beholding the wonders of Time.

October 23rd, 1682

A very large Globe opened to me, [with] which the worlds being compared were as Nothing.[25] It was Incomprehensible, not comparable to any thing; the best description I can give of it is that it seemed like still and circling round its own center. And in the round Globe I saw another Globe in the Center of it, which seemed to be the Deity, and from the sight or glance of the Deity shone a small globe of pure transparent Sight, or to express it more plainly, a Light like an oval Glass of sight. It seemed like Light, it was the Sight of Light. It was the Sight or Glance by which all things that are, appear to be.

This seemed to be the Eternal Wisdom of God, the Divine understanding; and by this Sight I saw, that without the Circle of Eternal Stillness was another Element of Light, that had neither Sun nor Moon nor Stars, but was like a white cloud of Mist, and this Sight like a Light enlightened it, and made it visible and Light throughout for there was no darkness at all.

The round Centrall Globe or Circle was the Deity, the Essence of all Essences, seeing all things in himself; but this Glance or Sight going forth from the Deity made things visible; for before the spirit of sight went forth, there was only a seeing in itself, but after this Sight had diffused itself into the majestik stillness; and about that circle the one elementary Nothingness (I call it so not because it is nothing, but because nothing is to be felt in it; this is elsewhere called the mist) then it was soon…by itselfe, as without itselfe; and this eseemed to be the still bond of Creating Power. Now finding such a…still moving power to draw me, I was through Infinite tenderness and Love caused to attend. This was thought and represented to me to be the State before Creation. 1. The Deity in the middle or center. 2. next to it, and around it (tho' here was neither first nor second) the great Abyssal Globe of majestik stillness, from which the Divine humanity took its birth. 3. was the outward Circle filled as with a Cloudy Mist. Now these made but one Globe, the latter still compassing the former. The Eternal nature, Essences, I mean the Divine Stilness was a pure white Essence like wool or rather Virtue and was virtually essenced from the Deity.

February the 19th, 1690

I am married to him. The Nuptials are come. I am my Beloved and my Beloved is mine who has had me into his Banqueting house, and hath filled me with Love.

O the fulness of Love! The Satisfactions of Love! We have enough if we have but the Thing loved. O thou Satisfactory Good satiate me with thyself for nothing save thyself will satiate the soul that is sick of love. I am sick, but thou hast made me sick; satisfie me in thyself O beloved! My Beloved is mine, he [is] among the Lillies; the Virgins love thee! Thy perfumes are those of the Merchants, thy perfumes make us love thee.

O for Union and Divine Communion to be full satisfied. It is enough Lord that thou [revealest] thy Spirit, O my Lord and my God! It is Love that is the staff, a Love of my Lord, a Love of Delights, fullness of Delights! O the fullness the soul is...Is this Lord thy manner to thy Friends? I am, as it were, how full for [thy] fullness hath filled me, wine hath satisfied me, and yet continue sick for love.

December 17th, 1691

Thy Names are wonderfull O God! Thy Sacred Names were in the pure wisdome of our first Innocency. We should know thee by Name. Thy very Nature would be felt & communicated to us in thy Names. We should understand thee, and be named upon by thee. O let us receive thy New Name, which none know but they who receive it! And the Name of my God and the Name of the City of my God; that I may be named into thy Nature, for thy Name and Nature is all one. Thy Names name Thee, He that hath one may understand. In thy Name thou hast said, we shall cast out Devils, we shall tread on Scorpions, and if we drink any deadly thing It shall not hurt us.

O Thou Conquering Life! when Thou comest into the Ship, the Storm must cease and be still at thy word. In the word of a King there is power. When thou speakest, thou castest out Devils, by the word of Power, and givest us strength to tread on serpents by the overcoming power. When shall we cease & be nothing at all, that thy Power may be all!...

O Thou Unknowable Good! Unfathomable Being! Untouchable—Essence! And yet how hast Thou manifested thyself as a Man to his friend, nay as a Beloved Bridegroom to his Delightfull Bride, sensibly to feel & enjoy to satisfaction, even to the Outward Man, and above all that ever was suitable under the Hall. Lord Thou art my fullness; I have taken in substance & it is enough....

How is it my Lord, that Thou comest vailed with so many vails! Is there so many vails to be rent away, as so many cloathings with skins, before we can come to see & enjoy Thee with vails away? O help us to get within the Vail, to know what it is that vails Thee! Is it—Prudence, preëminence, self-exaltation, &c. then rend Thou these away & speak plainly, powerfully, that we may know 'tis thou who speaks and not another.

25 December 1692

To burst forth, crying in Silence not willing to utter, hiding myself in the dust, getting into the bottom of the Sea, lying on my face, that he may be sounded forth, who is my *All in All*, and has so filled me as I am ready to say Words which you may say not lawfull to utter, because Ears are unfitt to hear....

But in the fullness, I say, *I am Goded with God*, he has filled and how else can I utter myself when filled with him? He speaks, not I: for I am no more I. For sometimes I am so bigg, as if I should be dilated in the Mistery. And sometimes so filled as if I should be nothing into nothing: But something cryes as a strong man by reason of much wine, I am all over filled with the fullness of Him, that filleth all; and I as all filled with him, and is not He then in me? And may I not say *I am Goded with God?* I have no other word to say for some dayes, for all in me, seemeth not to be me, nothing of me; I know not what to say, and am loath to say a little, a little of what I feel; but take me as one drunk with new wine, but take it also to be the wine of the Kingdom, which Christ Jesus drinks new with me in his Father's Kingdom, which Kingdom is within, when Christ supps, yea, and the Father supps, whose presence makes drunk and so annihilates and takes all of self out of us; which at last constrained me to write that which I long time doe but first mutter to myself, saying; How can I write *I am Goded with God!* Has He inrobed himself in me? And am I any other than he? I feel I myself all him! What then must I write? And how shall I utter, seeing I am not to be silent, but to express. O my friends! I ascribe not this to myself, as if I were better, and had merited this state. O no! But only to express a little what God is in his Saints and what I write is but to declare to you that such Honour have all the Saints.

You need not wonder how I came to this Ready liquor, if you read the precedent discourse of the Great Redeemed state of Men & Angels. Is there Joy in Heaven Among the Angels at the Conversion of one Sinner? And shall not there be Joy in our inward Earth, in our Inward and even in our Outward man, when we have heard and been enabled to declare, that the whole of Man must be restored: Poor fallen Man must be [brought] up again, the Prodigal to his Father's House.

Ah! and the Angels which left their first state, They, even They must come to their Father's house. And what joy does enter into the Soul in the sence of this, no tongue can utter, but it stammers as well as it can: But the headiness of this wine is inexpressible, unknowable, and gives me not leave to come within the Scent of it, for no language is given to utter it. But as David could dance before the Arke of his presence, which is returned to declare his Love, so could we with faith in this great Love declare the certainty of it, and proclaim on the house-topps that Men, Angels, and the whole Creation must come up to their first Dominion and primitive Glory: for God himself is come amongst us to dwell, the Emmanuel, god-man. And great was this mistery of Godlines, not fully to be known, till man and Angels and the Creation be fully restored.... But this is too strong a theme to be long upon, my strength would fail me to tell you of Love, the Love that shews this, and the Love revealed to me....

May 27, 1693

O thou deeper than thought! deep are the thoughts of thee O God! Thou Inconceivable Conception and Incarnate Word, incarnating thyself through thy own Conceivableness in us, and Love-Cooperating, multiplying Love; I have been in the Deep of the Love of God, and see the fountains of the Great deep broken up. O thou Song of Love, and deep wonder at the [song] sung in my soul!... When shall Sun, moon and stars worship thee? When shall principalities and powers fall down to thee and to the Lamb in us? O God of Truth! O God and the Lamb! Ah when shall Wisdom keep the house, and all be in peace O God within thy house and tumults cease? When shall divisions cease?

June 21 1693

This natural corrupt piece of mortality cannot doe his will; sometimes it is lame, diseased in its feet and full of aches and wekness, and tho it has been an instrument in Sin but not of Sin, sin being in the fallen Essence in us, and that wills and does, for the willing is the doing, as St. Paul sayeth, for if I doe what I would not (but hate) it is no more I, but sin that dwelleth in me; so that when this Receptacle or body falls off there must needs be a separation, and if the Will were before dead it can find then no longer place in him, for the will is not so depraved if it were out of the natural body to will evil; for most doe not love Evil as it is an evil, but as it is a mistaken good to them, they having so lost Reason's capacity that they take evil for good, and good for evil; and tho' they have in process of time found out the evil of their ways, yet have not thereby been enabled to choose the good, nay further have a long time [tried] to be in the performance of the good and have made strong resolution, yet have often found when they would the good evil was present, nay such a warr and hellish combustion, and the thing that they have hated, that through the strong powerfull temptation they have been ready to have consented to and some have been overcome...some more some less, ...But all must overcome through the Lamb and tho' some should dye in the wildernesss of temptation and not attain the bedewing of the Heavenly Canaan in this outward Manhood; yet know when they come into the Mount of God they shall have a Pisgah-Sight, and know that they belong to that place, tho' not bodily in it: but a Body there is for all souls gradually to grow up into the work of god, for were there not many Mansions Christ would have told us, but He goes to prepare a mansion, a dwelling house for every one according to their age and growth in the Inward man.

O Eternal Power wee wait for thy Time, when wee shall pass out of time into Eternity; is not time and Eternity in us in this our Life-time? and is not in all ages of the world, even after the body is laid down is not the soul remaining in the Essences of time? And was not Christ Jesus incarnate in all Essences to give up a body for the lost Image wee left in paradise? did not Christ Jesus come from all Essences of fallen natures to be restored? So that when Christ comes to give a Risen body to fallen Nature, all nature will be restored in and by his Living Essence dwelling in nature: for he by taking upon him, putting on our nature, cloathed his Divine Majesty with our flesh, and will he not give us then a body to cloath our Spirit with? Has He took such care to prepare for himself a body for us, and will he let any of his Creation want a body to praise him in?

January 9, 1693

Deep Sleep seizes, out of which opened time & Eternity. How vast were the spaces of Eternity! And time compassed, with all the works of it...so little, so inconsiderable as to be a small speck with a pen! that I was as one so narrowed into this speck of time & then separated & as if ready to be dilated into Eternity:

Some openings how that it is the living that prayse God; the dead cannot praise him. Dead works cannot praise God for if the spirit of life does not act & move us, we find we cannot praise God unless the spirit of life enters in. Sometimes we are like dead bones; our life is hid, now if the spirit of life flows upon us we revive, as it is this death to spirituals may be said to be dead. Now those dead cannot praise him, who are gone into Silence, for natural death...may not bring all into silence, but give a greater liberty to praise. I will not say much here of the dead & of them going to the grave and silence, for few know much of the dead as we call it, or rather the separation of Elements, but it shall be more known & be plain & easy, when we are come to the general assembly & church of the first born, & to God the Judge of all, & to the spirits of just men made perfect for the Spirit, God, and Christ dyeth not, neither is subject to changes, but the little speck of time may move. As the small cork that is held up by the waters so little a thing is time to be made mention of. But to think there is an annihilation or nothinging of man when he disappears from our outward sight, for man lives in his own essence, & the Essence praises God, though the manifestation lies dead, hid, & occult, but it is not hid to its own Essence and place of manifestation.

January 10, 1693

O the fullness! the feast!...imbib'd! As one drunk into the spirits penetrating! O for the faith of miracles which is the operation of God, the work of the spirit.

[full entry]
25 March, 1696

I am drunk of the Spouse. Say'th in the Canticles, I am drunk; I am caught away; if you know not this bewildering with a Soul and her Beloved, Judge me not till you feel like cases. Then you will say, Behold (with a note of admiration) the half has not been told of that which may be said in the house of wine with our Beloved, for his Love is better than wine. O how am I ready to reiterate my former expressions.

> Sick, Sick, Sick unto Death
> if God is not in every Breath
> and all in me offer'd thro' fire
> kindle thy live-coals, enkindle thy fire
> burn up all desire, if not of holy fire
> and all blow up by Divine Love's desire.

FINAL ENTRY
21 October 1696

I felt very distinct in me a Mist that arose in me out of the Inward Ground & fell down and watered my Earth in me. It was a sweet bedewing and meek water. The soul's solace with its Beloved; When I sent you without purse or scrip, lacked you any thing? I said, nothing. It was said to me, let alone complaint till there is need. O miraculous provider for all his Children!

Sometimes the Soul is fill'd with God. It feels his Love-sickness & dilating Love, having more than it can bear; It is overcome with Love.

All our Joys are not kept for fruition, but such as the soul cannot bear, being too full of Banquet & as drunk with Wine, crying out in its fullness,—Turn away thine Eyes! one look has ravished me.

O thou Fountain-Good! our words being so short we cannot speak the Deep of God unless we could meet with prepared vessels.
FINIS

Notes on the Text

Rawl. MS 1263 D Volume II. Note on inside cover: Mrs Ann
Bathurst's Writings vol II, from Ann. 1693 to 1696, n.p., which with vol.
1 contains all that she wrote.

Third volume copied by different hand, called *Mrs Bathurst's Visions*, from 1679, and on the back page is written, "These visions ware
when did live with dr pordich." Sometimes visions came when they
sang hymns, as for instance once a "small door" opened before her and
she saw a great light, and many colours within it [20th July; p. 25]. Or
Monday, July 21, when she saw a "beautiful landscape of fields," and
when she drew closer saw they were of pure gold. These visions in the
shorter volume are in the larger vol. I; see pp. 26-27, and addenda, p. 68

X

Friedrich Christoph Œtinger

The first German theosopher in the Böhmean tradition to be learned in Christian Kabbalism was Friedrich Christoph Oetinger (1702-1782). As a young theological student, Oetinger encountered Böhme's theosophy, and recognized in it "the true theology." His publications on this subject then followed for nearly fifty years, from his *Aufmunternde Gründe zur Lesung der Schriften Jacob Böhmes* (1731) to *Versuch einer Auflösung der 177 Fragen aus Jacob Böhme* (1777). But it is in his combination of various theological currents that Oetinger was most original, for he wrote not only on Böhme, but also on Swedenborg, alchemy, and various kinds of Kabbalism, of which he was made aware by Koppel Hecht of Frankfurt am Main.[26]

Oetinger certainly was not alone in his interest in Kabbalism, which was no doubt supported by such books as Knorr von Rosenroth's vast *Kabbala Denudata* (1677-1684), or Georg von Welling's *Opus Mago-Cabalisticum* (1735). Oetinger offers above all a confluence of Böhmean theosophy and alchemical symbolism with the speculative doctrines of Lurianic Kabbalism, about which he wrote in, for instance, *Die Lehrtafel der Prinzessin Antonia*, drawing attention to very abstruse doctrines, including the concepts of Adam Kadmon, or the universe conceived as a cosmic human being, and of the essence of the Godhead.[27]

A modern critic remarks on Oetinger's thought that his *naturphilosophie* "derives not from abstract concepts or bloodless ideas, but rather out of concrete reality. Against the rationalistic and idealistic thought of his time, his work provides an excellent and healthy sense of reality."[28] This sense of concrete reality, however, derives precisely from the nature-symbolism of alchemy inherited from Paracelsus, Weigel, and Böhme; it recognizes that nature is herself sign and symbol of the spiritual truths informing all existence. So even though Oetinger's work includes the heights of Kabbalistic speculative theosophy, it remains grounded in the cosmological insights of alchemy and spagyric medicine.

In Oetinger we begin to see a current that was to grow even stronger in Christian Kabbalistic theosophy: opposition to materialism, atheism, and mere rationalism, all of which are in fact linked together and emerge in Europe at precisely the time Oetinger was writing. Oetinger's use of Kabbalism was, like his use of alchemical principles, designed to show that Christianity was not a matter merely of belief as opposed to rational knowledge, but rather consisted in principles to be found "outside" Christianity proper in Jewish Kabbalism, and in the Hermetic disciplines traceable to Hermes Trismegistus as well.[29] In the following selections, we see that Oetinger wrote of Sophia in rather traditional terms, finding in Wisdom his inspiration and the secret center of his Christian Kabbalist theosophy.

Wisdom of God (Sophia)

Solomon describes her in his Proverbs, 8. Now one may ask if this Wisdom is a creature. No! She is the beginning of the creature, she is the Word from the beginning, the firstborn, gathered and particularized in God, to become creature in Mary. She is visible, in opposition to God's invisible being, and the fullness of heaven, creaturely in Christ and outside the creature wholly one with God in one spirit and one power. She is so great as the gloriousness of God and fulfills everything; certainly this everything is not so impressive as that which Scripture describes. Saint Paul says she is "the hidden, secret Wisdom, which God had demarcated and ordained before the world to our glory." (I Cor. 2.7) Solomon describes her very impressively in chapter eight; she portrays herself clearly in verses 22 ff.: "The Lord had had me from the beginning of his works; before he made something, I was there. I am poured out from eternity, from the beginning, from the inception of the earth. I was generated when the abground still wasn't there, when the great waters still weren't there, and when indeed no springs swelled with water." Because mountains and hills are means to collect the waters to such sources, she goes further and says: "I was, before the mountains were created, before the hills," the reason such springs are. And because the mountains must again have fields, so She says in verse twenty-six: "He had still not made the earth, nor the fields." Finally, because everything had a beginning, she says: "He had not yet made the beginning of the world's dust." This description will serve to explain Revelation 14, that God has made heaven, earth, and the sources of water. There one observes the backwards ascending steps that serve the other as instrumentality: namely, through abground, springs, mountains, fields, dust. Out of all illumined, so that She (Wisdom) is the fullness of all things and before the becoming-human of the image of divine being. Without Her God would not be revealed. But She is very hidden and is in man as in the body of sin or as in beast's stall, and warns man of sins. She is the mirror of God, wherein God sees everything before creation. On this account Solomon gave such a creaturely numbering of the main parts of creation; but in Christ will She be first truly revealed to us. In the humanity of Christ, God wants to image himself fully and bodily; there is the understanding of Wisdom first become rightly clear. "The mountains will proclaim peace and the hills righteousness." (Psalm 72/3) The ocean tumult, the earth, the water-streams and all mountains will proclaim it. (Psalm 98/8, 9)

The Wisdom out of God in Man,

Solomon elaborates in Proverbs. But because the Wisdom that Solomon had, still hadn't made him free from the Fall, so is She reserved for the faithful; these will be the first who know how to use the Wisdom of Solomon. She is described in all letters in different places. God opens her to the faithful. "Christ is for us Wisdom, Righteousness, Holiness and Salvation." These the spirit of Jesus teach, not out of books, but rather in the school of rebirth. In this book one finds occasion to consider ever more the precision of the words of Scripture, and if the spirit of Jesus opens itself to such, so one first knows what belongs to the Wisdom of Jesus. She instructs us to the denial of ungodly being, in order to live disciplined, rightly, and blessedly in this world and to wait on the blessed hope and appearance of Jesus Christ from heaven on the particular day of his future.

Desire

Man has so many inclinations and desires that he lacks things for his sustenance.

From the flesh arise many desires. Out of the imagination and reason arise much insidiousness, whence arise lusts and infatuations, so that the spirits without us see better than we ourselves. Hence Satan sets his snares in desires. When the desires are become customary, then they are passions. There we can easily be led to desire the evil (I Cor. 10/6).

But evil can turn itself around and be a impetus toward the good, and the reverse, too, in that the good can become a reason for evil. Solomon said: "When what one craves, comes, that's a tree of life." (Proverbs 13/12) One celebrates over some trifle, as if one had found the reborn salt of nature of the tincture of being. One must sit and be still. David said: "If I didn't sit and still my soul, I would be like one of the mother's separated and crying children." But all desires are stilled through knowledge of Christ. A Christ celebrates what he has in Christ so much that he hates his lusts and desires for anything else, according to Galations 5/24. Passions come from lust, that struggles in the members (Ja. 4/2). Desires from without fall through a glimpse of the world in the part of the soul where light is turned to darkness (Matthew 6/23). Away with desire, everything vexatious, for it is unfulfillable; choose the cross of Christ, and on this ground often do what is to you most sour!

XI

Louis-Claude de Saint-Martin

Louis Claude de Saint-Martin (1743-1803) was the greatest French theosopher, whose works were published under the name "The Unknown Philosopher," or *"le philosophe inconnu."* Saint-Martin did not come to the works of Böhme until relatively late in life; his early works were written from the perspective of his theurgic school, founded by Martinez-Pasquales, a sect that employed theurgic rituals and and "operations." This school, called Martinists, or later, *Elects Cohens*, fought vigorously the growing atheism of contemporary France, and in this battle Saint-Martin played a major role.

Saint-Martin's public role began with his books *Des Erreurs et de la Vérité, ou les Hommes rappelés au Principe universel de la Science* (1775), and *Tableau Naturel des Rapports entre Dieu, l'Homme, et l'Univers* (1782). In these works Saint-Martin explained the traditional doctrine of correspondences between man and nature, and the idea of man as a microcosm. He sought to oppose the reductionist atheist assertion—which incidentally has by no means disappeared since—that religion originated in mere delusion inspired by a fear of nature's powers. His works alluded to the scriptures, but were couched in a parabolic Hermetic language that, because it referred to God, for instance, as the active intelligent Cause, was designed to lead a materialistic, atheistic or scientist readership back toward authentic religion.

It was not until the mid 1780's that Saint-Martin was introduced to Böhme's works, but he immediately recognized in the theosopher "the greatest human light that had ever appeared," and the revelation *in toto* of what he had glimpsed in his earlier theurgic school. From this time on, St. Martin's works and life were increasingly informed by Böhmean theosophy, seen especially in such books as *De l'Esprit des Choses, ou Coup-d'œil philosophique sur la Nature des Êtres, et sur l'Objet de leur Existence* (1800), and *Le Ministère de l'Homme-esprit* (1802). In the latter book especially, one sees Saint-Martin emphasizing the necessity for human regeneration in the Logos, which is the Gospel way and the simple key to wisdom—something not seen in the spiritism of the day nor in authors like Swedenborg. In his later years, Saint-Martin learned German and translated several works of Böhme into French, not only as a service to French readers, but also to incorporate more fully those pivotal works into his own being.

If we were to characterize the overarching significance of Saint-Martin's work, beyond what we have here suggested, it would be to say that in him one sees how an extraodinarily chaotic social *milieu* like the French Revolution need not be a barrier to the theosophic path. This is a significance that ought not be overlooked in the present era, itself not the most stable nor the most spiritually inclined of ages. Indeed, while we may not be experiencing quite what Saint-Martin called a prefiguration of the Last Judgement—the French Revolution—still today we are faced with unprecedented ecological, social, and religious fragmentation. The serene spiritual path of a Saint-Martin has something to offer in such a time. And in the selections that follow, from *Le Ministère de l'Homme-esprit* (1802) [*The Ministry of Spiritual Man*] we see just how central Divine Wisdom is to Saint-Martin's gentle and profound spirituality.

The Ministry of Spiritual Man

Divine Wisdom and Spiritual Ministry

The original generation or formation of the planets and all stars was, according to our author [Böhme], according to the way that the wondrous harmonic proportions of Divine Wisdom have been engendered from all eternity.

For when the great change took place in one of the regions of primitive nature, the light went out in that region, which embraced the space of the present nature, and this region, which is the present nature, became as a dead body, unmoving.

Then Eternal Wisdom, which the author sometimes calls SOPHIA, Light, Meekness, Joy, and Delight, caused a new order to be born in the center, in the heart of this universe or world, to prevent and arrest its entire destruction.

This place, or center, according to our author [Böhme], is the place where the sun is kindled. Out of this place or center all kinds of qualities, forms, or powers, which fill and constitute the universe, are engendered and produced, all in conformity with the laws of divine generation; for he admits in all beings and eternally in the Supreme Wisdom, a center in which a sevenfold production or subdivision takes place. He calls this center the Separator.

He considers the sun as the focus and vivifying organ of all the powers of nature, as the heart is the focus and vivifying organ of all the powers of animals. He regards it as the only natural light of this world, and observes that besides this sun there is no other true light in the house of death; and that although the stars were depositories of some properties of the higher and primitve nature, and although they shine in our eyes, yet they are hard bound under the hungry fire of nature, the fourth form; that all their desire is toward the sun, and that they get all their light from it. (He did not know then the opinion that the stars are so many suns; which since it is not capable of proof by strict calculation, leaves the way free for other opinions.)

To explain this restoration of the universe, which yet is temporary and incomplete, he holds that, at the time of the great change, a barrier was placed by the Supreme Power between the light of eternal nature and the conflagration of our world; that thereby this world became a mere dark valley; that there was no longer any light that could shine in what was shut up in this enclosure; that all powers and forms were there imprisoned as in death; that by the great anguish they experienced they heated themselves, especially in the middle of this great enclosure, which is the place of our sun.

He holds that when the fermentation of their anguish in this place attained its height, by force of heat, then that light of Eternal Wisdom, which he calls Love, or SOPHIA, pierced through the enclosure of separation, and balanced the heat; because in an instant a brilliant light arose in what he calls the power of water, and lit its heart, which made it temperate and healing.

By this means, he holds, the heat was taken captive, and its focus, the place of the sun, changed into a suitable mildness, and was no longer a horrible anguish; in fact, the heat being kindled with light, deposited its terrible fire-source, and was no more able to inflame itself; the bursting forth of light through the barrier of separation did not extend further in this place, and on this account, the sun did not become larger, although after this first operation, the light may have had other functions to perform, as we shall see.... [30]

Dangers and Horrors Concealed under Divine Goodness, to Be Overcome and Dispersed by Charity

If we reflected on what is concealed under this universal material world, we should thank the display of divine goodness that it has been so active so as to hide this horrible sight from our eyes.

If we reflected on the unhappy condition of the human family, visible or invisible, we should thank the powers of nature for having spared us the sight of this heart-rending picture; and we should thank Supreme Wisdom for permitting that man and woman should now be able to join love and light in themselves, under the veil of the Eternal SOPHIA; because every holy marriage that is made is celebrated throughout the human family, and fills it with joy, as our earthly marriages give joy to families in this world.

If we reflected on what the anguish of the Word must be, we should thank it for its generous charity, in devoting itself to our peace; and devote ourselves to it in turn.

By thus walking in these ways of love and charity, we should ultimately banish all pain and evil everywhere, and recognize the immeasurable preponderance of good. It is quite true the devil is so wicked that, but for the divine ground or goodness which has come into man, we should not even know that there was a God; but it is also true that men are so surrounded with divine goodness that without the wickedness of man, we would not perceive the existence of the devil.

Different Hells and Wisdom

At first, when we cease to live our true life, that is, as soon as we cease to rest on the fundamental ground of our primitive contract, we at once learn by experience that there is a sort of passive hell, which may be called a divine hell, since, to us, it is like the struggle of real life against the inertia, or void, into which we descend through indolence.

But if we go further and, instead of resting on the ground of our primitive contract, we rest upon or unite with disorderly or vicious grounds, we soon come to a more active hell, which has two degrees: in one of these degrees, we must rank all those passions that bind us more or less to the service of our enemy; the other is the very portion or estate of the devil himself, and those who identify themselves with him.

The first degree of this active hell embraces, so to say, the whole human family, and there is perhaps not a single human who does not daily the devil's work, and perhaps that of many devils at once; though men do this work without suspecting it, unknown to themselves. For the demon keeps all men in his service, and makes them play whatever parts may suit him, and yet feign so well by keeping behind the curtain that he persuades them he himself does not exist.

This enemy, being spirit, drives all thought of an end out of man's mind, leading him from illusion to illusion, for he really works man in spirit, while he seems to be acting only in the outward order of things, and because man, who is spirit, naturally gives the color of his own boundless existence to everything he approaches.

This is the way the enemy whom he blindly serves leads him on, even to the grave, with projects and passions to which he can see no end, deceiving him alike in his real and in his transient being; this is also the reason why Eternal Wisdom, with whom we ought always to dwell, is obliged to withdraw so far from the infected abode of man.

How indeed could Eternal Wisdom dwell amongst them, seeing how they serve a master whom they do not know, and in whom they do not believe, seeing that in their blindness they judge each other, corrupt each other, rob each other, fight and kill each other? All these turbulent movements fill her with fright, who was ordained solely to watch and dwell with peace, order, and harmony.

In the second degree of this active hell, men also serve the devil, but not unknowingly, as in the preceding degree; they are no longer in doubt or ignorance of his existence; they participate, knowingly, and actively, in his iniquities. Happily, this class of traitors is in the minority, else the world would long since have sunk under the weight of the enemy's abominations.

The divine or passive hell comprises every region of sorrow except that of iniquity. Therefore, anguish succeeds anguish there, like waves in the sea. But there also, one wave swallows up another, so that none has entire dominion. Hence hope is still occasionally known in this hell.

In the first degree of the active hell, there is spiritually neither anguish nor hope at first; there is nothing but illusion; but under this illusion is the abyss, which soon makes the sharpness of its bitter sting felt.

In the second degree of this active hell there is only iniquity; there is neither hope nor illusion, for evil's unity is unbroken there.

Although to sojourn in the painfulness of the divine hell is a wounding thing, it is nonetheless a mercy of the Divine Wisdom to allow men who plunge themselves into it, to dwell there a little while. If they were not detained there, they would never know, or they would forget that even there the powers are still divine. Yes, this hell becomes one of the springs of our salvation, teaching us to tremble before the power of God, and rejoice all the more when we come to compare it with His love.

Supreme Wisdom also permits nothing concerning this hell, not even the two degrees of the active hell, to be concealed from the man of desire; seeing that he ought to be instructed in every branch of his ministry, since he later has to assist others, even those who, though still living, may have sunk into and naturalized, as it were, themselves into this abyss, or active hell.

For the existence of these walking associates of the devil is one of the frightful horrors that the Lord's workman has to know; and this is the most painful part of his ministry. For the prophet to take his place, must he not like Ezekiel, swallow the book written within and without; which means that he must be filled to overflowing with lamentations?

Yes, God allows even His prophets to be tried by the Wicked one, that they may learn to feel for their brethren in captivity, and redouble their zeal for the law.

Thus for the Lord's workman to fulfill his destiny, which calls him to be useful spiritually to his fellow creatures, above all he must beware of falling into the active hell; but besides this, he must labor to escape out of the passive or divine hell, if he has carelessly approached it, for so long as he is there, he cannot do the work at all.

Only according as he delivers himself from this passive hell do the riches of the divine covenant enter him, to vivify others, living and dead. Hereby one becomes not only the organ of praise (admiration), but even in some sort its object, when he manifests those inexhaustible wonders with which his heart may expand to overflowing; which in fact may come out of him, just as we see all manner of brilliant prodigies come out of light as it flashes from its fire-source.

Mirrors of Wisdom

So in our spiritual region there must be an active, vivifying Force, to decompose and rectify, unceasingly, all the false and poisonous substances with which we are filled daily, whether of ourselves, or by contact with our fellow creatures. Otherwise we should all long since have been in complete spiritual death.

This Focus is that universal principle of real and eternal life in man, which continually renews the divine contract in us; this is He who never leaves us orphans, if we accept His presents: but this is also that vivifying power that we disregard and pass by every minute, though it never ceases to be in close company with us. And it might say of us, as it is said in Saint John (13/8): "He that eateth bread with me, hath lifted up his heel against me."

Thus our conjunction with this vital and vivifying power is a radical necessity of our being; moreover, only this living and life-giving action can satisfy this urgent want of ours; it is also what contributes most to our true joys, by putting us in position to make, so to say, so many *wisdoms* spring up around us, which reflect the fruit of our works; and as Eternal Wisdom does to God, give us the happiness to see that they are good.

For all spiritual and divine beings need these wisdoms, to serve as mirrors to their own spirits, as they themselves serve the Spirit of the Divine, and only the animal material class has no need of these mirrors, for they have no works of wisdom to produce.

Now the power of the divine living action in us extends so far as to make us open the inmost center of the souls of all our brethren, past, present, and future, that all may sign the divine contract together, enabling us to open the interior center of all spiritual and natural treasures, disseminated throughout all regions; and rendering us, as it is itself, so to say, the action of all things.

Wonderful Revelations of Wisdom, Notwithstanding the Hardness of Man

There are such grand manifestations of the Word in the world, independently of traditions, and independently of the superb tableau of nature that, when I look at these grand openings which Wisdom in her bounty has disclosed to some of Her servants, I cannot contain my astonishment at so much prodigality! I might be almost tempted to believe that she does not know the state of brutality, ignorance, and gross hardness in which men are steeped in regard to the progress of truth and the spirit's fecundity.

In fact, in spite of her universal oversight, I believe she does not perceive the lapses and wickedness of men, till they fill up their divers false measures; because then this extreme deviation from right penetrates to the order of the Most High, and stimulates Justice, which otherwise would like to rest eternally in its covering of Love.

The habitual state of God and spirits, in regard to men, is to believe them less evil than they are; because since God and spirits inhabit the abode of order, peace, virtue, and goodness, they convey this coloring of perfection, which is their perpetual element, to all that exists. Though they be deceived, in some sort, continually by the oft-repeated abuses of mankind, they do not the less lavish new favors upon them the next minute; a truth of which the two Testaments of the Jews and the Christians present an uninterrupted chain of evidences; a truth which ceases to surprise when we gain an idea of the eternal generative Root, which never ceases renewing itself.

This manner of God and spirits towards man is not contrary to that oversight which they continually exercise over him to preserve, warn, and guide him in the ways Wisdom may open for him; because these are all works of love and beneficence, and their natural element.

They always begin with him in this way, far from suspecting evil in him; and he must be completely bound up in disorders for them so far to see it as to leave him to himself and the consequences of his faults; and even then they are not long before they give him fresh marks of attention and attachment.

XII

Georg von Welling

Born in Schwaben, Bavaria, in 1652, Georg von Welling worked as director of the Baden-Durlacher Office of Building and Mines until 1723, and died in 1727 in Frankfurt. Welling was primarily known for his book whose short title is *Opus Mago-Cabalisticum et Theosophicum* [1735], and which influenced numerous subsequent authors, including Goethe, who perused it during his alchemical studies. The title suggests a great deal about the contents, which certainly have a great deal more to do with magic than theosophy, more to do with Agrippa, elemental spirits, and arcane diagrams than with Böhmean cosmology.

However, translated here for the first time is not a selection from the *Opus Mago-Cabalisticum* itself, but rather an appended work on Divine Wisdom that was published along with the magical material: "A Little Tractate on Eternal Wisdom." As will readily be seen, this little treatise is very much a part of our Sophianic tradition, and it is interesting to speculate on precisely why it was appended to this work, so influential in the Gold- and Rosy-Cross movement in Europe. During this time, the eighteenth century, one finds close relationships between theosophy and the entire range of Western esoteric movements, and indeed the synthesis of all of these has been termed "pansophy." The following treatise on Wisdom belongs to the pansophic current of Western esotericism, but reveals how influential the theosophic tradition was within pansophy.

Eternal Wisdom

I. Of Who and What She Is

So speaks the wise king Solomon in his Proverbs, III/13: "Weal to those who find Wisdom," and those who receive understanding. Then [bandthieren] meeting with her is better than silver, and her income is better than gold. She is more precious than pearls, and everything that you might wish for is incomparable to her. Long life is at her right hand, and on her left is riches and honor. "Her ways are all lovely" and all who ascend to her are joyous. She is a tree of life to all that touch her; and "blessed are they who hold her." Now we must ask who this Wisdom is, whom Solomon so glorifies? So she answers herself, and says in Sirach, 24/4: "I am God's Word," and hover over the whole earth, like clouds. My tabernacle is on high, and my seat in the clouds. I alone am everywhere; so far as the heaven and deep as the all-ground, everywhere in the ocean, everywhere on the earth, among all peoples, among all the heathen. And Prov. 8/22: She speaks: The Lord has had me in the beginning of his Ways; before he made something, I was there. I am in eternity, from the beginning, before the earth. Where the deep were not yet, I was already there; before the well filled with water, was I already there; Before the mountains were born, before the hills was I ready. He had not yet made the earth, and what is thereon, nor the mountains of the earth. Where he prepared heaven, was I there; before he fixed the depths with his aim, before he made the clouds, before he made the spring of the depths; before he fixed the limit of the ocean and the waters; so that they never ignore his command; There he lay the ground of the earth, there was I the workmaster by him, and daily had my delight, and played before him all the time, and played upon his earthly ground: And my delight is by the human-children.

And the master of the Book of Wisdom writes, 7/24, Wisdom is the nimblest of all; she travels and goes through everything, so pure is she. She is then the breath of the holy power, and a ray of the glory of the almighty, and nothing impure can come to her: she is the brilliance of the eternal light, and an unstained mirror of the holy power, and and image of his goodness. She is one and does everything, she remains what she is, and renews everything, and she gives herself to holy souls, and makes God's friends and prophets. Because God loves no one, save he who remains by Wisdom. She is more glorious than the sun and the stars; and light goes forth from her; For [ordinary] light must yield to night, but evil overcomes Wisdom never more. She reigns to the end beyond all other force, and reigns everything well.

Now, out of this and other testimonies of the holy scripture it is more clearly revealed that Wisdom, our subject here, is something holy, yea, Christ, the eternal Son of God and first-born of all creatures, since of her the same is written as what is otherwise in other places written in the holy scriptures of Christ, or also of God himself.

In John 1 is Christ called the Word, and of him it is said that in the beginning was he by God, and that God has made all things through him. And of Wisdom is it also said that she is God's Word, and that she was by the Lord in the beginning of his ways, and that she was by his great creation-work the Work-master [Prov. 8/22, 31]. In Psalm 33 David speaks: Heaven is made through the Word of the Lord, and all his legion through the spirit of his mouth; and Solomon speaks in his Proverbs 3/19, 28: The Lord had founded the earth through Wisdom, and through his counsel prepared heaven; through his Wisdom are the depths parted and the clouds with dew made wet. Jer. 42/19 writes of God that he is "great in counsel and mighty in act." And Proverbs 8/14, speaks likewise of Wisdom: "Mine is both counsel and act;" I have understanding and might. [In] Rom. 13/1 writes Paul that no authority exists without God; and [in] Prov. 8/15, speaks Wisdom: "Through me reign the kings"; and the lords take their right. "Through me have the princes and all regents upon earth their authority."

Psalm 139 and I Kings 8 write of God that he is everywhere present and fills everything, and [in] Sirach 24, Wisdom speaks: I alone am everywhere, so far as heaven is and so deep as the abyss. [In] John 15/6 Christ says that he is life, and in Proverbs 8/35, Wisdom says: "Whoever finds me, finds life." In Hebrews I it is written of Christ that he is the brilliance of the glory of God, and the image of his Being, and likewise, in Wisdom VII it is written of Wisdom that she is the luster of the eternal light, an unstained mirror of the holy power, and an image of his goodness. In Isa. 11/2 it is written of Christ that in him rests the spirit of the Lord, the spirit of Wisdom and understanding, the spirit of counsel and the strength of the spirit of knowledge and fear. And Wisdom 7/22, says likewise of Wisdom that in her is the spirit of understanding, holy, one, manifold, sharp, nimble, eloquent, pure, clear, gentle, friendly, earnest, beneficent, steadfast, unerring, certain, and so forth. In Rev. 21/5 the Lord God speaks: See, I make everything new, and in Wisdom 7/27 it is written that she renews everything. In Matthew 2/28 Christ speaks: Come to me, all who are burdened, and I will enliven you. And in John 7/37, he says: You who thirst, come to me and drink. In Sirach 24/25 Wisdom speaks likewise: Come to me, all you who yearn, and satisfy yourself with my fruits. And in Proverbs 9/5 she speaks: "Come, take of my bread, and drink the wine that I offer." Which ought to suffice in demonstrating that Wisdom is Christ, the son of God, as he also names himself Wisdom in Matthew 11/19, Luke 7/35, 11/49. And also Solomon put this high subject well: Weal to those who find Wisdom. Since in Wisdom alone must our salvation, life, and blessedness be sought and found; And O woe to the men, who neither seek nor find Christ, Wisdom! Then such is and remains most unhappy and lost, until he seeks with his whole heart, and in her finds wholeness, life, and blessedness.

Chapter II
Of the Lovers of Wisdom, Who and How Fortunate They Are

Now after we in the foregoing chapter have seen something of the sayings in the holy Scriptures of Wisdom, we shall now say something of the *Philosophis* or Lovers of Wisdom, including who they are, how they are raised, and how highly fortunate they are. Hence we will briefly say that a true *Philosophus* or lover of Wisdom is such a man who "fears God, who eschews sins, who strives with his whole heart to rightly know the one true God as the origin of all life and being, to love, revere, and depend wholly upon him alone and to serve him in holiness and righteousness all the days of his life." And herein is grounded and revealed all heavenly and earthly Wisdom, so much as the creatures in and outside God may know and conceive it; in which knowledge the lover of Wisdom is able to attain through very high holy grace. Thus then the master of the Book of Wisdom writes 7: "God has given to me to speak wisely, and according to such gifts of Wisdom to think aright. Thus he guides us on the way of Wisdom, and governs the wise. And then are both we ourselves and our speech in his hand, there also all cleverness and art in all works. For he has given me knowledge of all things, so that I know how the world is made, and the power of the elements; of time, its beginning, end, and middle; the alternating seasons, and how the year's seasons change; the stars' cycles; the nature and kinds of wild animals; how the winds storm, and what people have in their minds; the many kinds of plants, and the power of their roots. I know everything that is secret, for I have been taught by she who is the artist of all things, Wisdom."

But what words are adequate to understand who is a true *Philosophus?* How such a one comes to be, and how very high such are in knowledge? Whereof already a part of this great blessed and happy condition is to know. Since it is already a great fortune to receive from God with such great Wisdom and certain knowledge of all things. If we proceed still further in consideration, we see what she herself speaks in Proverbs 8/17: "I love those who love me, and they who seek me, find me. Riches and nobility are with me, authentic good and righteousness; my fruit is better than gold and fine gold, my income better than silver; I wander in the right ways, under penalty of the law; I advise well those who love me, and make their treasures full." Of her Solomon writes in the Book of Wisdom 8: Are riches precious in life? What is richer than Wisdom, who creates everything? But do you [seek] cleverness? Who among all artistic masters is greater than she? If one has love of righteousness, her fruits are pure virtue: Because she teaches discipline, cleverness, righteousness and strength, most useful of all in human life; if one longs to know many things, she knows both what is past and what is future; she conceals herself in hidden words, and knows how to solve riddles; she knows signs and wonders; and how the times and hours should go. There is no annoyance or displeasure with her, but rather delight and joy. Those acquainted with her have eternal being, and those who are her friends, have pure delight, and infinite riches come from the work of her hands, and cleverness through her society and conversation, and peace through her association and talk. Indeed, I say: When we see pointed out this and much more which is found in the holy Scripture of the blessedness of the lover of Wisdom, in considering it we find that such things are so great that we cannot express it with a feather [pen] and we must be far more than foolish, when we do not also with Solomon decide to love her, to seek her, and to hold to everything that we attain in her company, and through her may be blessed and reach the highest blissfulness in time and eternity.

O! May then simpletons mark this, and fools take it to heart! Let your ears listen to Wisdom, and diligently open your heart! Take her discipline as dearer than silver, and attend to her teaching, more preciously than gold. Place yourself in her yoke, and let her lead you: one finds her near now. Delight in the warmheartedness [compassion] of God, and do not despise his praise. Do what is bade of you, because while you have the time, so you will be well rewarded in due time.

Chapter III
On the Means and Ways of Attaining Wisdom

It may come to pass by the grace of God that someone through reading the foregoing may be moved to seek after Wisdom and on this account ask: Through what means and ways is she most easily reached? We answer with the words of the Apostle James, who said 1/5: But if you lack Wisdom, ask of God, who who simply gives to one, and denies no one, so he will give her to you. And this is also the first and virtually only way that the wise have followed in every age, to attain Wisdom, clearly visible in their testimonies: Thus in Sirach: "While I was still young, before I was tempted, I sought Wisdom without fear with my prayer. I raised my hands to heaven; there my soul was illumined by Wisdom." And Solomon wrote: "Therefore I asked and was given cleverness; I called, and to me came the spirit of Wisdom."

But it behooves us to remark that this prayer for Wisdom: First, must be no mere mouthing, but must come from the whole heart; because thus writes Solomon [Proverbs 2/3, 4]: So you with diligence call and pray therefore; seek her like silver, and hunt after her as after hidden treasure; because so you will recognize the fear of the Lord, and find God's knowledge; because the Lord gives Wisdom, and from his mouth comes knowledge and understanding. And in Sirach: I long after her earnestly, with my whole heart: O God my father, and Lord of all good, you who have made all things through your Word, and have prepared mankind through your Wisdom, that he should be lord of all creatures, his might from you, that he should rule the world with holiness and righteousness, and direct with a right heart. Give me the Wisdom who surrounds your throne, and do not throw me out from among your children. Send her from your holy heaven, and out of the throne of your glory; send her, that she might be by me, work with me, that I may know what pleases you: because she knows everything and understands; and let her lead me in my work properly, and guard me through her glory, so you will accept my works. [Chapter 5] Second, such prayer must also take place in faith, as James writes: He asks but in faith and doubts not, because a doubter thinks he will not receive something from the Lord; on which account Christ also said: "Everything that you ask in your prayer, believe only that you will receive it, and you will." [Matt. 11/24] For without faith it is impossible to please God; because whoever wants to come to God, he must believe in that which he seeks in order to receive a reward.

Third, such prayer must be accompanied by rightly heart-felt love-longing, namely thus: that we imagine Wisdom in our heart and mind, as an infinite precious treasure, in whose lack we are most unfortunate, but in whose possession are most highly blessed and fortunate, and would remain so in time and eternity, and on this account our love and longing constantly leads us into her and our heart strives after her, so that we run after her as the noble treasure, in all our steps always wanting to come nearer, until finally she lets us find her, and our yearning longing after her is stilled; then this heartfelt request of the suffering is heard by the Lord. [Psalm 10/17] And this request has the holy one promised [to fulfill], that they should receive. [Matthew 7/7] But it is important here to know and good to remark that this prayer of the heartfelt love-request, or the longing, yearning, and groaning of the spirit in love (if I may express it so) is to be classed not so much with the mouth as with the heart. For this outward mouth-prayer can only take place in certain places and at certain times and hours. Only this inward spirit or heart-prayer can occur at all places and times and hours, at some times more passionately than others, according as God moves the longing and yearning of our spirit, and likewise come to adopt an exact collection of our minds and thoughts in solitude and stillness; then the solitude and stillness is a good helping-means to turn in toward oneself, and come to this inward heart and spirit-prayer, on which account then also the beloved holy one [Christ] asserts [lit: besohlen: to sole!] that when we want to pray, we should go into our little room and close the door and pray to our Father in secret, so the Father will see us in secret, and reward us openly. Hence he himself also often, when he would pray, retired to a mountain, into the wilderness or otherwise a solitary place, and there raised his heart to God. Which example and commandment of the holy one we must also follow, when we want to reach the true spiritual prayer and through this the true Wisdom. For God is a spirit, and those who pray to him must do so in spirit and truth. [John 4/24]

Out of all that is here said of prayer, certainly it is important to understand this part, referring in particular to seeking, which is required as another means of attaining Wisdom and all good. As God himself says: [Jer. 29/13]: So if you seek me with your whole heart, I will permit you to find me. And Wisdom speaks: I love those who love me, and those who seek me find me. And Christ the Lord says: Seek and you will find. But because so much [of import] is found here, it will not be unuseful to treat the subject in more depth.

The word "seek" means so much: that it means that one hasn't got something, and desires it, everyone knows; the more precious and costly a thing is, and the dearer we wish to have it, the more our earnestness and diligence in applying ourselves to seeking; and because Wisdom is the most precious and love-worthiest good, whose absence is the highest misfortune, but possessing her is and remains the highest blessed happiness in time and eternity, so we must then search with the greatest of earnestness and diligence; and now in order that this come to pass and our earnestness and diligence and longing be kindled, so we must 1. imagine in our hearts and minds the highest and love-worthiest good (as in fact it is) and hold and treasure her as riches, as Solomon did, as when he wrote: [Book Wisdom 7/8] "I hold her more precious than kingdoms and principalities, and riches I hold for nothing compared to her. She is comparable to no jewel, and all gold is compared with her less than sand, and silver cannot be compared with her. I loved her more than health or beauty, more even than light: For the illumination from her cannot be extinguished." 2. We must win her and her beautiful love, choose her for our own treasure, offer her our love and whole heart, with firm intent: in order to suffer and endure everything for her. 3. We must also really and in fact not only give up the world and its delights, but also ourselves, with all we have and possess, deny ourselves, and long to do only her will, and accept her in all ways, that she might be well-pleased, and, thus, 4. follow her completely, in order that we may lead a virtuous life and through holy grace rectify all our works and life, in order that we may do like her in each step, nearer and nearer, until finally after she has tested us enough, and has found worth, lets us find and takes us as a young beautiful bride of her bridegroom, and unites with us in eternal love.

Then certainly, whoever has love of God and his Wisdom or Christ, he also keeps the law, but where one keeps the law, there is a holy life. But whoever leads a holy life, he is near God, and such a man fears nothing more than offending God, and he would a thousand times rather die than do the least thing with knowledge and will against God; which is then a pure fear of the Lord, as glorified in the holy Scripture, in Psalm 111/10, for instance: The fear of the Lord is the beginning of Wisdom; the fear of the Lord brings life, and lengthens one's days. [Prov. 10/27, 19/23] The fear of the Lord is the true divine service; a blessed garden; a crown of Wisdom; a source of life. [Sirach 1] Which we then want to have the highest praise for. So this can be seen as an external means of the attaining of Wisdom, in so far as this concerns namely the knowledge and working of natural things, held and used in proper measure in the fear of the Lord: 1) Company and conversation with the wise, devout, learned. 2) Reading the books of holy, reverent and wise people. 3) A solitary, still kind of life free from cares and in this an exact observation and examination of nature and natural things, so that one, when opportunity is at hand, enquires and researches using different arts and ways to test; in which arts and ways then also the ancient Wise engaged, not only in all useful arts and sciences whose works and purposes in human life are not only necessary and useful, but also in research into the heart, or the most inward [aspects] of nature and natural things; thus nothing in all of nature remained hidden to them, as we have already pointed out in the description of the master of the Book of Wisdom, as written in Chapter 7. God has given me certain knowledge of all things, so that I know how the

world was made and the power of the elements; time's beginning, ending, and middle; how the day waxes and wanes; how
the time of the year changes, how the year goes; how the stars
appear; the art of taming wild animals; how the wind storms; and
what people have in mind; the many kinds of plants and the power
of roots. I know everything secret and hidden, for Wisdom who
is master of all arts, taught me. Indeed, see so far as the ancients
through prayer and diligence in the knowledge of nature were
brought; and because [they recognized] sickness and poverty as
the two aggravating evils that attach to human existence, they
sought to find in nature whether there might be something capable of overcoming such evil. And they found a certain thing
which they named their Stone, or the Stone of the Wise, with which
they could not only overcome all illnesses, and transmute all lesser
metals into gold or silver, but also worked other unbelievable wonders, and thus they attained the crown of all arts and sciences, the
prize of God and his Wisdom, as the Mistress of all arts and sciences.

Now after we have been briefly instructed in the means and
ways of Wisdom, so we encounter a very dangerous error-way,
in which many sincere souls may be caught. For when goodwilled
souls hear that they must seek God and Wisdom, they think that
they ought not seek and find this high good in themselves in their
own innermost soul-ground, but rather go out and seek God and
his kingdom here and there, by outward ceremonies and shadow-
works, in temples and among other men and books, and seek thus
the living among the dead, and want to have life from the dead,
which can never be found there, and so it comes about that they
never find what is right and essential in themselves, but rather
become exhausted in the struggle and become imprisoned by such
things, when such things if used rightly, could have served the
right life.

Now to confront this evil, people must think and believe, according to the testimony of the holy Scripture, that Christ and his
kingdom, as the kingdom of God, are not to be found in this or
that place, and is not attained by outward ceremonies and the
like, so that one could say: "See, here or there it is; but rather it is
inwardly in them" [Luke 17/21] and that it is not in eating and
drinking, but rather in righteousness, peace, and joy in the holy
spirit [Romans 14/17] and not in words, but in power [I Cor. 4/

20]. And consequently must they turn from the outward to the inward, as from the shadows to the body and essence that is in Christ, therein instead of seeking the outward temple, becoming oneself the temple and dwelling of God in the spirit; [I Cor. 3/13; Eph. 2/2] taking instead of the outward word and teachers, Christ, the living word, and his spirit, hearing it in oneself; instead of the outward Holy Supper, the inward Holy Supper of the Lamb; and instead of the outward books, becoming oneself a book in which God the Lord inscribes his holy heavenly love's-laws with living letters of the love-flaming spirit. [Jer. 31/33] One can only use outward things so long and so much, before one comes to the inward, in which could be advancement; but by the bodily one should not stay longer, lest one become an abomination before the eyes of the Lord, nor be led to mischief, a fall, and being cursed. Then likewise one can come to a place at which one on the way remains on a certain level; thus one cannot come to God—who dwells inwardly and there has his kingdom—when one always remains caught on the outward and holds such shadows to be reality. Therefore note this well, you seekers! and go into your heart, and there learn of God and his Wisdom, as is written: You will learn all from God. [John 6/45] But should this come to pass, so you must learn to be still, free from all sinful works, and with great watchfulness listen after the voice of Wisdom, and the gentle movements of her spirit, and also follow these. For although Wisdom will let her voice be heard everywhere in the alleys and streets, you will remain unknown and unreceivable, until you turn to her inwardly, and lurk by the doorpost of her house to hear what she wants to say and teach you. And it is necessary for the whole world to be still when the Lord should teach in his holy Temple.

And these are the easiest, most certain, and proven means and the correct way to attain Wisdom, which the Lord in his light has let be known, and through which all wise that have lived in the world have come to Wisdom: now anyone who treads this path and uses these means to come to Wisdom is certain not to rue his troubles; then Wisdom is beautiful and present and gladly lets herself be seen by those who love her, and lets those who seek, find, indeed, meet her, and gives herself to be known by those who gladly have her. Whoever would gladly soon see her will not have many troubles, and will find her waiting before his door. Yea, she gives herself, and seeks those who are worthwhile, and appears to him gladly along the ways, and looks out for him, so that she meets him. [Wisdom 6] Alone, without fear of the Lord, faith, prayer, love, and a holy life it is wholly impossible to gain her company. Wisdom does not come to a soul weighed down with evil, and dwells not in a body overcome by sins. [Book Wisdom 1/4] But she gives herself to holy souls, and makes God's friends and prophets. [Wisdom 7/27] She prepares them through her purifying love's-discipline, as God wants her to, and all are sent his good service and works: which she also wants for all those who read this!

We could here certainly still say much more: But because the kingdom of God does not consist in words, and we are certain that Wisdom will herself inwardly teach those who sincerely seek to follow her further everything else that remains to be said, so we want to advise the beloved and sincere reader with the cordial wish that he, with the clever salesman [Matth. 13/45] given the fine and precious pearl, may keep it in his eternal possession, to his great joy, enlivening, and delight in time and eternity. Yea! Amen! So be it. Amen!

FIN

XIII

Johann Jacob Wirz

Among the least well-known of our authors, Johann Jacob Wirz (1778-1858) is nonetheless one of the most accessible, and offers some of the most charming compositions in the whole of theosophic literature. Although Wirz is part of the theosophic tradition, he almost never cites or even alludes to other theosophers; Sophia herself has been his guide and companion, and he writes directly of her, in stories or parabolic teachings that are perhaps most paralleled in world literature by Sufi works, what Henry Corbin called "visionary recitals."[31]

Wirz's divine inspiration began around the end of 1823, and he soon gathered a small group, called the Nazarene community, which emphasized a simple, humble, and pure way of life. Wirz saw his group as incarnating an almost Joachimite "age of the Spirit" inspired and guided by divine Wisdom. He spoke of God as Father and Mother both, and held that this mystery was the secret of "ur-religion" from time immemorial. Central to his spirituality was this affirmation of the feminine aspect of the Divine, in connection with which he said that the Virgin Mary was the "spiritual-corporeal daughter of divine Wisdom." Wirz's major writings were published posthumously, and our selections here are those which focus almost exclusively on Sophia. My personal favorite is the story "The Wonderful Guiding of the Children of Wisdom," a multi-level literary parable well worth re-reading, and perhaps the closest in all of Christian mystical literature to the visionary narratives of Sufism.

From

Testimonies and Revelations of the Spirit through Johann Jacob Wirz

[*Zeugnisse und Eröffnungen des Geistes durch Johann Jacob Wirz*]
(Barmen: 1863-4)

"Teaching of Wisdom" (from the journals)

15 January 1835

Learn humility before you teach another.

Bring not another before the law.

Learn to bow your head there, where the door is lowest.

Keep watch over the manifoldness of your thoughts and over useless palaver.

Gladden your heart by contemplating God's mercy.

Be willing to go where you can assist someone; but ponder whether you are also serving God's honor.

An earnest word is good in its time; but who does not pray thereof, he makes it into a sharp, wounding sword.

Hinder no one on the way that he goes; he could otherwise go into error.

Give God the glory, where someone asks you about the truth, and do not be afraid (with all humility) to praise God's work and mercy in you, even if you are scolded by king Ahab as misleader of Israel. Think not that Elijah thereby will withhold his testimony; because God knows his time that He has seen for the revelation of truth.

Watch out for too many afterthoughts dwelling on the past.

When someone scolds you, bow your head, so that in the abuse the rose dew comes over you. Then only believe: Christ clarifies this as the salve and salving in the abuse that falls upon you. Thus watch out that you do not withdraw this salve. Amen!

Never become tired of keeping the goal in your eyes; because only the true, persevering soul can receive the gift of God's super-earthly grace.

Whoever is true will be truly rewarded.

The Heavenly Wisdom as Friend, Mother, and Wife

1 January 1837

Wisdom spoke: Endeavor to practice and hold what your mother, heavenly Wisdom, has said to you.

It is certainly difficult to travel forth in nature, wherein you dwell, on the superior way without interruption, and to make all hindrances into favorable circumstances; but faith, practiced in weakness, develops faith, until it finally becomes power.

You have last night, on the end of the year, engaged in a new promise for your heavenly Mother. This she has heard better than you hear your own voice. She has taken your vow and today answers you as follows.

Blessed are the souls that do not pledge alone to the holy Wisdom, but rather through the vow long to become wholly owned by her. To them she will be in everything that many theosophic authors have glorified as the heavenly Sophia. The masculine soul is to the kingdom of heaven what, in a weak comparison, an earthly, true, virtuous wife is to a man; the feminine soul, however, what a true, virtuous man can ever be to a woman.

First of all is this heavenly Sophia according to her motherly quality care for such a man also like an earthly mother, and grants him stay according to his individual situation and as is convenient for the furthering of this soul's health. Nothing should hinder him in his necessary needs.

The heavenly Wisdom is already in herself what God has promised to the souls that have forsaken everything to follow Jesus alone. She is the fulfilling of the glorification of God on earth and in heaven. But everything comes according to the degree which it can work in a soul.

Although there are always only very few men who love and seek the holy Wisdom, she has also in the great crowd of men on earth on the whole still a sizable number of friends. But there are always a few who really take her as mother and themselves as her children, and still fewer, one finds, who long for a true union with her.

Whoever has the mother, he is truly cared for according to soul and body. But whoever attains an authentic union with her, he possesses yet more, indeed everything which is permitted him in time and eternity, even coming to participating in the glorification that belongs to the image of God.

You ask in your mind: But how can a mother hold the same place together with a wife, for the relationship with a mother is far different than with a wife?

This question, my son, is not without ground. I will tell you how it is. At first to the soul desirous for holy Wisdom, She is only a girlfriend and fellow student, and then She, Wisdom, is the friend and teacher of such a soul. To take the soul to God, He gives it Her. This is also true of a people; God does the same with them, according to Holy Scripture. But if the soul is true to the friend of Wisdom, it in a childlike way bows ever truer in obedience under her, and longs to come nearer to Her; so Wisdom, according to the longing or desire of the yearning soul draws it in through her ever bearing motherly power. She then leads the soul into her Nothing, in which it finds itself as if closed in a stall. The longing of the soul now thus lies in the mother as an undeveloped seed. But by and by this seed develops in the heavenly bearing mother through the power of the holy blood of Jesu and the Holy Spirit, and if then during the development-time of the soul its will is not again drawn back, so the developed seed of the heavenly mother is born in the soul, from which it has received the desire as generation-seed.

Now begins the boarding and education for the child born of the higher mother, that now with heavenly food and drink must be nourished, in order to further its development. Then follows the education of the child through the instruction of its heavenly mother.

A soul that has received such a child from the heavenly Mother is to be seen as a Mary that as a nurse-mother bears this child in her heart. If the soul is true and holds out against all illicit intercourse and sensuality, which in this condition it must regard as enemies, then its child or new man from day to day wins more and more heavenly purity and similarity to the clarified image of God, until it arrives at the completed greatness of the holy child. One will encounter temptations from the devil, who as archfiend of all heavenly births, during the development-time of the new birth, seeks to awaken against one's will; and God protects the child in the soul against Satan's onslaughts. Without the hand of holy mercy not one single birth would come to pass through this particular trial.

As already the child carries this holy branch, the masculine son carries a scepter, which is given him as a power, his mastery over the will, the understanding, and the remaining qualities of the soul. This new birth, in which also lies a new will out of God, seeks with all its qualities by and by to draw and make subject the old man. Now as the first man from Adam obeys the second, new, spiritual Adam, so develops the child and ever more it comes of age.

Then the whole consciousness of the soul goes to further obey Wisdom in all things, in will and attainment, understanding and thought, as both twofold head-qualities of the soul, with which one is instructed by the outgoing spirits of the complete union with Wisdom, and of the essence of the new birth, like the holy sourdough once penetrated, so the motherly quality is transformed into a wife of the holy kind. In this way will Wisdom, through transforming the qualities of the soul, at last go from a mother to a wife according to the Son's will in the soul. All fiery qualities of the soul will through the water of life be overcome, and through the essential new birth now appears the authentic union of Sophia with the soul in power and effect.

Not with the old man nor the sensual nature, built of earthly dust and through Adam's Fall corrupted, comes to pass this union with the holy Sophia, but rather with the man newborn of God. Thus the new birth from time to time through the rebirth leads through the rebirth-spirit of Jesus; and also in the body of such men is an extract, that moves through all reborn parts, and the man in this way reaches the threefold rebirth. This last rebirth and transformation of the body is attained only very seldom, because only few can pass completely through the suffering-process and many on account of age and because of other weaknesses no longer possess the inward capital.

In this is already something great, if a man in the soul has a true authentic union with the holy Wisdom. She, the Wisdom of God, is the aim of all faith; She clothes Herself in the flesh and blood of Jesus, and God the Father sees and knows therein His Son. This new man, who is born of the first born Son of God as a holy Son, is the actual [rechtfertigung] justified manifestation out of God and the essential forgiveness of sins. God the Father plays in his love in this new creation and takes such a Son into his Fatherly arms.

Understand thus: the holy Wisdom is according to the first grade a friend and guide upon the way of life.

In the second grade is she a mother, the actual, true Mother of God, which the Catholics without differentiating recognize under the image of Mary. In Mary has Wisdom been personified according to her motherly quality; but because that which sanctifies is higher than that which is sanctified, so is Wisdom to be esteemed as higher than Mary. But both stand in exact union with one another, like soul and body.

In the third grade is the holy Wisdom of the soul a wife, through whom man first steps out of his separateness and becomes a whole man. Now, after again passing through this union with the heavenly Wisdom and the separation, the lost is again attained, and he may be called a completed man.

So take the little of the great mystery that you here participate in as a New Year's present from the heavenly Mother, and preserve it well in your heart. Amen!

The Highest Wisdom in the Profoundest Simplicity

8 February 1836

Beloved Mother, heavenly Wisdom, I presume once more to ask you something. What is one actually to understand by the true Wisdom? You have certainly instructed me often already on this; but I note that the sense of Wisdom's words may often be interpreted in different ways. Instruct me; I want to use my ears.

Wisdom's answer: Listen, my son: one has so many different, often erroneous ideas of the meanings and the essence of Wisdom because one does not obey Her commands. This is known by few. But whoever will do Her will, will inwardly become what She is, and will possess also the correct idea of Her names and being. Remain by what you have understood of Her teachings. You need to give the learned no reckoning of the idea of Wisdom. I see well that this thought is in your heart the actual reason for your question. You must only follow Wisdom and be true, and you will come ever closer to Her. Whoever requires a correct idea of Her will find it sung in the Book of Wisdom, [Ch. 7, 21-30].

She is, the kingly poet says, a breath of the majestic holy power and a ray of the Almighty. Therefore She cannot be grasped by the impure with sensual hands. She is by God, and God in Her. But if someone wants to know how to come to know Her, they will find signposts in the Book of Job [Ch. 28, 23], where it says: "The Fear of the Lord, that is Wisdom, and avoiding evil, that is understanding." And further, says the Psalmist [111, 10]: "The Fear of the Lord is the beginning of Wisdom." Without fear of God is the man who still would learn of Her a fool who has no true understanding.

But whoever would come to know Wisdom still more, or to be Her child and through Her to attain union with God, so She speaks to him nearer than his own heart, and repeats what once Jesus, in the Fullness of Wisdom dwelling incarnate, said to the rich youth: "Leave everything!" [Luke 18, 20-22] In these words of our adoration-worthy savior lies the most correct expression of the idea of holy Wisdom.

True Wisdom thus stands first in the holy contempt for oneself, and the world and in the disregard of all the glory of men [Job 5, 44]; second in the renunciation of all claims such that man could make with good conscience in the ways of righteousness [Matthew 5, 20]. This means that we should do more than observe the law. This is the true Wisdom of God and this rule of truth leads the lover of Wisdom, who sits by the throne of God, into Her sweet arms.

There is still another Wisdom, that is observed as an outflow of the constellations, and men partake with the constellation according to their affiliation. This illuminated much great knowledge and appears in many useful sciences and arts for this world, and makes a great appearance in the world. But this is, without the holy Wisdom, very dangerous, because its ground stands in good and evil and very near to the kingdom of darkness. This Wisdom, in which pagans can also partake, has before God no worth if it is not sanctified through the Mystery of the holy childhood of Jesus, through which man goes again into the kingdom of God as a child.

All Wisdom must be laid at the feet of the child Jesus. That we are given to know clearly out of the history of the three wise men from the Orient. They were drawn toward Bethlehem and to the child Jesus through their search in the astral spirit, and laid their knowledge, all their great expectations after the star, before the simplicity and lowliness in which the expected master came, before the crib in which the child lay. Truly only the character of the spirit of the holy child could rise above their expectations according to the astral spirit, as a consequence of the important and meaningful appearance of the star of the newborn king, and they celebrated, for they had not been deceived on their journey.

O my son, so ascend then ever deeper toward the simplicity here; then see how all great things outside the soul's simplicity, all great descending things before the eyes will deceive you. The greatest of all promises will come simply and in simplicity, and the fulfillment of the children of the new kingdom will be known and met with only in the simplest of all souls. Because the childhood of Jesus overthrows to the ground all that is great!

Song of the True Wisdom

25 October 1834, from the journals

> Turn to concentration
> Oft in your little chamber.
> Purchase, by turning inward,
> The fleeting time, my child.
>
> Why so frightened?
> Whoever borrows from God in faith
> Lives free from care and need
> In joy with God.
>
> Think how needful is
> Wakefulness, O Christ.
> Don't let precious time
> Be wasted by the Spiritus mundi!
>
> Only one day unwatched,
> Makes easily lost
> The work of many years:
> Be always wakeful.

Sell what you have!
He possesses true treasure
Who believes, hopes, and loves
And practices in patience.

Because if you hope much
Have much faith in the goal
And love much too
So you are truly rich.

That is Wisdom's teaching,
Worth more than gold and treasure
Even if it doesn't please
The wise of this world.

Many pious say:
The song doesn't please me.
Only a truly subtle mind
Possesses the spirit herein.

It reveals to you the riches
Of the Stone of Wisdom.
Only bow to the ground—
So is your Stone found.

The power of this Stone
Will be opened to you
If you to the Cross and suffering
Say Amen in all time.

Learn gladly this little song
So shimmers Jacob's star to you—
Springing forth clear and bright
The source of eternal light.

The Wonderful Guiding of the Children of Holy Wisdom In a Story

Conversation of a Friend of Wisdom with the Guardian of the City

A friend of Wisdom appeared at the gate to the city and asked:

Tell me, O guardian of the city, have you not seen my beloved? [Sol. 3, 3]

Guardian: What is your beloved's name?

Friend: Her name is—Wisdom.

Guardian: How is she clothed?

Friend: She wears the clothing of subtle truth.

Guardian: O my friend, I doubt that one would let into the city a person in such garb, unless she could produce a pass that she has studied truth.

Friend: O, by love, no! She has not studied, but rather she is so simple and uncultured as God had created her. What she speaks, she does, and what she teaches, she has done.

Guardian: I remember now; I have already heard of her. The name of this person is not entirely unknown.

Friend: The name is not the same. I would like to know whether you have seen her or not.

Guardian: No, I have not seen her, and must remark that your beloved would not be permitted once into the city. For we have only recently been given a sharp order to keep an eye out for her.

Friend: Why so?

Guardian: Because she, as one says, makes people crazy in the head, taking everything so exactly. We already have our rightful teachers, our high masters who are seen with the stamp of ordination. You have already made yourself suspicious, dear friend, because you ask after this person, and I'd recommend that you speedily get out of here; otherwise you might receive blows from the guardian of the city. [Sol. 5, 7]

The friend is of a mind to be on his way as a luxurious wagon comes under the gate, in which a very considerable, black-clad man sits.

The Guardian asks: Who are you?

Stranger: I am Doctor of R.R.

Guardian (With a deep bow): My dear sir, you pass freely

into this city.

And quickly rolls the wagon inward.

The friend, full of wonder of this, remained a few moments in deep thought, after the wagon rolled past into the city. Suddenly one of the guardians gave him a blow with a stick, and said: hasn't one of us told you to be on your way, and you still stand here? [Sol., 5, 7]

The friend went quickly forth. He was somewhat sad after this hard handling; but he was most hurt over the inconceivable difference between the treatment of his beloved and the doctor. In this he was soon animated again and thought: I want to leave this in God's hands in calmness [Gelassenheit]; because my beloved, Wisdom, has thus taught me.

After some consideration he came to a decision: I want to go to the villages; perhaps I will find my beloved among the people of the land. Yes, perhaps I shall find her there.

Second Section

Conversation of Wisdom under the Form of a Landsman with the Friend

The friend, thus talking to himself, came upon a countryman along the way, going straight toward the friend, greeted him and asked: How goes it with you, dear friend?

Friend: It must be good.

Countryman: Did you also know that you have a wound on your head that still bleeds?

Friend: I know that very well.

And now the friend told the countryman how he had asked the guardian of the city whether he had not seen his beloved, and how it went after that.

Countryman: I sympathize very much with you, dear friend. Where do you want to go now?

Friend: I want to visit the villages; because I believe Wisdom loves the land more than the city.

Countryman: The proof is in the testing. In this I don't want to hold you up.

Friend: Dear landman, where do you want to go?

Countryman: I want to go in the city in order to sell a book.

Friend: What's the title of this book?

Countryman: The truth, or the nearest way to God.

Friend: Why do you want to sell this book?

Countryman: My dear friend, there is a severe new law that one should need no more books that have even the slightest tendency of a so-called mysticism. Yes, the command goes so far as to say that we should get them out of our houses, which outwardly grieves me.

Friend: That is indeed a strict law. In this it appears to me that you should not, out of fear, travel hence to sell this book so quickly. There is still the question of whether someone in the city will purchase this book from you. I think you will still have your secret place in your house, where you can keep this book, as one once kept the little Pentateuch [Moses]. Certainly then we would not grieve over the loss of the written letters. O my dear landman, let us ask God in his mercy that he give us power to do the truth, for the highly learned men like to always quarrel over letters. We ought to in this be silent, suffer, be patient, and love, in which the chief character is my beloved. She is also to be held higher than gold and silver. Whoever has her for a friend, he possesses everything. She is a living book, which no one is worthy to use except herself [Rev. 5, 1-6].

Countryman: Dear friend, your words make my heart warm. I know that they are true. I am now resolved to go home again and to hold this book, disobeying the severe command; because we should listen more to God than to men. Dear friend, have you not a mind to go with me, and spend some time with me? I would be delighted if it were possible.

Friend: I accept your offer with thanks.

They now went a long way further in silence, and then spoke the landman:

Tell me, dear friend, you suffered hard handling by the guardian of the city, no? I for my part feel still not patient and strong enough to bear that in silence.

Friend: Yes, dear landman, I also do not have power over my old nature; but God gives such grace. It occurs to me at this point in the conversation that there's a verse in my heart in which Christ also once was in a similar situation. It goes:

Who God loves above all,
Will suffer his blow.
Who takes the least, without luxury
And alone is humble
Is God's beloved knight
When it still goes bad for him.

Now they wandered again a good time, silently near one another, until the landman asked the friend:

Dear friend, are you married?

Friend: O no, I am pledged to God; I may not be untrue to my
beloved.

Countryman: Thus you intend to marry?

Friend: Yes.

Countryman: How is your beloved called?

Friend: Her name is: Wisdom.

Countryman: Is this not the person that you now seek?

Friend: Yes, certainly, the same.

Countryman: If I am to trust your story, I must judge that this
person has many virtues.

Here spoke the friend with an eager tone, and with much
warmth of heart:

O my dear landman, where should I begin, in order to offer
praise worthy of her?—But I will have to give you a little description of her, out of the seventh chapter of the Book of Wisdom;
read from the twenty-first verse until the chapter's end. It is truly
a ray of the eternal light and an unstained mirror of the holy power.

Countryman: You don't appear to be so young any more, and
you speak so warmly and eagerly of your beloved. Tell me, dear
friend, have you already a long relationship with one another?

Friend: Yes, soon six years.

Countryman: That is too long, and against the customs of country people. What is the matter then, that you still are not married?

Friend: The guilt lies alone with me, because I am not true
enough.

Countryman: That should not be; but she is also perhaps suspicious?

Friend: O dear landman, that she is above all things; you could
hardly believe how suspicious my beloved is. In this one need not
wonder, because she possesses an extraordinarily pure, one may

even say a holy love; a love that is as strong as death, and an iron as firm as hell. [Sol. 8,6] She has clearly explained to me that our wedding will not happen until she has tested me through and through, through bone and marrow, to see whether I am true. I guarantee you, dear landman, my beloved does not permit one to play with her. That I experienced very shortly in a particular occasion.

Countryman: How so, dear friend?

Friend: I was newly in the land[32] and had visited the shepherd of my beloved, whereby I had experienced many blessings. I was refreshed by the green, beautiful meadows and the lovely pure country air. After some time I turned again toward home.

Now there came a well-clad man toward me, who inquired how I was. He had many similarities with the doctor who I had seen go into the city. I asked him: Why do you come here, my good sir? —He spoke: I come out of Asia minor; I have visited a trading post there on the midland ocean, and was also in a famous city not far from the Dardanelles.—I asked him what his trade was. He said in a lovely tone, but with a strong emphasis: I travel through the lands of the heathens in order to make Christians of them.

Now we engaged in a lively conversation. During this he looked strongly at me, and said finally to me: Dear friend, it seems to me I should know you. If I am not mistaken, you have visited my school many years ago. I answered: That could well be; you look familiar to me. Then he asked me what I was doing here. In the middle of the conversation he glanced down at my feet and saw that I wore torn, wornout shoes. Then he said to me: dear friend, it appears as you presently wander on a wholly different way than I formerly knew. I tell you, dear friend, that the way that you now go is a very dangerous way, as one can see from your torn shoes and your wounded feet. Come with me, he said further, and I will again set you on the right way, that the other true Christians also walk. I replied to him: Forgive me, my dear sir, but I believe that the way upon which I now go is the right way. It is certainly very narrow, rough, and thorny, and very lonely. —Indeed, very lonely; I feel the weight of the world, because only crazy, single-minded heads wander there, imagining that they know the right way, but they certainly do not know it.

They go gladly on such a concealed, slippery way, so that other men should not see what they do. Do you not also know that I have made this claim to you because you bear a sign for me? Therefore follow me willingly; I will lead you on a more comfortable way, where your feet will not be torn and you won't undergo such great humiliation.

This man through his penetrating words made so strong an impression on me that I trembled in all my joints and was stunned, frozen for in this astonishment I no longer knew what I should do; because I was as if bewitched. In this condition he took me by the hand, and I was ready to follow him.

At once as I remained standing, I looked on my breast and glimpsed the cross, which my beloved had given me instead of a ring of troth. I took it in my hand, and hardly had I grasped it when my beloved appeared.

But, my dear landman, can you imagine it? She appeared with a helmet on her head, and her visage was as she is described in the Revelation of John, 1.14,15. Now was I doubly thrown to the ground; because never have I known my beloved from this side. She, whose mouth tastes of honey [Sol. 4,11] whose eyes shine like those of a dove [Sol. 5, 12] stood at once in a warrior aspect there before my eyes. Out of her mouth went a two-edged sword; her eyes were like fiery flames and her otherwise so delicate feet glowed like an oven. But she drew the truth in order to hold the poor and miserable to the right [Psalm 45, 4, 5].

Now imagine my condition, dear landman! I, poor and weak, not accustomed to war, had just angered my beloved; then she struck with the sword of her mouth at this former companion, that had once hired me in his vineyard. This man also had something attractive for me in his manner. He was clothed in black, like a spiritual man, but wore a white veil over his black garment. And then, O wonder, was it my Beloved who unveiled this man, black like a Moor, hidden under this white veil; which came to pass. Then in the struggle a strong wind wailed, that evidently came out of the mouth of my beloved, so fell from his body the white veil. There my eyes were opened to something. Strange it was, that this struggle was waged for the castle of the holy Michael. And I saw that Michael and his angel struggled, and the dragon and his angel struggled also.

Suddenly this man was distanced who menaced me by the way, who brought account against me and would struggle for the remainder of my seed [Rev. 12].

Countryman: Dear friend, you have undergone very difficult temptations on your pilgrim's way. I pass over the struggle that you have told of; but one thing has me bemused, and seems a great mystery. You said namely that as soon as you grasped the cross, your beloved stood before you. How did this happen?

Friend: Yes, certainly is that a great mystery, of which David also spoke [Psalm 25, 14]: "The mystery is by one who fears the Lord." This mysterious cross the Beloved engraves in the breasts of all her lovers with a fiery touch; because it is the troth ring she gives to her betrothed. From this bridal ornament alone can one know the true friends of my Beloved. I must note that I made a great mistake, because I did not look to see if this masked Moor had the same on the breast, whether he also had this cross, and was deceived by the white veil. I am now ashamed of my blindness, through which I was made a little shaky in my vow, on which account my Beloved also looked sharply at me. From there has she kept a close eye on me.

Countryman: Will you, dear friend, do me the favor of allowing me once to see this cross?

In the warmness of his heart the friend grasped at his breast and drew forth the cross. But in the same instant the landman before his eyes disappeared, he who had been clad in a green garment, more a gardener than a ploughman, and he who had for more than two hours gone with the friend. Instead was revealed his Beloved before him, who now said to him: O you indolent and weak believer, must such not come to pass? [Luke 24, 26] Be now another time true, and hold what you have, that no one takes your crown from you. Because many are called, but few are chosen.

Third Section

Wisdom Gives Her Friend Further Teachings

Now after the friend had thus again found his beloved, she instructed him with her motherly Wisdom:

Wisdom: God is Wisdom and the true Master of Learning. He

says: Come to me! I want to give you understanding and show you the way you must walk. I want to lead you with my eye.

Go as a child in my hand; be gladly unknown, forgotten, and regarded as nothing. This is the narrow way that the many despise and the few love; and there are few souls who find it. This anonymity and this forgetfulness is the stall in which the holy one was born, whom neither the King Herod, nor the Pharisees and the learned in writing, nor the high and learned in Jerusalem have found. Only a few wise heathens found him, who followed as children of the star, which led them to the child Jesus; and poor simple shepherds, who were neither masters nor book-learned, neither scholars of a highly regarded university nor officials of the king of reason.

Then Wisdom revealed to the friend how she will lead him further. She said to him:

I will now name you friend no more, but rather because you are following me into the stall, so will I give you a more precious name, namely the name of a child.

Fear not, dear child! I want to lead you still deeper into the stall of secrecy. You should according to your nature again in your mother turn in to your Nothing, and be therein born anew. Note, beloved child of the higher Wisdom, in this stall is hidden yet another stall, and that is the immaculate, modest, chaste body of the pure Virgin Mary,—for the earthly reason a wholly dark stall, darker than any stall in the world. To this stable is all earthly desire forbidden entrance; because this Mary is, as her name gives you to understand according to the nature-language, conjoined with the higher powers of her soul in God. Therefore could she also, according to the qualities of her nature, become a mother of the Lord. To such exaltation in God no Pharisees or booklearned in Jerusalem can reach; and were she not exalted to God in her heart, neither the shepherds in the field nor the wise men from the Orient could see the star and the door to the stable.

Mark well, dear child: in this stall you should mortify the sensual desires of your old Adamic nature and your selfhood and nourish the little mustard seed of your pure, supernatural longing, sinking deep in me, in the mother of the soul, this still Mary.

In this stillness and hiddenness will I unite with your pure longing through my spirit, my blood, and water. Then will the little mustard seed enclosed in me grow green in a new life and you will as a new man in the light come forth, through the narrow way, that for the human reason is a supernatural way, because this birth is itself supernatural.

Then you must remain for a long time in the stall of secrecy and are not permitted to go to Jerusalem in order to, in your former character of a friend, ask the guardians at the gate of the city whether they have seen your beloved; for it may well go still worse than before....

Out of my gentle-hearted nature will I lead you over plants, sticks, and stones. These all should only touch the feet of your earthly man. Fear not if you must wander in the dark night on the narrow way in dark faith. For see, Wisdom is your mother; she is the true woman clothed with the sun; her face glows brighter than the sun [Rev. 12, 1].

This motherly Wisdom will not forsake you so long as you only hold fast to her and love her [Wisdom Ch. 8 and 10, 9-21]....

Fourth Section

The Flight into the Wilderness and What Came to Pass on the Way

Now after forty days the faithful one [Joseph] found it necessary with mother and child to flee into the wilderness. It was given to him to know in his heart and through outward conditions that Herod* sought after them, in order to kill the child and thus had ordered that the residence of the stepfather [Joseph] be searched.

The faithful one thus saddled his ass and made an escape by night with the mother and child. By daybreak they arrived at a little city, on whose gate was written: "Hurry from here and tarry not." The mother of the child (Wisdom) made the faithful one, who was inclined to make a little residence there, take notice of this inscription. He listened to the voice of Wisdom and love; because obedience and love belong together and make a beautiful married couple. And so they went forth from there....

---

*With this word "Herod" understand: the man of proud, sensual reason, who gladly appropriates everything to himself, brother of the evil self-will as the red fiery dragon.

Once the child asked Wisdom: Why must we flee into the wilderness, where are only such folk as heathen and idolators with no Christian religion? Couldn't we have stayed in our land and with our fellow believers and found a place where we could hide from our persecutors?

Wisdom answered: Dear child, I will not reject this question, although it comes out of the ground of your old nature, but rather will only say to you that I must lead my newborn child thus, because in your delicate childhood you are much securer by raw worldly people who have no concept of religion and therefore less to brood and search over regarding the birth and the ways of my child and to mislead you than if you are among such men who only have false concepts of the principles of religion. Because these latter, who have false concepts of truth and hold fast to them, are from a spiritual perspective interested only in public worship and in their unreborn condition in moralistic accounting, works according to the law, and public services worshipping images chosen by men. They are to be regarded as only cultivated and civilized heathen, who seek salvation through works, or only through works of the ancients and through religious practices without spirit, like the people of Israel in the desert, who worshipped the golden calf. These are they who act under different and varied leaders, and who I would keep away from my newborn children, for they measure, judge, and criticize according to the concepts and images of their reason. For the reason, which is under the constellation of this world, is blind to the kingdom of God and cannot conceive of the birth out of God's eternal spirit, because it is a mere temporal power that cannot see the eternal, glorious, and holy mystery and does not want to grasp it; reason should be, without any speculation on its own, like the moon under the feet of the woman clothed with the sun [Rev. 12, 1] as the true holy reason beneath Wisdom, which flows primordially out of God and from which the earthly reason must receive its light, if it should stand in its proper place. Then can we through it, in the light of holy Wisdom, know aright the things in this world according to their qualities and properly differentiate everything. And to this end is it given to us....

There is then still one other reason why, dear child, I led you into the desert and into secrecy, namely in order to protect you from the Worldspirit and sensuality, which transform one into another, and are very destructive to the spiritual rebirth, yea even a death. This Worldspirit is these days very dangerous, because he has wrapped his class of men in a moralistic robe and a great many of these "Awakened" hide behind the Bible and all sorts of pretences and grounds....

Sixth Section

Conversation with Mother Wisdom, under the Form of a Travelling Salesman

Our friend [having again taken on his former persona] was approached by a man who had the appearance of a travelling salesman, and carried a case on his back. He came up to him and greeted him in a friendly fashion. But our friend, who was deep in thought over his situation, did not notice the man or his unusual greeting: Jesus Christus be with you!

But then he raised his eyes and returned the graceful greeting weakly: I thank you. They looked on one another for some minutes, without speaking a word. Finally our pilgrim asked the unknown wanderer: Who are you, dear friend, and where do you hail from? The unknown one answered: I am a travelling salesman and came from the Orient.

Pilgrim: What do you carry on your back?

Salesman: I carry treasures from the Orient, which one cannot find in the Occident.

Pilgrim (who with these words had begun to awaken from his melancholy, asked now in a livelier tone): Dear friend, would you let me see these treasures?

Salesman: Permit me first a question that you may well find unexpected: have you means enough that I can let you see the treasure?

With this question the pilgrim was very perplexed and thought it over. Finally he said in an eager tone: Dear man, you make yourself very big with your treasure. Concerning my means, I believe I have plenty to be able to pay for seeing your treasure. Perhaps I am also in a position to buy your treasures; because although I don't possess great means myself, I have credit with other people who have means.

The salesman, who during this speech stepped backwards, blinked with an keen eye on our former friend and smiled. In this position he listened patiently to the pilgrim. Finally he spoke in a slow tone: So, my dear friend, you have thus still credit in the world and rely on it. That is exactly what I wanted to know. You cannot see my treasure yet.

Pilgrim: Why not?

Salesman: Dear friend, I must explain to you that by this question I did not mean your temporal means, which you understood me to mean; rather I understand with this question the means and condition of your soul, in order to know how far you are awakened in grace and are become strong. You have but betrayed yourself, and what I wanted to know, that I discovered through my question; namely, that you stand in credit and indebtedness to the world, which you showed all too well. Therefore I know that you cannot yet see my treasure, although I would gladly point it out to you. Because you must know that this treasure is of a kind that only one who possesses a subtle and simple eye can see, and for its real worth can value and treasure it.

My dear friend, I must openly confess that position, birth, and credit in the world, so soon as a man is seized thereby through dependency, makes the soul's eye blind and hinders it from seeing the treasures with the rising of the sun. And not only that, they are also a hindrance for the heart, that cannot experience the dawn which comes from the quality of the holy name of Jesus, in union with his purple-red blood that flows in the soul, which with a subtle eye sees its beloved bridegroom and goes out to him in holy jewels and with burning lamps [Ps. 110, 3; Matt., 25]. These souls, because they abandon everything earthly to do Christ's will, possess a wondrous illumination and an agility of motion, like an eagle, and the woman clothed with the sun, through the twin wings of faith and love sweeps into the heights, and in the beautiful morning dew with burning, true love goes forth to kiss the soul's bridegroom and to prostrate itself before him.

O dear friend, believe certainly that trust in the good of this world and what is good in the sight of men darkens the eye of the soul. Because thereby is it drawn to the earth and according to the descent of the sun, in which region your eyes have been only all too strongly turned away from the truth, on which account the soul wails and despairs that it stands in a completely outward condition, unable to see the oriental treasures of Wisdom and to know itself as the holy mother, that would lead it in the dawn's dew [Ps. 110, 3] by her true and unknowable hand.

My dear friend, I must speak with you according to the measure of my knowledge, and tell you that the tears you have wept are truly not tears of the poverty of the spirit. But only such poor are promised the kingdom of heaven, so also the sorrowing and crying sinners have the holy promise that they will be consoled. [Matt. 5, 3-5]. The tears of the poverty of spirit cleanse our eyes, so that we may be in a position to view the mysteries of holy love; by contrast, the tears shed in regret for the world darken the eyes and finally give birth to death.

May you repent of such tears that you have spilt in valuing the world, which has no real value against the worth of an immortal soul that has become precious to its creator and savior through a newbirth of its childhood. May you, I say, repent these tears, so will your eyes again be cleansed, to see the holy mysteries of love in the cross of Christ, the symbols of whose order are described to the children of Wisdom of the heavenly Father, who has engendered them in his son.

With these words our travelling pilgrim in the desert stood there as if an electric shock had touched him before the unknown one. This unexpected realization penetrated to his innermost core. And now he looked the unknown one up and down and finally stammered out the words among tears of the most intimate feeling: O my dear friend, you seem to me very wonderful. What is your name?

Salesman: My name does nothing for the main point. But if you want to know: I am "Oftenheim." And as he said this, he disappeared.

Seventh Section

The Child Explains to the Step-parents the Incident with the Traveling Salesman. The Mother Elucidates This Incident. New Battle upon Departure.

Our pilgrim was quite dismayed over this event, and as he still thought over the wonderful appearance, there stood his step-parents before him. The Mother Wisdom (so will we from now on call her) asked the child in sharp expressions about the reason for his long disappearance from the house.

The child, or the former friend, explained to the dear mother with tears in his eyes the state of darkness in which his heart had fallen through considering his former condition and through consideration of the situation; and also in hindsight recognizing that the narrow way had become dubious to him. The child further explained what had come to pass with the travelling salesman, and how he now in an instant had disappeared. He could not say enough of the conversation that he had held with this man, nor convey his astonishment over the wonderful events and their conclusion.

The mother, who had heard calmly the story of the child, spoke finally to him: Dear child, that the way to the heavenly fatherland became suspicious to you, this came from your sensual nature, your old man, which wraps you like a cloth with which you let in too much, and lures you too much toward flesh and blood. This old nature will sometimes call you still into the world and vanity. Yes, if you are not more diligent than before and wakeful and not earnest in your renunciation, so you have reason to fear that your old nature through your dependency on the world and your old friendship will still lead you toward the untrue. Thereby would you then lose your childness, and I would have to cease being your mother. Because you must know that I am only a mother for simple children, and not for the wise, clever, and rich of this earth that take the spirit of this world for a father, and their old nature for mother. They do not want to go in me, as in the upper mother, and through me again to be born as children of Wisdom. It cannot be denied that many are children of the old nature, and earnestly try to be holy and with this in mind do many good works, whose good results God and no one else knows. But by them one finds no children of Wisdom according to the upper birth; because their works flow only out of a good intention, and in order to become holy thereby, and are thus not working out of the spirit of God, and bear no fruit of the spirit of childness, but rather act out of an awakened natural good will out of the old nature, wherewith such people seek to please God, even though in essence they only mean themselves....

My dear child, the conversation with the travelling salesman and the wonder of his sudden disappearance before your eyes has distressed you. You forget your trouble and your doubts were thereby assuaged. But do you believe that even this wonder, if you had subtler eyes, would be still necessary? Because if you had faith, Wisdom would not find it necessary to work wonders. In this you can draw out a teaching and know how God's Wisdom in all things knows how to serve her children, in order that they, and indeed all men, might be taught and know. Yes, Wisdom calls, as scripture says, in the streets and lanes, and clothes herself in poor, childish, simple people. She serves often like a poor farmer's wife, in order to tell the great teachings of truth, that one has sought for years in high universities, and that one without prejudice against the low condition of such poor and unlearned person as Wisdom can receive as a great blessing.

After this teaching the mother with the child and the stepfather went back to their quarter, for their time of residency there was at an end...Our faithful one stood at daybreak and saddled his ass. The travelling family, with heartfelt thanks for the friend and love they had experienced, took their leave of the innkeeper and his wife....

Eighth Section

The Journey in the Wilderness. Important Conversation between the Mother and the Child.

Our family now travelling in a few minutes were on the border of a great kingdom. Thick clouds bedecked the heavens, but the weather was rather good. By and by they lost sight of the mountains and hills of the fatherland, toward which the eyes of our fond former friend often looked back. Thereby was a kind of homesickness in him awakened, in which he remembered the heights and the hills where he had worshipped the father [John 4, 20, 21].

The land where now they trod was very flat and like the Russian steppes, or a sand-desert of Egypt. They glimpsed only a few villages in the distance, and these too were soon lost from sight. The uniformity and monotony of this landscaped filled our dear friend with homesickness, because his eyes had grown used to the changing beauties of nature, which held much attraction for him. This mood of our dear old friend did not long escape mother Wisdom and by evening's rest they had this conversation:

Mother Wisdom: My dear child, tell me what's wrong? You appear to me as if you have been sunk in a deep melancholy all afternoon.

Child: Dear mother, I don't myself know what is wrong with me; but I do know this much, that I am bored and plagued with homesickness, which began when our beautiful mountains of home were lost from view. Here I see nothing other than an eternal monotony, and instead of the beautiful flower-rich meadows of our land there is nothing before my eyes but a sand-ocean, that with each blast of wind blows its grains in my eyes. That is certainly not the kingly way of which you earlier told me, is it?

Mother Wisdom: This complaint I expected, dear child. Certainly this is the kingly way; undoubtedly not kingly for your old nature, that must be led through it in death, but certainly for your spirit that rises over sensuality. Because, mark it well: this land wherein I lead you is a land of death for your sensual nature, whose thoughts and images in you are like dustclouds in the desert, rising high. You spoke already of the boredom that you have, hardly in the land of contemplation,* having left the amusements of senseworld, and are hardly stepped into the unknown land, which is still not the only desert in which we must take up our residence. For this land, about which you begin to complain, will unveil the whole condition of your heart; it will reveal to you

---

*We here refer to the enjoyment which the high mountains offer the eye of the lover of nature, in which the mind amuses itself. But such expressions must, though we here speak in terms of images, be understood spiritually.

how you are still with the outward men of nature and are dependent on much comfort. Likewise, it will reveal the unrefined condition of your faith, according to which you still hold many high ideas of a sensual service of God, which are the high mountains in you rising and hindering you, hindering the worship of the pure, essential Godhead in the spirit, and in truth as it truly stands in itself. Because the sensory-world cannot conceive God, even though it strives with its sensual clinging after this holy, essential good of all goods to know and to grasp this independent Wisdom in her Ur-light.

If you, my dear child, contemplate this holy Ur-essence as is proper and worthy, so you must go into the dark and confine your natural understanding powers. Your sensual imagination must, as once the folk of Israel at Mount Sinai did, remain behind; because the eternal Godhead dwells in a supernatural—inaccessible to the sharp reason—light. And here appears in an exalted sense what the Apostle Paul said: the dark man does not hear or understand what the spirit of God is [I Cor. 2, 14].

Child: O dear mother, what a light strikes me from your words; a light that divides the darkness in me, as now the sunbeam above penetrates the lowering clouds. Your teaching words remind me of the Sun-woman who is described in the Revelation of John [Ch. 12]. Yes, it appears to me as if in my heart the ray of essential light breaks forth to illuminate the dark letters in me. Now can I understand how this Sun-woman reveals herself in each reborn soul and clarifies it, and so we through this quality must be raised over ourselves and all earthliness, and thus may stand as conqueror on the heights of Mount Zion with the great number of the elect that the Lamb has purchased from the earth and the influx of the elements, that then, like the Sun-woman, they will have beneath their feet the transformed moon and stars with their fiery working.

O dear mother, your words have made so deep an impression on my soul that I have strong enough faith in this instant to bring me over all hindrances and over all earthliness. Now I saw clearly how this our way is the right way, even if it sometimes goes against my reason.

Mother Wisdom: My child, now you believe [John 16, 31, 32]. But see, the time comes that your soul will be dark and you will seek to leave me, your mother. The enemy will in the hour of darkness on this way make you suspicious through subtle methods that you now do not suspect. Then you must hold, hold, hold what you have, in order that no one takes your crown [Revelation 3, 11]. But if I in my power withstand, so will I in this my spirit power go before you and with this renewing spirit give you new strength [Matt. 26, 32].

During this conversation it became very dark, because night had fallen. They neared a hamlet, or at least a few outlying houses wherein they could seek night quarters. But the people would not offer them any, so they had to travel further. This rejection struck the child deep in the heart; thus he spoke to his mother and said: dear mother, is this not nasty and uncharitable of these people that they offered us nothing?

Mother Wisdom: Dear child, we will not permit this to enter our hearts, but rather think what is written in the evangelio, that no hair falls from our head without God's will.

Child: But this pains me so much that I would like to pray to the heavenly Father to make fire from heaven fall and burn this house up.

Mother Wisdom: Do you not know which spirit's child you are? Think that the Son of Man is not come to damn men's souls, but rather to save them [Luke 9, 53-56] and that He not once had somewhere to lay his head.

Child: Dear mother, I must say to you that I have a great fear of these people who dwell in this land. Their great stature and their raw looks make me anxious and fearful.

Mother Wisdom: Dear child, these are the Moabites, a great and strong race, like the Anakims. Of this spoke the Lord to the children of Israel [Deut. 2, 9] that He will give them no land of these folk to possess; and they should also not fight with them. Therefore be still and don't let in the fire that falls from heaven into yourself. But fear not. Be faithful and not unfaithful, for you will inherit the praised land of joy that the Lord your God will give you. You should overcome all these clouds through faith and love in order that you may go through the gate of the city of God with the righteous folk that preserve their faith. Amen! [Is. 26, 12]

Ninth Section

Stopping in the Huts of Love and Warmheartedness That Later Are to Be Met under the Names Zacharias and Elisabeth.

At the end of this conversation, in which the faithful one had revealed his fear and anxiety, and the child after his old nature revealed his impatience and weakness—while the mother bore everything with great patience—they glimpsed in the distance a light. The mother Wisdom gave the faithful one a sign to turn sideways and go toward this shining light. Soon they came to a small hut, in which this light burned still, late in the night, and the hut was like a little night-hut in a gourd-garden. They stood a while before this hut, which was made of boards and bedecked with straw, hesitating, unsure whether it would be a good idea to knock. Finally Wisdom gave the faithful one a wink, and he knocked. They waited there not long, and someone opened a little window and asked: Who knocked in the midnight hour here? The mother Wisdom answered: It is the voice of the friend who has stopped before your hut in the midnight hour, and asks you whether love and warmheartedness are home here, and might take a travelling family under your roof?

The man, a venerable grey, who according to his character really was called "Warm hearted," was quite astonished to hear this name, as was his wife, who according to her character was really called "Love." When they heard this, he pushed aside the straw and spoke: Dear wife, wake up, for here is something for us to do. Love was also awake and ready—so she went quickly to the little window, in order to see who was there; and there she glimpsed the little child by the mother, covered under the one coat. Love hurried to the little door (which was indeed quite narrow) and flew to the ass, asking the mother: How comes it that you are out so late with a child and still not in an inn?

The mother Wisdom spoke: We knocked more than three hours ago at a rather well-built house to ask for a night's rest; but they would not take us. We were forced to travel further and finally saw your little house.

Love, overcome by pity, asked no more who they were or where they came from, but rather bade the Warm-hearted one, her husband, to be of one mind with her, and to take the faithful one and Wisdom, with the child into the house. The Warm-hearted one motioned that the mother and the child should dismount the ass, and led it immediately into a stall that lay behind the house. Then he led the family into the room, which was narrow and very low, so low that the the faithful one, who was still not used to bending, hit his head very hard. They set the pair at a little table, and prepared a bed for the child, who was not in the best of humour. Love, or the mother of the house, prepared something for the family, in order to liven them up. But so poor was the house that Love and Warmheartedness could only give them what they had, namely, bread and milk.

While Love hurried to the fireplace to warm the milk, Warmheartedness drew close to the faithful one and asked him whence they came, and where the aim of their journey was. The faithful one explained this in brief, as well as he could. Soon appeared the housemother again, set the milk on the table, and Warmheartedness laid the guests' bread there too.

After they had eaten and were strengthened, Love and Warmheartedness prepared a bed of straw. They laid down on it and soon slept peacefully. At daybreak Love and Warmheartedness awoke, but did not hurry because they did not want to disturb the peace; then Love and Warmheartedness sacrificed the usual and only worked so soon as something useful and necessary called and conditions required it. Mother Wisdom soon woke up, because Wisdom did not sleep long, and whoever is early up, finds her, as the Holy Scripture says! But she also was still, as others wanted. Finally by and by all were up from their beds. Soon they united for a morning prayer, which Warmheartedness, Zacharias, in a patriarchal spirit, led. After this morning offering was finished, Love hurried to the fireplace in order to prepare a breakfast for the travelling family. During this time the young son, Hope, also awoke, and as soon as breakfast was ready, the housemother set the table and after a short prayer all ate.

After they had eaten, they rose, and the Warmhearted one, or Zacharias, spoke a prayer of praise and thanksgiving for the blessings they had received. But he dwelled particularly on behalf of the guests, even though he did not know them well. After this prayer and thanksgiving the guests, and also old Zacharias and Elisabeth were sunk in a deep stillness, for a still adoration of

God had overtaken all of them, of such a pure and high kind that not even subtle words could express it. Mary particularly considered in her heart the words that Zacharias in the praise-giving had spoken, and brought them to the eternal as an offering, asking that He only according to his will may fill them with holy Wisdom, and she spoke in her still, God-given soul: "Lord, let come to pass what you will." But this did not remain only a still prayer, but rather arose as a speaking Word out of the depths in Mary, and emerged through the power of the Spirit from her tongue, so that it arose out of the stillness, and she had to call out: "Yes, my soul exults in the Lord and celebrates God, my Savior; because He has seen the lowness of his maid and filled my soul with his eternal Word. He, the eternal, has moved himself in the virginal power of his Wisdom, that was by Him in the beginning; yes, when the world was made, was she by Him as the Word, through which All is made. This Wisdom is a reflection and a pure mirror of the glory of God. In this newborn power she gives herself forth to the soul that hungers for her, and has love for her, and creates God's friends and children of Wisdom.

"Also you, Elisabeth, has the Lord blessed with your son [Hope], born in your old age. He will go before the Lord and become great in his grace."

And there Mary* ended, so Elisabeth arose in spirit and spoke:

"How is it that you, blessed of the Lord, come to me and speak to me, unworthy that I am, with such words? My nature sinks in the dust, but the spirit moves and ascends into God, and is strengthened in the power of your words in the living hope that unfruitfulness will be transformed into a happy child-mother [Psalm 113, 9]. For He has not despised me in my lowness and weakness, but rather considered me in his compassion. And you, my friend, you daughter of eternal Wisdom, you are blessed, for you have believed in the creative and imaging Word. Now you are prized as blessed children of the upper Wisdom, who are born out of the holy Seed. Yes, you are prized as this blessed holy seed

---

*Mary is in this writing also named Wisdom, but it should be remarked that she must be regarded as only a vessel in which the upper Wisdom can transfigure herself according to her nature in a higher degree.

from generation to generation, and will know all that the Lord will offer his elect in the future. A sword is brought through your soul, when you will see the Son of your body derided and mocked by those who say "you must be Jews." A sword is brought through your soul, when you will see how finally your Son will be hung on the wood of the curse and as a testimony to truth must suffer the martyr's death (namely the spiritual, after the magical).

This confirmed Zacharias, and he spoke in the spirit of Simeon: "Yes, this is the fall and resurrection of many in the spiritual Israel. Because the Word moves forth out of the depths of Wisdom, and through his mouth speaks forth, even though many do not understand him, but rather will rise up angry against him."

The faithful one, who had remained silent through all of this, did not know how it was that he had still not had such greetings, brought forth words of bewilderment and spoken in a naive tone: These beloved friends here have known the right religion, because they understand us without words; yes, the beloved friends from whom we yesterday departed, by all their spiritual knowledge and good intentions, would have not understood us when we were so tired. One feels here so completely at home, and it is so inwardly well here, that one would gladly build such a little hut. This little dwelling is built too low because one knocks one's head on the ceiling; also it is made too loosely, beacause the wind penetrates through the walls, as my stepchild has well experienced what effects frosty winds can have upon his weak body. But this I would like to disgregard, and gladly stay longer here. Yet too, it would be a good time now, the faithful one continued (in which Wisdom confirmed him with a wink), for us to move on further, even though we still don't know where we will in the evening lay our heads.

Tenth Section

Longer Stay by Zacharias and Elisabeth. Mary Instructs Her Child That Now God Requires an Offering of Isaac from Him.

As the faithful one in this way had expressed his heart's perceptions, Elisabeth rose and spoke to him and to Mary: Listen, God has here presented you a dwelling for your residence before you must travel further. Come and see, behind this room is hidden still another chamber that you still haven't noticed. This will be your space. It is small and low; but we hope that the dear friend will gradually dwell in our humbleness; because the faithful will endure all trials. And whatever the dear stepchild requires, so we will care for him as best we can, so that he lacks nothing.

Zacharias also added a word, and bade the dear guests to stay. Mary looked over the offered room and took the invitation with much thanks, and as this was the guidance of Wisdom, the true souls were gladly led by her in humility. They knew that a particular grace lay in this offer. They saw namely that neither the child nor the friend, according to his old, infirm nature, nor the faithful one were already strong enough to bear the many sacrifices that would await them in the wilderness. They knew well that the holy Wisdom of these two could gradually prepare them for hardships and profundity, and they would educate them in the life of the spirit.

Zacharias and Elisabeth were delighted that Mary had accepted their offer and had decided to stay a little longer with them.

When they went into the little room, Wisdom turned to the faithful one and said "Bow, bow!" But the faithful one, who still wasn't accustomed to bowing, did not pay enough attention and hit his head in the corner. This reminded him strongly that he still had a stiff neck and ought to bow more, but he trusted in the hope that things would gradually go better.

It was a stormy day, because the weather had changed. Rain and snow flurries alternated, and then snowflakes came in through the little window, which wasn't completely shut.

The child of Wisdom noticed this evil-condition, but outwardly did nothing, even though his old nature nonetheless was frightened that they would suffer here. But the mother Wisdom, or the mother of the new birth and creation, consoled the child with the reassurance that everything would be well; they only needed patience.

The child grew daily in grace, wisdom, and power. The faithful one practiced daily his bowing, and grew in spiritual life. He learned much from Zacharias, who taught him from the Holy Scriptures, and spoke with him about various aspects of the future of the Lord.

Mary and Elisabeth were daily bound inwardly in the spirit with one another, and did everything together as one family, indeed, one church that was in God himself, a temple of his spirit.

Elisabeth and a maiden, named Service-ready, untiringly cared for the child of Wisdom and spoke much with him so that the young son John evermore grew in the power of the spirit. Thus they quickly neared the end of the time of their residence there. Wisdom reminded the faithful one from time to time, and also the child to prepare for the important step with which they would resume their journey.

Mary had by night often carried on important talks with the children and the faithful one. She reminded them that God would now require of them a greater offering than they had earlier brought. To the children she spoke: See, the time is here, that God will lead us deeper into the desert. I, Wisdom, will certainly not leave you, but will stand by your sides, for we must take hidden ways that will not be perceptible to your nature. But listen, my son, the life of your old nature, wherein your I and Self is rooted, must you bring as an offering to your Lord, creator of your life. It will be difficult to bring this Isaac to the foot of the Moriah mountain as an offering. But listen, you son of Wisdom, so long as you do not do this, the temple at the Moriah mountain cannot be built; because the old must be overcome and die before the new can arise.

Note well: until now the Lord has asked only a tenth of your income from you; but now he asks everything—yes, you yourself. Therefore hurry, my child, go to the Lord, and bring yourself to Him, albeit late, as an offering. The wood of the burnt offering you must carry on your back; that means: you must take up your cross, and carry it patiently, when your body is often subject to weakness and fragility. Take this wood of suffering patiently and carry it like Abraham, the father of strength, indeed, of supernatural faith, the faith that renounces everything visible, and hopes in the living God alone, who can alone call the dead again to life, because He is a God of the living and a father of life.

Prepare yourself, my son, and renounce your old robe, namely your old customs. Go naked before your fiancé. He carries the right knife in his hand; because he is called blood-bridegroom, and uses it in a very exact cutting, because he permits nothing uncut in the new community. But fear not becoming naked. He will heal you after the cutting and will clothe you with the clothing of righteousness and with the coat of holiness. Hope only in the Lord's mercy, because the grace-bond that the Lord has made does not waver. Do not permit the spirits of darkness to make you err, or become fearful, when they seek to make you suspicious of the wonderful guidance of the Lord, as if God had forgotten you and did not have you in his sight [Is. 40, 27-31]. Hurry then and save your soul up on the mountain. There, there is the temple of love, the city of peace. There your spirit is collected in God. Do not grow tired nor fearful of following the narrow way, that winds up the steep mountain between fire and water. On the one side of this narrow way is a vast depth filled with the black-grey water, called the water of anxiety; on the other side is the immeasurable depth filled with fire. Out of both depths will the Enemy arise, plague you through anxiety and fear, then through fire-spirits, and seek to hinder you in your aim.

So do not make an error, but rather be manly and strong! Arm yourself with the helmet of holiness and with the shield of faith; be booted, to tread on scorpions and fiery serpents that lie in your footpath already, and will strike against you. But when you, as has already been said, have brought the offering of yourself to the mountain, so your way of ascent up the mountain will become lighter, because you will then have given up the heaviest weight, namely your own I, thus becoming freer and able to breathe easier.

Here, my beloved, you have a song that the spirit of dawn and the rising light, the knight of the holy cross, has given me this very night for you. Learn it by heart and carry it deep in your heart; close it not up in a cupboard, but rather use your youthful power in struggle and war, that which is ordered on this your resourceful course.

The song goes thus:

Bow, you poor, weak striver
If you want to as victor, as conqueror
Go into the hall of the holy Guardian,
There, where all the cross-strivers stand.

Keep courage; you have begun the struggle
So strive until it is won.

Soon will strike the critical hour
That leads you to the holy bond....

Now it begins in earnest; he who does not win now
He must then lie in the fire.
Now it begins in earnest; O let everything stand
You don't want to go under in Sodom.

Many souls are now attacked
By the fire that they themselves have awakened.
Left and right is it now enkindled
Burning in all souls that find it....

This fire no soul escapes
That does not attain the living water
That out of Jesus' side-wound wells
Clear and bright, stilling all burning.

This is the bride, chosen of God.
Jesus has born her out of suffering;
His heart is her newly arising
As blood and water flows from the cross.

Holy are those who as the Lamb's children
Through his blood gain victory. As conqueror
Will they with Him and with His
Joyfully be united in Paradise.

You should go still further
Where Jesus has gone before:
To the Godhead of innermost holiness
To His glory, yes, to the Father's glory.
Amen!

Eleventh Section

The Time of Parting and Journeying is at Hand. Mother Wisdom Leads an Earnest Talk with Hers and with Zacharias and Elisabeth.

The son of Wisdom (who we will now name him after his awakening of the spirit) had carefully listened to the instruction of mother Wisdom and also the Son: "Bow, bow," that she had given him, and read it with much consideration. Thus he spoke:

Dear mother, in the spirit I can grasp well this all, and I am completely convinced that one must go this way if one is to reach the true goal. But I must note that this way seems to my natural, outward man as a wonderful way that he cannot conceive, that indeed, terrifies him. Ah, dear mother, I fear that I may not want to hold to the way you have pointed out in your talk and in this song. My stepfather and I have hardly recovered by these people and from our fatigue; hardly have I been able to enjoy my play with the son Hope, and you speak again of separation and stripping away, of cutting and blood-bridegroom. Ah, well is it that a blood-bridegroom separates me from my dear little brother Hope that I love inwardly. But, dear mother, if it should be so. I obey.

Now the faithful one began to cry too, and said: Yes, dear mother, I must say that it seems to me also hard. I believed that we would be permitted to remain longer here; I began to have hope that we would remain here a long time, with these beloved souls, Zacharias and Elisabeth, together with their son, making one family. Thus I have submitted myself to many, and so much as it was possible, gone through much discomfort that I was not formerly used to, and dwelt in this low room. At least I had the hope that this family could go with us into the desert as one band, indeed, would be a church with us. Ah, he sighed, it always goes differently that we had thought. In the end you will also forsake us, and then we stand alone.

The mother Wisdom heard this with much patience and spoke finally: listen, the ground of your hope should not be despised; but Isaac, Benjamin, must be offered. Isaac must be offered on the mountain Moriah, and Benjamin must go into Egypt. Do not make the son of Hope, as your Benjamin, into a Golden Calf, as you have done here, which you have courted according to your nature, so the temple that you have here dreamt of is become a great height on which you worship your self-made God according to your sensual concepts. You have certainly begun to become accustomed; but this accustoming to many things that before appeared uncomfortable is in the end to become wholly customary, and your nature has found, through renunciation become customary, a good replacement for everything that you have given up.

See, dear son, see, dear stepfather, this is how things stand. If you want to be further developed in the holiness of your souls, if you want to see the temple of love and truth on the mountain Moriah, so offer Isaac. If you want to arrive at Solima, the city and land of peace, so your Benjamin must wander in Egypt; otherwise God cannot lead you to the goal. For the family with whom you wish to make a caravan in the desert is available another time. God will permit you to stay a little longer in this lonesome valley until you are more prepared to give up the old in favor of the new. In this you must also bring an offering, namely the offering of your son; because he is named Hope in that you cling fast to your hope. He must wander on your behalf in Egypt and through the courses of the dark world.

But, said the faithful one, all this you, dear mother, did not say so clearly in the beginning. In the end things will be still again wholly different.

Admittedly, replied Wisdom, it is true that everything has been already said in my earlier talks and instructions with you, some things clearly, some more hidden; you have only understood it incorrectly. And by the way, God cannot open everything to you at once, but rather only according to the substance of your needs in the life of renunciation and according to your understanding, which comes only from experience.

Now spoke the son of Wisdom: dear mother, I now want to follow you wherever you go. But I cannot promise that there won't come times when I'll again want to turn back, if it becomes too hard for my nature.

Wisdom spoke: Beloved son, since you want to follow me, I'll make you ready; for already dawn is breaking, and a longer stay here would only give you cause to discuss further with flesh and blood.

The faithful one also decided finally and spoke: Dear mother, I too want to follow you, although I have nothing but darkness before me. But it occurs to me that I do not have my tools here, which I need for my work. How could we build a decent house in the wilderness?

Wisdom spoke: Worry not over that, faithful one; God will care for us. But take a sword, namely the sword of the spirit, wherewith you can withstand the onslaught of the king in your reason, that reasons so against the way of God, and can strike against the fiery serpent in your temperament. In this work you oughtn't lack it in the desert. It is also necessary that you take a sword with you, in order that everything be fulfilled; because we must also still reckon with evildoers.

Mother Wisdom now gave notice of their departure to the dear Zacharias and the good Elisabeth, to whom this news came like a lightning bolt, and they did not know what they should say. Finally Zacharias spoke: But how did you come, dear friend, to this decision? Is this really God's will? How does it fit with our Hope and with the promises that God has given us? I at least believed that you would remain long enough by us for your son to grow big and he and my son could go forth together as two true witnesses. That was my hope, which I kept in secret with me. Your son, if you lead him forth, is according to my view still not strong enough to bear the difficulties in the desert.

Now Elizabeth, who had held something back, began to speak: I must say according to the truth that your arrival had given us the expectation that your residence will be only so long as God's will didn't lead you further. Alone out of some conversations, particularly that of one morning—I believe it was in the past month of July—that you had with us, led me to have the hope that you according to the will of God would remain longer with us. In this we want to send you on the inconceivable ways of God. Finally this also stirred Zacharias, who said: God's will be done!

But it hurts me very much, said Elisabeth; indeed, it seems too in this moment unbearable in my heart. Wisdom spoke: What then, dear friend? Ah, replied Elisabeth, my son, my hope. He had through your and your son's company won very much in the spirit, and this he will lose through your departure.

Dear friend, responded Wisdom, what he has won in the spirit, that he has alone through God's mercy won. The mustard seed can bring forth no fruit until it is buried and died in the earth [John 12, 24].

Elisabeth asked: What do you want to say with the words "buried, died"?

Wisdom spoke: Do you really want to know, dear, precious Elisabeth, can you bear what I want to say to you?

Elisabeth stood still, and it was so difficult a revelation for her that she couldn't ask further, fearing that she really could not bear it. Finally placing all her confidence in Wisdom, she stuttered:

What is it then, that you want to say, dear Mary?

Wisdom spoke: Keep your soul in patience, dear Elisabeth; because the Lord wants your son, Hope, to be taken away.

These words made gloomy the faces of Zacharias and Elisabeth, and a black, shadowy foreboding curtain came over their souls as the glorious outlook for the future sank. They stood a while, regarding one another, as if made of stone. Finally Zacharias spoke in a melancholy tone: O Mary, dear friend, you are with your prophecies become a riddle for us. Where now are the promises that once were given us? Dark bedecked are now our earthly kingdom and our hearts. Everything appears to me now a contradiction; especially the enthusiasm in which I have spoken a song of praise with you at each first intimate morning meal! What an impenetrable curtain!

Wisdom spoke: Have courage, beloved, for God is called Wonderful! [Is. 9, 6-7]

Twelfth Section

(Afterword)

3 December 1835

Still is the dense and dark curtain before this guidance not lifted. The previously marked souls that should follow the guiding hand of the heavenly Wisdom in Jesus, have still not prepared to go the narrow, subearthly, or still more, super-earthly way. They have not seized childlike and simply enough the word in the Evangelium: Who will not forsake everything for me, cannot be my disciples.

That is the subterranean, unknown way travelled by few, that goes not over the heights but rather through the humblest depths.

My chosen son is terrified by the death-gate that on his journey back he must pass through. He has brought a difficult offering, and that will in future open the gate and ease the way. Amen!

Come, souls, all! Yes, come, you who thirst for Jesus! He alone is the true Wisdom that is spoken of in many images in this little book. Whoever drinks a drink from Him cannot do other than despise the world, and the world will in turn despise him. These expelled sons and daughters are then my brides. Who is wise enough to learn and to practice this?

7 December 1835

Come, souls, who thirst after Wisdom; come to Jesus, who has cleared the way to true Wisdom. He had nowhere to lay his head. He was poor, scorned, and mocked by the wise of this world. He died by the ignominious death of the cross. Therein lies the true Wisdom, that is revealed in the images of the mother and the children of Wisdom and the faithful one in this little book.

Die, son of Wisdom, and the curtain will be raised from above to below. Then will the holiness in you be revealed and everything become clear, what God has permitted to be veiled in you.

Die, lower your head, and the headman will strike his breast, and your crucifier will go home.

Die, in order that the stone be broken and the graves open, in which so many souls lie enclosed.

Die, in order that the old earth in so many brothers shatters.[33] Die, give up your life, so that God may again take it. Amen!

Question: Lord, how should this go, and how should I die? asked a Nicodemus, to whom everything here is still night.

Answer: Wait, you for whom night comes, and remain by Jesus until day comes again. He will make death into day, night into light, your why and wherefore and your no into yes!

FINIS

XIV

Franz von Baader

Franz von Baader was born in 1765 in Munich, the son of a physician, and although he was originally trained to take over his father's practice, he went on to study minerology and the other sciences under Alexander von Humboldt, and spent four years in England beginning in 1792, where he came to see at close hand the results of the industrial revolution, especially the appearance of a proletariat class. In 1796, he returned to Germany, where in addition to working in quick succession in a series of ever higher official positions, he was able through various chemical experiments to develop a patented formula for glass fabrication that brought him a substantial income. Thus Baader came to theosophy from an unusually scientific viewpoint.

Having spent years studying Böhme and Louis Claude de Saint-Martin, as well as other mystics, including Meister Eckhart, Baader was termed by August Wilhelm Schlegel "Boehmius redivivus," or "Böhme reborn," a complimentary designation still indissolubly linked to Baader's name. Baader is most famous as a theosopher, but his theosophic writings encompass an extraordinary range of subjects, from religious eros to the political concept of "theodemocracy" to the meeting of Catholicism, Protestantism, and Eastern Orthodoxy.[34] In particular, Baader's emphasis on "erotische philosophie" and on furthering a religious rather than merely materialist science call for much deeper scrutiny than they have yet received.

Unlike some theosophers—like Wirz, for instance—Baader is above all a scholar and intellectual; he founded no gnostic community or circle, but rather reveals yet another aspect of theosophy: how it can illuminate every aspect of modern life, from politics to literature, from science to philosophy, from religion to art. The following selections were chosen because they illustrate Baader's characteristic emphases upon love, upon developing a Christian "erotic philosophy" that by definition does not reject but rather embraces the feminine in daily life as in religious philosophy. We begin with his letters to his second wife, Marie Robel, a twenty-five year old woman whom he married (in his seventies) after the death of his first wife. We then turn to a work discussing Sophia directly, and finally to an essay that illustrates the almost incredible density and brilliance of Baader's writing. We should note that for Baader, Sophia also means "Idea." These are to my knowledge the first works of Baader to be translated into English; we hope more will follow.

Letters to Marie Robel

München, 16 Sept. 1839

What, beloved Marie, yesterday I could not say with the presentation of rings, I want to tell you now in handwriting with more certainty. I recognize, namely, your great friendship and the inclination, in which you influenced me, as an indication of caution on my part for you. But in the conviction of this given ring you should value it as our engagement ring, linking you and I in complete earnestness. And I have given it to you as a sign of my conviction, for you as my fiancée, in order to provide for you in life and in case of my early death. In engagement one cares for one another more tenderly than during matrimony, and one may say what one wishes, but this is still the rule (which also I experienced) that the condition of engagement is the spring of love, while marriage, when it is good, is Love's autumn, albeit for most it is winter. Thus you still have the advantage over me, in that you remain less outwardly free, while I am bound to you, and you, if you want to marry someone else, still may remain certain of my conviction, through which I feel bound to you, not through earthly desire, but rather through authentic love, which truly marries the lover to the beloved, and which for me is the true sacrament.

München, 23 Sept. 1839

The more I come to know you, beloved Marie, and the more your profound, at once tender and strong heart opens, the more I love you, and you are like a Nightviolet whose aromatic fragrance breathes not from the open market, but only in the stillness of my heart.

> Blessed, who before the world
> Opens without hate,
> Holds you to his breast
> and with you enjoys
> What among men remains unknown
> Or unthought,
> [What]through the pure still breast
> [passes] in the night.

You are right, beloved Marie, that the heart of man, as that alone undying in him, ages and grows wintry if the sunshine of eternal love does not shine within, and the eternal spring or eternal youth does not awaken in him. But have you not brought this sunshine again to my heart, are you not the messenger of this eternal spring? Recognize here your worth and that my gratitude is yours.

München, 25 Sept. early, 2 am, 1839

The little rose blooms still on my writing table in fresh water. So blooms and wakes pure love in a still, gentle heart, whereas wild and impure passion burns the barren heart to ashes.

München, 26 Sept., 1839

You are quite right, beloved Marie, of late, in saying that the two love-bound rose-buds—in the interpretation of the mysteries of love—protest against a third. It is not that you must keep your union secret, but rather only the feelings, sensations, and convictions of love, because to divulge these is an uprooting, even a prostitution and a betrayal of love. And if Jesus said of holy love that one should not throw a pearl before dogs and swine, since they would trample it underfoot and rend us asunder, so we should value also the inner, true love, whose feelings one should not reveal to unbelieving souls, to gabbling geese or mimicking parrots, who would then divulge them.

Love is summer in the heart, but the world outside is wintery;

should I open the door, that we might freeze? The world not only disbelieves in love, it despoils, despises, indeed hates it, and the devil, who rides the world, rushes after love to kill it, like Herod killing the innocent children. You need only listen to how the world speaks of love, which it doesn't really know, any more than it knows the aim of union, which it knows rather as bare means to a bad end, for example naked sexual lust, or money, or position, or protection, and so forth. Love should be for us a house devotion, and be as Christ said of prayer, that man ought not go into the open market to pray and cry out, but rather that one should close one's door and should pray to the Father in secret, who will openly reward us therefore. If two, Christ said further, become one, whatever one asks me, so it shall come to pass. We two are now become one, and no third should intrude on this unity. If we cease to be one, we would be loveless; were we loveless, we would also be Godless or God-empty. This, beloved Marie, is to me the sacrament of love.

München, 1839, late, undated

When Christ warns us that we should not throw the pearl before hounds and swine, for they might trample it underfoot and rend us asunder, so is this particularly true of the pearl of conjugal love and loving marriage, from which one can also say that it does not suffice to celebrate one's possessions, but rather one is never in this world lacking inner and outer temptations to try one, hence the keywords:

> Hold what you have,
> For Want [Poverty] is a bad guest!

The devil, one says with good reason, is an enemy of love and marriage, and because he had realized in himself the birth of these heavenly children, and to be near them is painful to him—like a blind worm near light—so he seeks through his Herod-servants, who plan like common children of the world above all to strangle these innocent children. If it is folly to wish to demonstrate love and religion to the world, so is it cowardice not to defend them against attack with good and blood, and whoever cannot remain constant in the war with the world, cannot live in joy.

> Blessed is one who closes ears and heart
> To the world's venom,
> Holds love still in his heart
> And through this takes sustenance,
>
> What is unknown to people
> And despised by them
> In the breast closed to the world
> It shines through the night.

If one contemplates the inner unholiness and the outer unhappiness, in which for long or for short, sins or infractions ruin or entangle one, so can one not ward off the conviction that the commitment of the sin itself is already divine punishment, or the beginning thereof—and, as the folk saying has it, an abandonment by God, inasmuch as one inwardly has abandoned one's God, and one's heart has already turned from Him. Though it only appears to the creature that God has abandoned him, much like an immovable rock in the ocean appears to flee a ship, which is distancing itself from it.

Now this inner divine service is alone authentic, and every outward service only has meaning insofar as it serves and conduces to the inward. So we see that the greater part of humanity acts as if merely the outward service were significant, and as if each inner holy service of the heart were dispensable, in which all true religiosity is made into fundamentally spoiled superstition in the clutches of a degenerated priesthood, and the common rabble are daily encouraged, in order to gain through the priests' holy-appearing comedies much entrance money. One but need only to read the gospels, the apostles' histories, and their letters, in order to recognize how far modern Christians are from this primordial simplicity, tenderness, and fullness of heart, replacing it instead with these dog-and-pony shows and often heathenish worldly luxury.

On the Relationship of the Logos to Sophia in God

The author has through the publication of this work [*On the Identity of the Idea of Wisdom in the Old Testament*, by Stadler, (München: Bayer, 1832)] gained the profit of having brought a subject of religious science again into consideration, which, inasmuch as it in earlier times was brought fully into clarity, in latterday theology appears to have been lost. But on this account even the expositions of the Trinity have been for a long time so inadequate, not to say flat, because the concept of Sophia of these theologians has been wholly absent, and because any theology or religious science that lacks this concept is like the relationship of common geometry to the higher or analytical.

The author believes that the problem is to be solved by the identity of the Word (Logos or Son) with Sophia (Wisdom) as mere (tautological) monotony. But no ancient theologian has denied my knowledge of the identity of Sophia with the Son or the firstborn Word, just as no mystic is subject to the accusation—in the completely erroneous way of this author, who attributes this error to Böhme, Pordage, and others—namely that Sophia is seen as the fourth person or as hypostasis in God. What is more, Substance, as fully attested in church dogma and in classical church word-usage, should not be spoken of as the author does here and there in referring to the holy Persons as three Substances, but rather as substantial qualities (*in personis proprietas*) of a single Substance, which makes itself known as *personans* (*persona*). Hence, for example, one can in no way assert of Sophia or Wisdom without the creating Word, whose Adjudicator she is.

Now the author cites more writers as well as places in church teaching whereby he believes himself able to show the unity of Sophia with the Word, which certainly proves nothing of this unity, but rather the opposite, demonstrating that these topics cannot so briefly be covered, and on another occasion may be explained in much more detail.[35]

On a Lasting and Universal Spiritual Manifestation Here Below

München, 22 Dec. 1832[36]

While at your excellency's request I offer here my views on what comes ever more frequently into discussion—placing the magnetic or somnambulistic in a category of spiritual manifestations—permit me first to point out the irony that lies in naturalists or rationalists having made the charge against each spirit that one should not place faith in such irrational appearances and events, attacking even more the fear of ghosts, when they also won't confess to or avow the fear that some of these events might be undeniably factual, upon which fear their entire naturalism or rationalism is grounded. This *petite santé* [poor health] of our modern rationalism is understandable if one recognizes that it is nothing more than old, massive materialism, of which these humans or humanoids are able to convince themselves; it is in fact more a mere reminiscence or a spectre of materialism. But it is also not to be denied that we have become much less at home in nature and with spirits than our forebears; we are in fact to a certain extent in nature in a sublimated or precipitated spectral realm, and one can say that we are like light-shunning moles burrowing ever deeper into the material realm, so that whereas before all spirits were *above us*, by burrowing through this material realm, we have hereby begun to root up spirits *under us*.

Setting aside these somewhat sinister spirit-appearances permit me now in this writing, your excellency, to discuss a great, joyous, true, secret and permanent spiritual appearance, on which I offer the following few suggestive words in the conviction that herewith we have a key to knowledge, which our theologians, philosophers, historians, nature-philosophers, and aesthetes have forgotten or mislaid, and for a long time have had no use; whereby it would be not the least bit unexpected that in many cases the religious and unreligious, the educated or uneducated, and even perhaps for the most part those occupied with public education would cry out to me: "Paul, you rage, your art makes you mad."

When the poet says:

> Only phantasy is eternally young
> What never and nowhere has appeared
> That alone never ages.[37]

so appears the troublesome dualism of the Ideal and the truly corporeal asserted as necessary and permanent. And if we correct this verse with a little addition, namely:

> Only phantasy is eternally young
> What never and nowhere *in the earthly life*
> Has appeared
> That alone never ages!

we can as an explanation of this dualism place this claim also by the following words:

> If a bad dream in waking is dissolved
> The truth is flown away from you to heaven
> To incline heaven's truth downward to you
> It may first reveal itself
> Nowhere else than in the dream.

Thus is such an explanation introduced, but certainly not wholly completed. An explanation—which unites it in optative and imperative—cannot yet be seen clearly here. Some tell the story that the distancing or separation of the beloved from the lover was first noted by poets and artists, and that in this way poetry and art or sculpting may have been founded.

But in fact we are in this fable given the key to understanding the true meaning of both; indeed, it is the key to understanding our collective lifetimes and the work at hand. If namely, through our guilt, Idea [Sophia] is removed, remaining disembodied or incorporeal, so incorporeal spirit[i] in the night of our earthly life appears to us as a heavenly star. Even if at first in the unreachable distance or height, it appears[ii] to us again as Ideal and similar to a Revenant [the tarnished image of God], so is this truly not spirit, but rather spirit-appearance [Erscheinung]. The word "Spirit" [Geist] here can be taken to mean Sophia or Idea, and certainly Sophia is still incorporeal in relation to us, her incarnation still an aspired-to condition, a free Gift to us. This nostalgia is due to our exit from on high, which we forfeited and have not earned, but also represents a Task, carried out through actual operation or formation in us of her Body as her [Idea's or Sophia's] Periphery or Brideclothing, her descent and actual dwelling in us.[38]

Thus the center realizes itself through dwelling in its periphery, or perhaps better, one enters them only together in their reality or concreteness, and the complete periphery is the same as a magical circle with its center.[39] [When] this morning-star in eye and heart is grasped and held, all our images and works in time have nothing other than the pronounced aim of—or the imperative like the optative in time is none other than—the realization of an Ideal [Sophia] out of the whole soul, from the whole heart and with all one's powers.

But each attempt, one might say, to make ready these bridal gowns or veils, makes us sensitive or painful, because we likewise must break through each lie-layer [Lügenkleid] or again cut through it [zerstechen]; this destruction of ourself [as our own products] therefore takes place together with the production[iii] of our light-clothing or light-body. *Destructio unius generatio alterius,*[40] or, as Paul said, the origin and waking of the new light-man takes place together with the death and dissolution of the old, dark man.

From this transformation, it follows that each who experiences this is really a Christ, in whom now has begun this inwardness in a limited form or inform of Sophia, or, as the apostle said, in whom inwardly Christ [in whom alone and above all each light-spirit again becomes corporeal] has begun to win a form. We must contemplate this immanence or inform not only as revealed in the highest poetry and painting, but also in itself as the hearth or focus, out of which all working poems and artworks derive, and to which they should again lead us back.

I will say yet more. This inner image and cultivation of man, this striving after the primal inner realisation of an Ideal or this endeavor or aspiration should be according to the Kingdom of God in us [as the Scripture says]. It should be the focus for all outwardly effective creations of poetry and art of man, but also it should be the regulative principle for its collective correspondence with outward nature, likewise the principle of physics[iv] as the science and art of the illuminating Idea. Of all this, our so called nature philosophy barely has an idea any more because, having lost what the man of nature should be, science has also lost what the nature of man could and should be; consequently his true *imperium in naturam*[41]—something other than the Baconian—is wholly lost.

Thus these nature philosophers for example are no longer capable of understanding the first elements of physics, according to which, [after Genesis] the origin and continued existence of the outward [material] nature comes about through the separation of the lower waters from the upper.[42] Through this separation not only is the benediction removed, but also the curse was nearly brought about; whereupon man only acts as master and sovereign in this nature by his first act, because *in him alone was opened this otherwise closed source of the upper heavenly waters*. For this reason, we still [like a clockwork and horary] see and feel unfolding in man the outward nature [with its seven interrelated outwardly impelled Forms] in order to encounter within, as is hoped, the three higher Forms [in Descensus], out of which we can again experience the missing higher, sweet Waters, so as to be free of the inner fire- and time- fever. For the fiery fever of time makes it so that the Seventh Form never can be brought to a full conclusion [Sabbat], for the cycle never lacks a continually renewed start.[v]

But if already the outward nature has not achieved its aim, namely, the indwelling of the Idea, [Virgin]—[because earthly flesh and blood are not able to inherit the Kingdom of God] and if from one day to the next a creature in reproduction only passes down and furthers the unsatisfying mania or the unsolved problem— so nonetheless the *Idea* arrives at the goal of its realization through Nature via intermediate ways. If, in other words, works and images in time, like the notes of a fleeting lute, arise and fade away, and the individual work is immediately removed from our eyes, nonetheless that work does not disappear, but rather comes [the time-stream left behind] immediately into good custody. There, our individual work [as image or figure], looks like it was drawn with a sympathetic ink of all elements and regions of the world, coming to production in the glow of the world's judgement fire, each of us creating a collective *tableau* of our temporal works either as *Glory* and *Holy-manifestation* or as *Fire-circle*.

And through this hardwon insight, the problem of the relationship between the Idea [Sophia] and the real herebelow can be clearly solved: namely through the conviction that *the temporal-earthly forms and acts do not themselves realize fully the Idea [Sophia], for their realizing [Incarnation] is but conditional—or, as the apostle says, the temporal and transient scaffolding of our lives is and should be a permanent building.*[vi] Through this saying one understands well, by the way, why every true poet and artist never escapes a doubled affect or emotion. Each yearning after the manifestation or incarnation of the *Idea* in any case has the complementary effect of pain and even anger against the refracting Substance.[vii] From this one understands the threefold ways according to which people value and are impelled to create poetry and images. One way is merely as a time-waster, in which the allegedly educated or cultured take delight, much the same whether their intention is to go to church or to the theater. The second, less common way is in the high, lastingly earnest and truly religious sense, namely in order—not without labour pains—to manifest the bridal gown of the heavenly *Sophia* herself. And the last, an equally little-known way, is to manifest the black scream of Hekate.[43] For it is not merely frivolous poetry and imagemaking that is the direct opponent of religion, but rather the truly infernal or demonic.

And hereby I believe we have arrived at the goal of this communication, namely *to have recognized that and how all people are obliged—each united in this—to bring about the Incarnation of manifesting Spirit.*

Notes by Baader

[i]Because the bodiless spirit is not completed, but rather the body is to be raised up or, as St Paul says, to be spiritualized, meaning corporeal spirit. In the lack of this understanding man falls (*ut historia docet*), into bad spiritualism and bad realism, bad supranaturalism and bad naturalism. The Greeks were acquainted with what we call spiritual manifestation, referring to *eidolon*, and so forth; hence they didn't place the incorporeal as an object so much as a subjective comprehension (Erfassung). If one were permitted to do the impossible, and out of the completedness of being allow to completely manifest what is in fact closed to manifesting, the spirits would have every bit as much right to regard us as incorporeal phantoms and phantasy. There too we would be just as unwelcome, an idea that Goethe already expressed in these words:

You are the same as the spirit you conceive, not me.

[ii]The instant in earthly life becomes transfigured;
     No more peering with hollow eyes in the dark
     A ray of the higher sun
     Penetrates the earthly dark out of Love's source.
     And *this* ray glimmers through the whole world,
     And *this* ray illuminates history—
     Where only for an instant its glance falls,
     All the grey of shadows are suddenly illuminated,
     All swims in the bright glow of lilies and roses
     Suffused in the hope of the angel's gaze.

[iii]I say: "production" [Herstellung], not restoration, [Wieder-herstellung], because in the case of the God-image in which and to which we were created, were it prepared through human "fixation" [corporealization], its resumption [Wiederentleibung] could not take place. Still, I remark that the redemption or annulling of the dark man likewise only comes about through the removal [entleibung] from the spirit of sin. Thus for men the corporealization of *Sophia* that has not yet come to pass became knowable through the incarnation of the Word.

[iv]I take here natural science in its higher and universal meaning and not in its lower, in which it should merely serve industrial purposes. Our atheistic and deistic nature philosophers must necessarily give way to a Christian [that is, a religious] nature philosophy, of which I long have been conscious, and for which for a long time I have had a delight in preparing the way.

[v]On this relationship of man to outward nature Saint-Martin writes in *Ministère de l'homme-esprit*, p. 56, to wit: "*Oui, Soleil sacré, c'est nous qui sommes la première cause de ton inquiétude et de ton agitation. Ton oeil impatient ne cesse de parcourir successivement toute les régions de la nature. Tu te lèves chaque jour pour chaque homme; tu te lèves joyeaux dans l'espérance qu'ils vont te rendere cette épouse chérie our l'éternelle Sophie dont tu es privé. Tu remplis ton cours journalier en la demandant à toute la terre avec des paroles ardentes où se peignent des dèsirs dévorants. Mais le soir tu te couches dans l'affliction et dans les larmes, parce que tu as en vain cherché ton épouse; tu l'as en vain demandée à l'homme; il ne te l'a point rendue et il te laisse séjourner encore dans les lieux stériles et dans les demeures de la prostitution.*" In this work is treated, incidentally, the threefold ministerium of man, which as suffering in nature—of the ordinary man of the creaturely soul—has to eventually yield (finally, to the master) i.e. to the suffering of holy love or of the holy heart, in which the master partakes. Relative to the aforementioned drive of outer nature or of the world-spirit, to appear in man and through him to be integrated, I would remark that the spiritual fairy tale of Comte Gabalis [namely, that which refers to

the mortal elemental spirits seeking marriage with immortal men, in order to become immortal] bears a deeper truth than one might think. Jacob Böhme writes, in *Three Principles*, 14 §32, "Because the spirit of the soul is out of the eternal, and had the Virgin before the Fall, therefore now the spirit of the great world continually seeks the Virgin in the spirit of the soul, and supposes that she is there still, as before the Fall, where the Spirit of the great world appeared in Adam's Virgin with great Joy, and desired also to live in the Virgin, and to be eternal. Because he felt his corruptibility, and his own roughness in himself, therefore he wanted to partake of the loving kindness and sweetness of the Virgin and live in her, so he might live eternally, and not perish again. For by the great longing of the darkness after the light and virtue of God, this world has been generated out of the darkness, where the holy virtue of God beheld itself in the darkness, and therefore this great desiring and longing after the divine virtue continues in the spirit of the sun, stars, and elements, indeed, in all things. All groan after the divine virtue, and wish to be delivered from the vanity of the devil. But seeing that cannot be, all creatures must wait until their dissolution, when they shall go into their Äther [eternitas] and take their place in paradise, but only in figure and shadow dissolved, the spirit fragmented, which here has been filled with such longing." One can therefore liken this spirit of the world, or spirit of the age [which as *spiritum mundi immundi* our nature philosophers take for the Holy Ghost] to an outbreak of a fierce thunderstorm and its persistent howling gale, which finally again ends, as an old and beloved myth has it, with an untameable unicorn that eventually lies at the feet of the Virgin. [J. Böhme, *Three Principles*, 14 §38].

[vi]It is the same way with the whole of outward nature and its works, and one must produce this general, but false image, as if for example in time all propagation had only the aim of [continuing] the line of sexual reproduction. This is to say, namely, that in time, these and many more enumerations can only endure so long, until the activities of all creatures are completed outside of time. [Editorial note: In other words, the holy place of humanity in creation derives from our partaking in the "sympathetic ink" Signature or "Inscription" of all creaturely being in Sophia. We exist in time, but our existence is consummated outside of time, in Sophia.]

[vii]Hence in art, science, morality and above all in life-experience we want to make things easy, as if we can dispense with this pain, which one finds nowhere better illustrated than in new politics, which is to say, in the corruption or gangrene of the radical means against revolutionism.

XV

Leopold Ziegler

Leopold Ziegler (1881-1958) was one of the most important theosophers of the twentieth century, similar in scope to Graf Hermann Keyserling, but much more well read in and influenced by Christian theosophy, and instrumental in what has come to be called "East-West dialogue." Born in Karlsruhe, Germany, and a student at the University of Heidelberg, Ziegler's first major published work was *Die Metaphysik des Tragischen* [*The Metaphysics of the Tragic*](1902), in which he discussed the significance of suffering in human life. But his characteristic themes were struck more clearly in *Gestaltwandel der Götter* [*Transformation of the Gods*] (1920), *Überlieferung* [*Tradition*] (1936), and *Menschwerdung*, [*Becoming Human*] (1948); the latter two his main works, illustrating his preoccupation with Buddhism and Christian theosophy, and charting a course out of existentialism and nihilism into a renewed and primordial spiritual revelation that affirms the whole of life.

In the selection that follows, from *Spätlese eigener Hand* [*Late Harvest From My Own Hand*] (1953), on the occasion of the Roman Catholic Church's *ex cathedra* proclamation of the Virgin Mary's corporeal ascension to heaven, Ziegler discusses the spectrum of Sophianic spirituality, including the Russian Sophiology of Soloviev and Bulgakov, and ties it in with fascinating speculation on the possibility for Asian-European linkings through the figures of the divine Mother and Virgin. Ziegler is undoubtedly one of the most intellectual of all our authors, and his range of reference is vast. Here we have a modern overview of the Sophianic tradition within Christianity with an eye to a Roman Catholic perspective, yet remarkably aware of and open to the full range of the Sophianic tradition.

On the Mothergodhead

On the occasion of the new *ex cathedra* as proclaimed to the faithful as binding church teaching of the corporeal ascension of Mary, I find myself called by my venerable sirs and by some friends to make some remarks. With inner conflicts and only obeying a certain urgency, I venture today to fulfill your and my friends' wish. At the same time, I share the doubled reservations against criticizing the new dogma, which I honor and regard as the exclusive concern of the Roman Catholic church. Nor do I want to have a position on a problem of Mariology that, on your part, has been given a new impetus by the papal decision, whose force can hardly be appraised. For if the proclamation of a dogma for some was the treasured and bequeathed verities that sealed many years' movement—the dogma fixed and defined in the literal sense of both words!—so under the circumstances even this, a past, foregone event, may bring about about future occurrences. First reactions on the evangelical side appear to confirm this; the reactions in the Eastern church remain to be seen. To be awaited in particular, whether the dogma here in question will be held as a step toward their own Mariology, or as a further distancing from it, if not to say an estrangement. But one thing must be conceded in evangelical as in Orthodox places of the youngest dogma—namely the genuine Roman consistency. For the teaching of the corporeal ascension of Mary bespeaks more exactly than its predecessor of the immaculate, unstained reception. It bespeaks, completes, and crowns her insofar as both together make understandable the fundamental exception of the Godmother's belonging to the Adamic, and thus to the original sins of sex and seed. Exactly here is my doubt whether the Eastern church can accept the second Marianic dogma, after they were convinced that they must negate the first.[44] But Mary raised up out of the unbroken ancestral ethnic line of Adamic man contradicts this. And that is certainly ground enough to think that the likelihood is small that the Eastern church will agree with the second dogma rather than the first.

Yet ignoring this, I will constrain myself alone to a spur of the moment attempt to bring to speech the great and eternal desire in and behind the new teaching. I mean the matter of the

Mothergodhead as such, on this side or the other, of individual creeds. Incontestably this matter is numbered among the oldest and most penetrating in the religious consciousness. But in the disorder of the Reformation, where it was not exactly forgotten, it was pushed aside by the now burning wars of faith. Evidently at times even the very serious attempts of Wittenberg could not change anything about the fact that there could be no closer ties with the eastern church, where the mother remained truly the unforgottenhood-unforgettableness in the full sense of the Greek 'aletheia.' This certainly is remarkably different from the the historically now dominant world of Protestantism, where the forgetting of the Mother resulted on the one side in the soul of the people in a grasping overestimation and overvaluation of everything manly, willful, active, and on the other side a denigration of everything eternally-feminine, bearing-receptive, waxing-ripening. In the soul of Western humanity, the hard key had triumphed, so to say, over the tender. Renaissance and Conquest, Reformation and Counter-reformation, Calvinism and Capitalism, absolute and natural states are ideas that demonstrate in different ways this diagnosis.

And certainly this enkindled war in the European soul over 'the Mother of the illuminated inward image' was a temporal-historical innovation. But the theme reveals itself in the sharpest way merely as the repetition of an age-old war that Christendom had already in its origin, and because of its origin! Undeniably, Christianity breaks forth as the Evangelium of the Son into the world of the old folk, the world of the heathen, that essentially is a world of the great mother. People do not recognize enough that with the ascent of the Roman republic came first of all the victorious patriarchate. In the midst of this motherworld a way must have prepared itself for the Evangelium of Jesus Christ: he came from the Father, the uniquely generated one-born from all beginnings, all origins, but received in temporality and borne by a human mother's love on behalf of the unique becoming-human [Menschwerdung].[45] The manifold difficulties here we may divine if we give up our reckoning, so that on the Father's side here the Son is accepted in faith as a true *Metaphysikum*, or, if you will allow me the word, as a true *Ontikum*, that fundamentally in his double quality as bearer of the revelation—Logos means

"Opener"—and as savior-god from the beginning there with the original creator and maintaining-God "of co-essence." Both are indispensible key-signs to the meaning of certain perspectives on the being of Being [des seienden Seins].

How different is the Mother of Jesus in the Gospels! Two exceptions we can disregard, namely the proclamation of the angel and the description in the secret revelation, where, when the adversary chased the bearess of the God into the wilderness, Mary lived, still and unostentatious in the ordinary space of history. So quiet, so unostentatious, that the hard words of Jesus, that would appear to signify an unbridgeable cleft between Son and Mother, still today gives sensitive hearts pain. But in any case this stillness and unostentatiousness of the commonplace of Protestant spirituals at least doesn't contradict the expression of this statement: In the documents of the new proclamation Mary is given neither face nor mouth. In this statement there resonates an undertone of sadness, probably because in this glimpse one feels an oppressiveness, what an ill-considered theology puts into play if it insists on "demythologizing" the Evangelium and to shut out the Mother-milk out of which the Crystal grows.

Thus the Mothergodhead of the Palestinian neighborhood to the Mediterranean or the Nile was nothing less than demythologized. She teems, nonetheless, with the riches of the ur-images that are still there. Even where she is not represented symbolically as a *Metaphysicum* or *Ontikum*, always authentic Arche- and Prototypes remain, and stand symbolically for the truth. On the other hand, one easily understands that this or that Motherform carries in her train characteristics that make her unacceptable to the Evangelium. Here we may number the Aphroditic-Erotic, even where it is by Greek philosophy transposed from the sphere of a fully desensualized beauty to the eidetic. In the same way a Hekate is consigned to hell, and hence one may be permitted to surmise her kin to the much greater Kali of the Hindus, who on her side gives the sinister name to the slow fading of the era Kali Yuga. Plainly the people-strangling Anti-mother, if we may call her so, must certainly be closed out of the Evangelium. But one is dealing with nothing other than the Apocalypse. The Anti-mother of the Whore of Babylon, who comes out of the ocean of rising wild animals, the Abgrund-dragons, and such have also their place in eschatology and Satanology. It would be controversial whether one has the right to reckon the glorious Pallas of a late Athens as part of the authentic Mothergodhead. In a deeper degree unmistakable are the still impersonal fateweavers like the Parze or the Norn, who step with their motherly train more and more behind the austere Virgin. And because she, masculine-feminine, combines the means of peace and art with wars and the weapons, she moreover supports her favorites with a decided practicality, indeed a political-tactical worldly-cleverness that is also unthinkable under obedience to the Sermon on the Mount.

Always it has been a goad in my spirit and heart that the outward parallel of the most sublime mythologem of the Mediterranean Mothergodhead in the double form of the earthly-subterranean Demeter-Kore has found entry through no door into the Evangelium. Or perhaps an entrance through a door that no one noticed or doesn't want to notice? In any case it is without doubt that the Greeks were led to the evangelical Lord before the beginning of his suffering—which necessity wanted to make them wish for such an approach with such irresistibility. He spoke thus deeply personally to the Greeks in the similes of the Eleusinian Mysteries, and married this "until the end of time" with the Mysterium of Golgotha, indissoluble-salvation.... Out of unlike pale and harmless places in the Scripture, so it appears to me, derive consequences of a wide-ranging kind, while here a sign of Jesus is left ignored. He invites us to make the broadest use of the promised freedom of the children of God, namely, from their commonality to ultimately reconcile antiquity and Christendom in the truth of their mysterio-mystical Mother-root. [Merely in brackets and by way of example I toss forth the question—is the step from the Earthmother Demeter to the Mayqueen Mary in truth impossible?]

Remaining is still a last appearance of the Mothergodhead in the Eastern and Mediterranean lands. It is the God-bearer, the *Theotokos*, who has indeed been mentioned in relation to the Apocalypse of John. The Adversary and Abgrund-dragon, also named the thrower-apart or *Diabolos*, persecutes the Mother, after the child's removal to heaven, until the earth rescues her from his deathbringing engulfing maw. So is she pointed out to us as entangled in a war that plays itself out on many levels of being, eschatological, historical, and mythical, and the Mary of the Gos-

pels throughout is metaphysically-ontologically as profound as
she is high. Is she only outwardly in the center of being of the
Evangelium, the Apocalypse and Eschatology, more or less the
power of a soulish-spiritual Osmosis, as she can not seldom be
observed in folk-life? Or might it not reflect the not wholly incon-
sequential facts of the case that the Ur- and inward image of the
Mother also isn't lacking or dropped out in the God-world-con-
sciousness of the Hebrews? Must we not in consequence subsequently correct our former supposition that she, the Mother,
should have been holy alone to the heathen, but to Israel and Judah
a vexation, an unknown, an unrecognized? We may then believe
the Great Mother as mythologem dwelled chiefly in Mesopotamia,
in Asia Minor and Egypt, in Hellas and Rome—not to mention
the numberless earlier peoples who dwelt upon the earth. But
also in the Bible we meet with the Mothergodhead. We meet her
in the books of the Old Testament in the full meaning of the Word,
Metaphysikum without any trace of doubt.

The two deciding hieroglyphs for the *Metaphysicum* of the
Mothergodhead are *the Ruah Elohim* of the "Book in the Beginning" and the *Chokmah-Sophia* of the "Book of Wisdom." Whether
and insofar as they both, spirit-breath and Wisdom, point to a
being in itself, I cannot trust myself to judge, and in the same
way, whether and insofar they both are merged in the Theotokos
of the secret revelation of John. Enough that the Apocalypse always again offers the until now all too little used occasion for a
Mariology, in which the historical, mythical, eschatological and
mystical sides of the mysterium are rendered even. What I take as
true in this is the astonishing circumstance that Ruah Elohim and
Chokmah-Sophia can in no way be put out of the Hebrew nor the
Christian theology: but the religious consciousness of the Occident in spite of this has not been impressed with the Ur- and inward images of the Mothergodhead. It is as if the oldest trace of
the mother, always again lost in our holy Scriptures is, in a long
stretch, comparable to a Persephone-Kore, who is entrapped now
and then by the prince of death in the circuit of time. Now dis-
solving into unreadability, soon the trace of the mother merges
again into supra-meaning and her scent is never lost. Here for me
are the most exciting adventures of the Godseeking spirits. You,
the editor of the *Merkur*, partake in this quality, if merely in ab-

breviated keywords, by now still venturing such an attempt. Its presumption also cannot frighten you as severely as it frightens me. You will thus have to be content with five or six attempts that I, so to say, picked up from the floor, so that as with a sling they might be thrown to the goal.

First: The very old Hebraic *metaphysicum* of the Chokmah-Sophia—possibly with the, where not exactly alike, so still synonymous *metaphysicum* of the Ruah Elohim growing out of one and the same root—finds entrance and shelter, appreciation and authentication in the Jewish mysticism of the Kabbala. As the authentic secret transmission of Judaism, its parallel is put forth in the Apocalypse of the secret revelation of Christianity.

Second: Given the historical peak of the Kabbalistic mysticism for the high middle-ages, hardly in accidental contemporaneity with the fullness of the shining summer of Christian mysticism, then it came to pass at the beginning of the modern era that the 'teutonic' theosophy of Jacob Böhme united both these great kingdoms of western mysticism. His unique synopsis succeeded in shifting from the church-formed theologians, be it overlooked, be it passed over Chokmah-Sophia in the midst of the world-history, in that he let Wisdom be vowed to man in himself, or to the first Adam as his once and future ordained bride.

Third: If the West [in a narrow definition] could be remonstrated for its all too untroubled overlooking of the Biblical Chokmah-Sophia, this is in no way true of the East, [in a narrow definition]. For the essential Sophianic did not finally differentiate the Christianity of Eurasia from that of Europe or America. The advancing estrangement of both is still furthered outside this, so that in Russia, the Mother, the Chokmah-Sophia of the Bible inserted a still unexhausted Demetric, indeed a sinister, menacing Chthonic, whose fearfulness embodies itself in Gogol's wellknown legendary villain of the Wij. So there flows in the orthodox Mothergodhead Sophianic, Demetric, and Chthonic source-powers together, penetrating and mixing in unique ways. Sophia is and remains also here Wisdom, the Queen of heaven, the Virgin on high. But as Demeter, Earth-mother, and Mother Earth She receives and bears the holy child. In this last connection, rarely have I been more strongly touched than in Fedor Stepun's memoirs of his life and times, recording the confession

of a Moscow actor upon departing his friends: "But I believe with
Dostoyevski and all my predecessors that the earth is the bearer
of God." Again the old Russian lamentation of this same
Mothergodhead in her dark underworld relative as a 'dark Ma-
donna' who attends in the kingdom of the dead. This embraces
everything, graded in layers, of the inward concept of orthodox
Sophianic teaching; this saves, conceals, and disposes [entbirgt]
of it.

Fourth: Although I cannot wholly verify it, according to many,
Böhme's Sophianic mysticism, if I may so say it, did not remain
wholly unknown in modern Russia. But its historical importance
was first with its involvement in some 'Romantic' reservations,
including so-called German philosophy. For mediated through
Oetinger, who tried to make it a home in his Swabian country of
Swedenborg, the Sophianic mysticism of Böhme attained [this] in
the circle or horizon of Baader and Schelling. With them then it
acquired its passionateness and enduring nature, which it adopted
respectively where soul-transforming spirits meet one another.
Hence when Baader in the twenties of the nineteenth century
sought to make the leap to St. Petersburg, rather like Alexander I,
his goal was not attained in the last instant out of misfortune,
perhaps also imprudence, whereas Schelling, without any work
on his own, had all the good luck. Or more exactly said: not as
much Schelling himself as his late philosophy of mythology and
revelation. This was practiced still more with an uncontradictable
attractive power by Sergei Jurjew, the old friend of the great religious thinker of Russia, Vladimir Soloviev, and indirectly also
soon in this [Soloviev] himself. Outside the example of Baader's
actually peerless struggle, Schelling too had travelled in the
Cabirian and Kabbalistic Mysterium as well as in the Sophianic
mysticism of Böhme, having here access to the holiness of the
Mother. And were a paradox permitted me, so I'd not shirk the
assertion that he, with this Sophianic mysticism, restored in the
highest degree the metaphysical-theological sense of the Russians
Jurjew, Dostoyevski, Soloviev, to what was its original peculiar
position. Alas, certainly with the events of 1917 this development
was cut off or, perhaps only pushed aside and diverted, no one
knows to what hour. Enough that the souls seek and find the
Mother in the Fatherland of Böhme, Schelling, Baader, Goerres,

Bachofen, in the Mother of Matuschka Russia by the power of inalienable "Mother's rights": Europe's Great Mother of Eurasia. Once such an event is come to pass, one indeed well maintains not without justification it is forever...

Fifth: As I see it, Schelling's Sophianic mysticism in its main characteristics was primary for that of Soloviev, but permit me to offer a few further observations. In three ways, this mysticism of the Mothergodhead certifies her metaphysical rank. First of all, the cosmogonic, provided that the Mother is in the form of the Chokmah-Sophia or Wisdom, who by Schelling was posited as the long absent 'mediator' and medium between the still-unrevealed creator God beyond his own creation in himself, and the creation unsealing and manifesting him. This faith in the literal cosmogonic performance of the mother-Wisdom—that according to Schelling's judgement herself never fully clarifies her repeated question of the "so that" of a world, but always approaches nonetheless an answer—appears still interwoven with an eschatological performance. For one and the same Wisdom, who calls the world into being [Dasein] will one day in the "youngest day" bring it back to her Creator, and this in the style of an Origenic *apocatastasis panton* or Restoration of the All-Whole in the All-Whole. For the Orthodox thinking, feeling, and believing, this state of affairs, even this apocatastasis, even this restoration, is at all times much more acceptable than the Catholic view, with its historically documented aversion against all that is admonished even only in the most distanced way as Gnosis and Gnostic. A third completion still applies, that of the Chokmah-Sophia then as a consistent gradual metamorphosis, in German "Überwandlung, Höherwandlung" [transmutation] of the world in the complete sense of the apostolic "We will be changed"—be it charismatic, be it mystic-alchemistic. This is the steep path of the world, that holds in its balance the fall from God's heights into the anti-god's Abgrund. According to Böhme's teaching, this path one must here have always before one's eyes, the path which the first Adam certified and warranted, so that he already was married from the beginning with Wisdom as his bride. Despite his "broken oath" in world-time, Adam will ripen inevitably toward the holy wedding with Sophia. She, Sophia, Wisdom, not Eva Chawa, that is 'Life', will be offered his hand in bond in the days of the restoration, as the heavenly Virgin clothed with the light of the Sun, as Soloviev's ecstatic vision glimpsed.

So far as I personally am concerned, I harbor no residual reservations about this thought of Böhme, Schelling, Soloviev as regards taking the dogma of the heavenly ascension of Mary as one concept of this exceedingly high symbolism. For taken as symbol, it is incontestably one of the Mother, of Wisdom herself in the work of the sober 'heavenly ascent.' There is a metaphysical-mystical over- and higher-forming of the world. It is her clarification and refinement in the sign, namely, of Sophia! In this case we stand in an outward half of the mystical body of Christ, above all a member of the Christian revelation's truth. That is, in the assumption—but not finally in regards to the century's deeper and deeper soul-consuming conflagration and its all-melting power— I venture to hope also in the merging together of the Eastern Sophia-mysticism with the Western Mary-mysticism.

Is it necessary to append still a sixth? Necessary, to confirm that from here the lamentably broken West-eastern dialogue could be begun again? To confirm that the house of the Mother thus, that, to speak with the Kabbala, is not only the place of the broken oaths, but rather also the domain of the reconciliation? That any other attempt to bring new things into flow must be damned to be sheer balderdash? That it under no circumstances is to be done by power, but rather essentially out of the full authority of the Exousia? That always only where the Word itself holds full authority will the souls of people learn from one another and so open together their common truth? That living in the signs of the World-reconciler, Wisdom and Mother are the means to discuss what today irreconcilably separates Europe from Eurasia? I mean a Communism that pretends to be a *communitas*, and is indeed no *communitas*. Enough, and more than enough. For exactly this path is the riskiest and also the most necessary, it goes without saying, which is somewhat conveyed with Plato's train of thought on the 'Ur-society' 'underground.' And on this the writer of these lines has devoted also a bit, a study on the Platonic and Christian state....

With some reservation, indeed, with some aversion we may touch on a last [point] still, that in evangelical circles excites concern and has engendered controversy. I refer to the repeatedly expressed opinion that the corporeal heavenly ascension of Mary produces a detrimental competition with the heavenly ascension of Jesus and compromises the plainness of the Christian holy gospel.... For if one concludes thereby that Mary in truth corporeally ascended, then she fundamentally surmounts with her own heavenly ascension that of her Son! Then she places the infallible salvation-act of Christ in question, even if she doesn't render it exactly superfluous.

Whatever has to do with this train of thought, but isn't handwaving, I will let alone. Against this I could think with no less right that one would have to reach the opposite conclusion. It more or less then certifies that the heavenly ascent of Jesus has even now in its inalienable assumption exactly what the heavenly ascension of Mary's clear teaching lacks. Namely the temporal 'death-performance,' to employ here Albert Schweitzer's coined expression regarding the Christian baptism. The nature of the heavenly ascension is not decisive for holy history as such, whereas the death-performance of the crucifixion, burial, and resurrection is decisive. But so far as what concerns this heavenly ascension, she can be spoken of as having a corporeal ascent only in a unique sense, while Jesus also overcame precisely by freely suffering his death in bitter necessity. I want to say that he overcomes the mortal inherited corporeality of the first Adam in the immortality of the second, and thus also 'transfigures' it. In truth, not accidentally or incidentally does the Gospel have the resurrected wait forty days longer on earth and what belongs to each according to choice and will appears. In the world beyond, the graves are opened and one is clothed with another corporeality just as the coarse or grossly sensual receive what is theirs. With high consistency proclaims the Orthodox priest in Easter midnight—not yet on the day of the ascension—to the congregation as unique holy message: "*Christos voskres mjortvi*," "Christ is risen from the dead." In such a way the subsequent "heavenly ascension" receives its whole meaningfulness from the "crucified, dead, and descended."

In summary, it is said that in the inner kingdom of the triune God there is neither struggle nor contradiction. There is thus also no struggle and contradiction between Mother and Son, and seen aright, understood "in the spirit" and not according to the letter, no contradiction between the heavenly ascensions of both. In eternity Jesus-Christos-Theou-Hyios-Soter rescues the world, in that he dies its death and world and death are hereby conquered and overcome. In eternity the Chokmah-Sophia, the Theotokos-Maria, bears the Helper and Rescuer, her Son.

XV

Nicholas Berdyaev

While Leopold Ziegler's work is important and has been unjustly neglected, without doubt the most important and original theosopher of the twentieth century in my view is Nicholas Berdyaev (1874-1948). Although Vladimir Soloviev and Sergei Bulgakov—also known as Russian Sophianic authors—are significant writers to whose work some attention was given by scholars at the end of the twentieth century, of these three authors Berdyaev is by far the most enduring and vital, his importance far out of proportion to the neglect his work suffered after his death. Berdyaev's writing is vivid and lucid, and emerged out of a fiery creativity that sometimes outstripped the speed with which he could write. Exemplary of this creativity is Berdyaev's early and central work, *The Meaning of Creativity*, written in a time of "well-nigh intoxicating ecstasy" in 1914. In this work, he revealed, he said, "the theme of my whole life."

Berdyaev was born into the Russian nobility in 1874, and came from a family of military men. His aunt owned the Russian town of Belaya Tserkov, and about 150,000 acres of land near Kiev; he grew up accustomed to great luxury.[46] In 1904, he moved to St. Petersburg, where he and Bulgakov published a journal entitled *The New Way*. During this time Berdyaev formed his thought, and became involved in the lively religious ferment of the time, meeting all of the major Russian members of the "New Religious Consciousness" that had emerged in people like Dmitri Merezhkovsky and his wife, as well as many others. Exiled in 1922 by the Communists, Berdyaev remained independent of any specific literary, political, or religious movements or organizations. In 1922, he and his wife, Lydia, moved to Berlin, and in 1924 they moved to Paris, where they were to remain thereafter in exile, and where Berdyaev was eventually to die.

Like Soloviev and Bulgakov, Berdyaev was deeply influenced by the Sophianic tradition of Jacob Böhme, and in many respects Berdyaev was the most faithful of the three to this tradition. Berdyaev recognized, as perhaps no other philosopher has, the immense importance of Böhme's concept of the *ungrund*, or the spiritual un-ground prior to being, and how the *ungrund* is the origin of human freedom. He discussed this idea in numerous places, including most notably his book *The Beginning and the End*, but it informs virtually all of his writing. In his book *Freedom and the Spirit*, in fact, Berdyaev directly asserts that he sees himself as a theosopher in the tradition of "Jacob Böhme, Louis-Claude de Saint-Martin, and Franz von Baader"—in other words, precisely in the tradition from which all of our selections are drawn.[47]

The selection that follows is taken from the center of Berdyaev's pivotal book *The Meaning of Creativity*, and certainly shows the degree to which, even at this early period, Berdyaev was indebted to the Sophianic tradition. Here, he discusses the central question of eros, one that had begun to be investigated by Franz von Baader, on whose work Berdyaev is explicitly drawing. The Böhmean idea of the androgyneity of Adam before the fall is also central to Berdyaev's perspective here, one that given contemporary interest in questions concerning sexuality and gender, certainly presents fruitful possibilities for further inquiry. Berdyaev is unquestionably the best author with whom we could conclude this anthology, and in this selection he draws together themes that have recurred from the beginning to the end of this anthology.

From
The Meaning of Creativity

Jacob Böhme's teaching of the androgyne and Sophia is very profound. "You are a youth or a maiden—but Adam was both in one person," [writes Böhme]. "Out of his lust, Adam lost the Virgin [Sophia] and in his lust he received the woman. But the Virgin still awaits him, and if he only should desire to enter into a new birth, she would receive him again with great honor." Böhme distinguishes between the Virgin and the woman. The Virgin was the Sophia of the first Adam, whom he lost in the Fall. "Eve was created for this corruptible life, for she is the woman of this world," [Böhme continues]. "But the Wisdom of God is the Eternal Virgin, not woman: she is immaculate purity and virtue and stands as an image of God and a likeness of the Trinity." "This all-Wisdom of God, who is the Virgin of beauty and an image of the Trinity, is in herself an image of man and the angels, and has her origin in the center of the cross, like a flower springing forth from the spirit of God." The Sophianic quality of man is connected with his quality as androgyne. The fall of the androgyne meant the loss of the Virgin Sophia and the appearance of the woman, Eve. [Hence Böhme writes that] "The Virgin is eternal, uncreated, and unborn: She is the All-Wisdom of God and a likeness of Divinity." Böhme's mystical doctrine of man as androgyne makes it understandable why Jesus Christ, the absolute and perfect man, never knew a woman and in His own life did not realize the sacrament of marriage. The first Adam, also, did not know a woman and was not married.

[According to Böhme,] "Adam was a man, and equally a woman, and yet neither, but rather a Virgin full of virtue, purity, and incorruptibility, as an image of God. He had within himself the tincture of fire and the tincture of light in the gleams of which there rested his love for himself, as a sort of virginal center, like a beautiful rose-garden or pleasure-garden, in which he loved himself. And we shall resemble him after the resurection of the dead, since according to Christ's words there they neither marry nor are given in marriage, but live like the angels of God." [Thus, Böhme continues,] "Christ on the Cross liberated our virginal image from both man and woman and in divine love transformed it with his heavenly blood." Christ restored the androgynous image of man and returned the Virgin-Sophia to him. [Böhme writes that] "The image of God is human-virgin, not man or woman." [Accordingly] "The Fire-soul must be tempered in the fire of God and become brighter than pure gold, for it is the husband of the noble Sophia, out of the woman's seed. It is of the tincture of fire, just as Sophia is of the tincture of light. When the tincture of fire is completely purified, Sophia will be restored to it, Adam will again embrace his supremely honorable Bride, who was taken away from him at the time of his first sleep, and will become neither man nor woman, but only a branch on the jewelled tree of Christ that stands in God's paradise."….

For Böhme, the distinction between Virgin and woman, between Sophia and Eve, is important. His doctrine of Sophia is deeper and more complete than the cult of eternal virginity which we learn from Dante, Goethe, or Vladimir Soloviev. Even the cult of the Mother of God as illuminated womanhood is not ultimate, for the Mother of God is still in the line of Eve, and is spiritually like her. The cult of womanliness corresponds to man's passivity: in him the anthropological consciousness has not yet awakened. The cult of womanliness after all remains within the limits of the old man, from whom the womanly has been separated and set over against him, that is, until his new birth. Elements of a religion of feminine divinity slip into this cult. Into the pure cult of the Virgin Mary it is easy to mingle the idealization of the woman, Eve. Christian mysticism still remains in a sexual polarization. But the consciousness of the anthropos must attain complete liberation from its immersion in the feminine sexual element, in this attractive and absorbing sexual polarity. The cult of the pure Virgin, carried out logically, leads to the cult of the androgyne and to Böhme's doctrine of Sophia as the divine Virgin immanent in humanity. Böhme's doctrine of Sophia had as its objective the virginity of the soul, man's lost *Jungfraulichkeit*. We find the doctrine of the androgyne already in the Kabbala. And in their own ways, certain of the Church Fathers had a foretaste of it, for example, St. Maximus the Confessor.

In the nineteenth century, Franz von Baader revived Böhme's doctrines of the androgyne and of Sophia. Baader says that the idea of the androgyne should not have been foreign to the theologians, "least of all should the idea of virginal androgyneity have been strange to the theologian, since Mary gave birth without having known a man." [Baader continues]: "The nature of the soul is virginally androgynous, that is, each soul contains its nature (earth, bodiliness) within, and not outside itself." Baader sees the purpose of married love in the restoration of man's lost virginal nature, an androgynous nature. "Thus," [he writes] the secret and the sacrament of true love in the indissoluble bond of the two lovers, consists in each helping the other, each in himself, towards the restoration of the andrygyne, the pure and whole humanity, which is neither man nor woman." "The androgyne conditions the indwelling of God in man. Without this concept of the androgyne, the central concept of religion, that of the Image of God, remains uncomprehended," [Baader affirms]. [Hence] "The divine Sophia (Idea) was the helper of the virginal human who was neither man nor woman: this human being, through his connection with her (Sophia), a connection that could not be sexual, should have confirmed the androgyneity and thus eliminated the possibility of becoming man or woman. And even now, after the human being has become man and woman, this same Sophia, as soon as anyone turns to her inwardly, makes both man and woman participants, at least inwardly, of the androgynous, angelic nature."…. Humanity's rebirth as androgyne will mean acceptance within oneself of the whole of nature, the genuine revelation of man as microcosm. In the true birth of the integral human, both God and nature will be within and not outside him….

Deliverance is possible only through the new Adam, who comes into the world through a new womanliness…. With the Virgin Mary began man's liberation from that natural power. In the Virgin Mary, the earth takes into its bosom the Logos, the new Adam, Absolute Humanity. *And if the fall and enslavement of the old Adam, the old man, confirmed in the world the rule of natural-racial birth through the sexual act, the new Adam, the new man, could be born only of a Virgin who conceived by the Spirit.*

AFTERWORD

Sophia Today

What are the significances of Sophia now? Above all, the Wisdom tradition is more suited than perhaps any other aspect of the Christian tradition to our post-traditional era, in which doctrine or dogma alone neither convinces nor is adequate for many people. For by contrast, the Wisdom tradition affirms not only doctrine, but rather teachings founded in direct experience. In a time when many people are searching for ways to connect their own longing for direct spiritual experience with their inherited spiritual traditions, Sophianic spirituality offers a unique opportunity.

All too often, the Christian tradition has been depicted as simply a social phenomenon, as hypocritical and cut off from authentic spirituality. The sense of many that Christianity is spiritually bankrupt—a charge echoing from Nietzsche to the present—helps account for the growing popularity of Asian religions and the 'new religions.' There seems an historical inevitability to such events, but the Christian tradition is far vaster and deeper than such a depiction might suggest. Recent years have seen the publication of countless mystical works from antiquity to the present and the works included here reveal that there is still much more beneath the surface.

One can understand why traditionalists—and I use the word here in the broadest possible sense—want to preserve religious forms, and additionally, why some of them would feel threatened by the advent of religious hybrids like Christians who practice Buddhist meditation, or syntheses of Christianity and Native American or other indigenous traditions. But despite their dangers, such syntheses are undoubtedly going to mark the post-traditional world, and what is more, may well be seen as manifestations of the need for renewal in what would otherwise become moribund traditions. Indeed, it makes more sense to recognize tradition as a current than cling to a fixed image of it, more sense to recognize that at the center of one's tradition is divine Wisdom, and that the important thing is to reverence this Wisdom of which the changing panoply of symbols or forms are manifestations.

We have already entered into an era in which whether we like it or not, the forms and structures of the past are being discarded, and in which we are challenged to live a direct relation to the divine. The artist Cecil Collins wrote in his wonderful book *The Vision of the Fool* that

> If I may make use of a simile, the Trinity, I believe the age of the Father is over. The age of the Son is over. This is the age of Holy Spirit, this is the age of the universal principle—the open, flexible field of consciousness, the understanding of the unity of life in the multiplicity of human experience, so that we find in our culture again that hidden unity which transcends the fate of multiplicity and nemesis.[48]

In this new era, all doors are open, the doors to hell, and the doors to paradise. Indeed, even this language is too constrained to express the full import of our situation; perhaps we could say that we are each faced with the *nihil* and the *pleroma,* with destruction and with transcendent fulfillment. A post-traditional world reveals choices of unprecedented gravity, whose outcome can be either dissolution, fragmentation, nihilism, and destruction, or a miraculous ascent across the abyss on a mysterious bridge that appears only to those who have faith. There are only a few who have already dared to step across, among them artists like Rilke and Collins.

In this new and unprecedented situation, we need guides, and in it we will have to draw upon aspects of traditions that previously have remained largely unknown to the general public, and even to most theologians. Among these the Sophianic tradition is of special, and perhaps even paramount, importance within the European inheritance. For although the Sophianic tradition incorporates the many threads of European esotericism, including

Hermetic, alchemical, and gnostic elements—and might well be termed the *summa* of these streams—its primary significance is in its continuity as a living manifestation of direct gnostic experiential praxis. Our challenge these days is to enter into this living immediate relationship to divine Wisdom.

For the truth is, from one perspective, everywhere we look in contemporary society we see a crying need for Wisdom; everywhere we see her lack. Certainly in politics we find little sign of her guiding hand; neither in economics, in the relentless pursuit of money and power and consumerism; nor in education is Wisdom often evident; and for all its technical prowess, science is not gifted with a surfeit of Wisdom. Indeed, in every sphere of life it would seem that the ancient prophecies of a coming dark age, an era of cultural disintegration and spiritual eclipse, are coming to pass around us in awful clarity, like a vivid nightmare from which one cannot awaken.

But from another perspective, of course, one can awaken. Indeed, the Sophianic tradition is precisely *about* awakening; it is experiential rather than intellectual, the vision of the heart's eye, not just reason's measure. Awakening here means integration of the whole being, illuminated by the supernal light of the holy spirit, a becoming-complete, what in German is called *Menschwerdung* (becoming-human), a term that applies to Christ's incarnation and to our becoming truly human, which is to say, realizing Christ, an archetype of realized, illuminated humanity.

The Sophianic tradition insists that Sophia gives birth to Christ in us, that only through Sophia, divine Wisdom, can Christ be born in and through us, for incarnation is not simply something that happened once in the past; in the Sophianic tradition, we are all born to incarnate the divine, to follow Christ in the most profound sense of the words, and one may even say, to embody Christ. If the incarnation is to have a more than historical meaning, this meaning can only come to be in each of us, time and again, and not just once, millennia ago.

I believe, like Leopold Ziegler in the mid-twentieth century, that the meeting of the world religious traditions we are experiencing is the single most important historical event of the present era, and that central to this meeting will be not only the encounter between Buddhism and Judeo-Christianity, but even more specifically, the encounters and, yes, even the syntheses of Asian and European esotericism or experiential spirituality. Of particular import will be this Sophianic tradition, perhaps most because it is the syncretic, multitraditional Wisdom tradition of the Occident and represents the conjoining of all the major esoteric traditions of the West. Further, is it not significant that Prajñaparamita (Transcendent Wisdom) is the Mother of Buddhas, and that Sophia is the Mother of Christs?

For we are discussing here the future, and what can be born anew—not the past, nor its forms, but rather what has informed the past and can inform the future. Who can deny that in our era, however much we admire or cling to the forms of the past, it is ever more difficult to hold on to them? There is a principle of dissolution at work in the world, whether we want to see it as good or as evil, and perhaps in some respects it is neither, but simply necessary so that people go beyond ritualism for its own sake and confront their real task: to realize that which the rituals bespeak and signify.

In our present era, confronted by the apparent dissolution, dispersion, and synthesis of historical forms, we will increasingly find ourselves returning to the primordial, to the origins of traditional forms, for only this can revivify those from which life has been withdrawn, and create new ones. In either of these cases—revivification or creation—Wisdom will be central, for through Wisdom do all things in the cosmos come into being, and only through Wisdom can life flow forth and manifest. Since humanity has fallen from Wisdom, the return must be through her. Could there be any other way?

Suggestions
for Further Study

What follows is not a comprehensive bibliography of works of or about Christian theosophy, chiefly because such a bibliography already can be found in my book *Wisdom's Children*. Here I am offering a brief annotated selection of books that readers may find of use in coming to understand more deeply the nature of the Wisdom tradition represented in these pages.

There are countless lines of inquiry for the interested reader to pursue. One could turn to the many works of Jacob Böhme, which represent the fountainhead of the entire theosophic school represented in this collection. There are many various editions of Böhme's works available in English, chiefly through used book dealers. And I intend to publish a few more works by some of the authors represented in this collection, including work by Johann Gichtel and Franz von Baader. One can also pursue further the twentieth century representatives of this tradition, including Sergei Bulgakov, Vladimir Soloviev, and above all, Nicholas Berdyaev, whose extremely important works have been unfairly neglected in past decades by scholars and publishers both.

For scholarly background, one can certainly turn to the numerous works in both French and English of Antoine Faivre. A primary resource for scholars in the field is Faivre's extraordinarily erudite survey, *Access to Western Esotericism* (Albany: SUNY, 1994). Useful as an introductory collection of scholarly articles is *Modern Esoteric Spirituality* (New York: Crossroad, 1992), edited by Faivre and Jacob Needleman. Faivre has published numerous books in French on Western esotericism and in particular on Christian theosophy, many indispensable. Among those that may interest readers here are the brief introduction *L'ésotérisme* (Paris: Presses Universitaires, 1992), and the extensive study *Philosophie de la Nature: Physique sacrée et théosophie*, (Paris: Albin Michel, 1996).

There are numerous other works available in both French and German that are of great value for the scholar. The books of Pierre Deghaye and Alexander Koyré are very helpful in approaching Böhme's work, and there are also important works by Serge Hutin. Those who read German may be interested in the works of Ernst Benz, a wide-ranging scholar; Will-Erich Peuckert, who wrote several major surveys of various esoteric currents; Karl Frick, who produced a massive multivolume survey of esotericism, part of which is entitled *Licht and Finsternis* [*Light and Darkness*]; Gerhard Wehr, who has written extensively on the history of theosophy and mysticism; and Peter Koslowski, who applies theosophy to contemporary philosophical issues.

Unfortunately in English as yet there are relatively few books available on theosophy. The first introduction in English to the full theosophic tradition is Arthur Versluis, *Theosophia: Hidden Dimensions of Christianity* (Hudson: Lindisfarne, 1994). And the first extensive survey of the major figures and characteristics of the theosophic tradition is the companion to *Wisdom's Book*, entitled *Wisdom's Children: A Christian Esoteric Tradition* (SUNY: 1999). Also of interest to readers may be Versluis's *Gnosis and Literature*, and *The Mysteries of Love: Eros and Spirituality* (St. Paul: Grail, 1996), both of which include discussions of theosophy referring to aspects of the tradition not discussed anywhere else in English. Finally, readers may be interested in Versluis's book *Western Esotericism, Literature, and Consciousness*, which offers a survey of Western esoteric currents with an eye to their emphasis on a mysticism of the word.

Notes

[1]See Saint-Martin, E. B. Penny, trs., *Theosophic Correspondence* (Exeter: Roberts, 1863), Letter XXX.

[2]We find a parallel tradition in Buddhism: a Buddha is an anthropomorphic manifestation of immanent transcendence, of the indescribable nature of all things. A Buddha is dynamic awareness, but even so, we can see and experience a Buddha in art or ritual, and in life. Since we are human beings, is it surprising that transcendent Wisdom should manifest in perfect human form? Indeed, all the countless sacred images of Buddhism reveal not historical figures, but transcendent principles that we human beings can actualize in our own lives. There are many such parallels between Buddhist and Christian esoteric traditions.

[3]Kurt Rudolph, *Gnosis*, R. M. Wilson, ed. (New York: Harper, 1983), p. 76.

[4]It was Hans Jonas who made popular the modern notion that ancient Gnosticism resembled nothing so much as secular existentialist philosophy or even nihilism, but as Jonas himself remarked, his work on Gnosticism struck a chord with the popular imagination and might very well be superseded by later scholarship, as indeed has proven to be the case. See on this topic Arthur Versluis, *Gnosis and Literature* (St. Paul: Grail, 1996).

[5]'Imagination' here does not refer to fantasies,but rather to direct spiritual perception through what Henry Corbin called the 'imaginal faculty.' See Corbin's *Creative Imagination in the Sufism of Ibn Arabi*, R. Manheim, trs., (Princeton UP: 1969) as well as Corbin, *The Man of Light in Iranian Sufism*, N. Pearson, trans. (Boulder: Shambhala, 1978).

[6]For a discussion of what I call "Christian Tantrism," see Versluis, *The Mysteries of Love* (St. Paul: Grail, 1996).

[7]See for instance the collections at the Gotha and Halle libraries in Germany.

[8]I would add to this list the eccentric work *Sophia und Logos oder die Philosophie der Wiederherstellung* [*Sophia and Logos or the Philosophy of Restoration*] by Otfried Eberz (München: Reinhardt, 1967), a massive book full of rather unusual interpretations of history and literature. Eberz's primary thesis is, roughly, that the suppressed Sophianic spirituality is now finally coming into its own.

[9]See Versluis, "Christian Theosophic Literature of the Seventeenth and Eighteen Centuries" in *Gnosis and Hermeticism*, R. van den Broek and W. Hanegraaff, eds. (SUNY: 1997), pp. 217-236; see also Antoine Faivre, *Access to Western Esotericism* (SUNY: 1994), pp. 10-15 for a different list of characteristics pertaining to Western esotericism more generally.

[10]See E. Schüssler Fiorenza, *Jesus: Miriam's Child, Sophia's Prophet: Issues in Contemporary Christology* (New York: Continuum, 1995); see also Susan Cady, Marian Ronan, Hal Taussig, *Sophia: The Future of Feminist Spirituality* (New York: Harper, 1986). Much of feminist Sophianic scholarship has focussed on the Wisdom literature of antiquity. A good example is Claudia Camp, *Wisdom and Feminine in the Book of Proverbs* (Decatur, Ga.: Almond, 1985). For a study of Sophia and goddess traditions, see Caitlín Matthews, *Sophia: Goddess of Wisdom* (London: Aquarian, 1992). The only such book to take into account the theosophic tradition is Susanne Schaup, *Sophia: Aspects of the Divine Feminine Past and Present* (Nicholas-Hays, 1997), which also emphasizes the idiosyncratic work of Otfried Eberz.

[11]Jane Leade, *A Fountain of Gardens: or, A Spiritual Diary of the Wonderful Experiences of a Christian Soul, under the Conduct of the Heavenly Wisdom; Continued for the Year MDCLXXVIII* (London: 1700), III.324

[12]Ibid., III.327.

[13]Ibid., III.329-330, III.335.

[14]For a more extensive discussion of this disagreement, see Versluis, *Wisdom's Children: A Christian Esoteric Tradition* (SUNY: 1999), pp. 69 ff.

[15]See for instance Basarab Nicolescu, *Science, Meaning, and Evolution, the Cosmology of Jacob Böhme* (New York: Parabola, 1992); and Peter Koslowski, *Die Prüfungen der Neuzeit: Über Postmodernität, Philosophie der Geschichte, Metaphysik, Gnosis* (Wien: Passagen, 1989).

[16]On Böhme see Pierre Deghaye, *La Naissance de Dieu* (Paris: Albin Michel, 1985); Alexander Koyré, *La Philosophie de Jacob Boehme* (Paris: Vrin, 1979 ed.); Andrew Weeks, *Boehme: An Intellectual Biography of the Seventeenth-Century Philosopher and Mystic* (Albany: SUNY, 1991); on Böhme's predecessors see Alexandre Koyré, *Mystiques, spirituels, alchimistes du xvi siècle allemand* (Paris: Gallimard, 1971).

[17]From Böhme, *The Three Principles*, ch.xiv.§51-53, 84-89.

[18]See Serge Hutin, *Les disciples anglais de Jacob Böhme* (Paris: Didier, 1960), p. 82.

[19]See Rawlinson Ms. 833, Folio 63.

[20]Ibid.

[21] These paragraphs appear as follows in the *Theosophic Correspondence* of Louis Claude de Saint-Martin (Exeter: 1863), pp. 92-93;

Happy are they who hunger and thirst for Sophia, for they will see, in the following treatise, that she promises to descend into them with her divine principle and her World of Light. A considerable time may pass, however, sometimes twenty years or more, before the eternal Wisdom really communicates and reveals herself so as to shed tranquillity and peace in the soul of him who desires her, for, after vainly seeking different ways to get to her, the soul, disappointed in its hopes, falls at last, without any strength left, in lassitude and discouragement. If then, neither fervent prayer nor religious meditation can do anything, and no entreaty, however earnest, avails to induce her to come down and abide in our souls, we are then convinced that, by our own efforts, our acts of faith and hope, or by the activity of our mind, it is utterly impossible for us to break through the wall of separation that is between us and the Divine Principle, all these keys being powerless to open the door to this principle. And when our soul then finds that, in hitherto following the road of *Ascension*, it has always missed its object, it concludes that this was not the right way (even though it may have been treated on the way with communications and heavenly revelations), but that the only path to arrive at Divine Wisdom and her principle, is by *descending*, to sink inwardly into one's own ground, and look no more without.

When the soul takes this road, and sinks into itself, then the gates of the depths of Wisdom open, and the soul is introduced into the holy eternal principle of the world of light; in the new magical earth, in which the virgin Sophia, or Divine Wisdom, shows herself, and discloses her beauties.

But if the soul here is not sufficiently watchful, and firm enough to concentrate itself continually in its center of nature (Centrum naturae) and, through the passive tranquillity, it does not so sink into this abyss, this chaos, out of which the new paradise is formed, as to rise again, and fly up on high, it is then in the greatest danger of being surrounded, and cruelly tempted by a crowd of innumerable spirits, from either the dark world, or from the elementary astral principle. But in its extremity, its heavenly protector appears again, to strengthen it, and repeat and confirm the first lesson.

[22]*Abfall*, meaning secession or apostasy, and a term distinctly Gnostic in flavor.

[23]Gichtel VII.341 ff.

[24]See for more on Gichtel's monumental project, Bernard Gorceix, *Johann Georg Gichtel: Théosophe d'Amsterdam (Paris: Delphica, 1975)*, pp. 33-34.

[25]Here Bathurst's vision is strikingly similar to that of John Pordage, in particular in his *Theologia Mystica, or the Mystic Divinitie of the Aeternal Invisibles, viz. the Archetypous Globe* (London: 1683), and in his *A Treatise of Eternal Nature with Her Seven Eternal Forms* (London: 1681).

[26]See G. Wehr, *Die Deutsche Mystik* (Bern: Otto Wilhelm Barth Verlag, 1988) p. 290.

[27]Friedrich Christoph Oetinger, in his *Die Lehrtafel der Prinzessin Antonia* (Tubingen, 1763, eds Reinhard Breymayer and Friedrich

Häussermann, Berlin: De Gruyter, 1977, 2 vols.), I.131 ff.

[28]W. Hauck, in Wehr, op. cit., p. 292.

[29]See Ernst Benz, "Die Naturtheologie Friedrich Christoph Oetingers," in *Epochen der Naturmystik, Hermetische Tradition im wissenschaftlichen Fortshritt*, A. Faivre, ed. (Berlin: Erich Schmidt Verlag, 1979), p. 275.

[30]From Louis-Claude de Saint-Martin, *Man: His True Nature and Ministry*, E.B. Penny, trs. (London: Allan, 1864) pp. 110-112, 188-194, 461-463.

[31]See Henry Corbin, *Avicenna and the Visionary Recital*, W. Trask, trs., (Princeton UP: 1960); see also *Spiritual Body and Celestial Earth*, N. Pearson, trs. (Princeton UP: 1977).

[32]See Pordage, *Sophia*, chp. 22, regarding this "new land."

[33]The original reads: Stirb, auf daß die alte Erde in so manchen Brüdern sich spalte.

[34]Franz von Baader, *Sätze aus der erotischen Philosophie* (Frankfurt:1966).

[35]From Baader, *Werke*, F. Hoffmann, ed. (Darmstadt: Scientia, 1987 ed.), X.342-343

[36]This work bears the subtitle "From a letter to the Gräfin Wielhorski, born Princess Birron von Kurland. Baader had close relationships with a number of Russian nobles.

[37]The conclusion of Schiller's poem, "An die Freunde," 1802.

[38]In other words, we should separate ourselves from the spectral nature of the world, for only thus can we realize the true spiritual manifestation of Sophia. To us as human beings, Sophia appears at first like a revenant, spectral, and like an image, but in fact is more real than what we take for granted as real in the physical world.

[39]Baader is alluding to the practice of magic, about which he wrote in more detail in his essay "Der verderbliche Materialismus." There, he was drawing on the Paracelsian tradition of stellar and elemental spirits.

[40]"The destruction of one is the creation of another."

[41]Bacon's *imperium in naturam* represented the division of science and religion, whereas Baader's goal was the reuniting of science and religion. For Baader, Sophia, or Idea, meant the union of science and religion through Wisdom.

[42]Gen. 1, 7-10, referred to in the Zohar, in which is elaborated the difference between the upper (heavenly) and the lower waters. Böhme also alluded to this distinction, in *De Signatura rerum*, cap. 10, §13. Cf. also Baader's "On the Biblical Concept of Spirit and Water in Relation to the Trinity," *Werke*, op. cit., x.1

[43]Hekate was the goddess of sorcery and spectres in antiquity; she was connected with the Underworld. She is the antithesis of Sophia, the Heavenly Bride. Just as there is a heavenly or inspired poetry (a modern

exemplar of which is Rainer Maria Rilke) so to there is an infernal or demonic poetry or prose.

[44]For a perspective from the "other" Orthodox side here see the selection from Berdyaev that follows. What Berdyaev denies, from a Böhmean perspective tinged by his Eastern Orthodox background, is precisely what Ziegler affirms about the uniqueness of Mary.

[45]Ziegler's magnum opus was his book *Menschwerdung* (München: Summa Verlag, 1948), a book dedicated to Böhme, Kierkegaard, and Baader.

[46]Nicholas Berdyaev, *Dream and Reality: An Essay in Autobiography* (New York: Macmillan, 1951), p. 9.

[47]Nicholas Berdyaev, *Freedom and the Spirit*, O. Clarke, trs. (London: Bles, 1935), p. xix.

[48] Cecil Collins, *The Vision of the Fool and Other Writings* (Ipswich: Gologonooza, 1995), p. 101.

List of Sources

Arnold, Gottfried, *Das Geheimnis der Göttlichen Sophia*, (Leipzig: 1700).

Robert Ayshford, *Aurora Sapientia, that is to saie, The Daiebreak of Wisdome Of the three Principles and beginning of all in the mysterie of wisdome in which the ground and key of all wisdome is laid open, directing to the true understanding of God, of Man, and of the whole world, in a new and true triune wisdome Physisophie, Theologie, and Theosophie. tending to the Honour of God, Revelation of the true wisdome and to the service of the Sixt Church att Philadelphia* By Her Minister called by the Grace of God to beare witness of God and of Jesus Christ, 1629, Ashmole MS 858, Bodleian Library, Oxford.

Baader, Franz von, *Sämmtliche Werke*, Franz Hoffman, ed., (Leipzig, 1851-1860).

Bathurst, Ann, *Journals*, 2 vols., 1693-1696, Rawl. MS 1263 D, Bodleian Library, Oxford.

Berdyaev, Nicholas, *Smysl tvorchestva. Opyt opravdaniia chelovieka*, (Moskva: Izdanie G.A. Lemana, 1916); translated as *The Meaning of the Creative Act*, D. Lowrie, trs., (New York: Harper, 1955) [selection substantially revised and augmented by the editor; permission to publish this selection gratefully received from *f*ditions YMCA-Press, Paris, France].

Bšhme, Jacob, *Theosophia Revelata*, Johann Georg Gichtel, ed., (Leipzig: 1730 ed.); available in reprint as *Sämtliche Schriften*, 8 vols., Will-Erich Peuckert, August Faust, eds., (Stuttgart: Frommann, 1955-1961).

Bromley, Thomas, *The Way to the Sabbath of Rest, or the Soul's Progress in the Work of the New Birth*, (London: 1655). [Reprinted 1692, 1710].

Gichtel, Johann Georg, *Theosophia Practica*, 7 vols., (Amsterdam: 1721); cf. MS English translation by Charles Heckethorne, Walton Collection, Dr. Williams's Library, London.

Leade, Jane, *The Laws of Paradise*, (London: T. Sowle, 1695).

Oetinger, Friedrich Christoph, *Sämmtliche theosophische Schriften*, (Stuttgart: 1858); see in particular, *Biblisches und emblematiches Wšrterbuch*, (1776).

Pordage, John, *Ein gründliche philosophisch Sendschreiben vom rechten und wahren Steine der Weissheit*, (Berlin: Christian Ulrich Ringmacher, 1779).

_____, *Sophia, das ist, Die holdseelige ewige Jungfrau der Göttlichen Weisheit*, (Amsterdam: 1699).

Saint-Martin, Louis-Claude de, *Le Ministère de l'Homme-esprit*, (Paris: 1802); cf. English translation by E. B. Penny as *Man: His True Nature and Ministry*, (London: Allan, 1864).

Welling, Georg von, *Opus Mago-Cabalisticum et Theosophicum*, (Frankfurt/Leipzig: 1735, 3rd ed., 1784).

Wirz, Johann Jakob, *Zeugnisse und Eröffnungen des Geistes durch Johann Jakob Wirz*, (Barmen: 1863-4).

Ziegler, Leopold, *Spätlese eigener Hand*, (München: Kösel, 1953), selection translated by the kind permission of the Leopold Ziegler Stiftung and Kšsel Verlag.

Index